英雄

HERO

D1440493

Author:

Wing Shing Ma

Translator:

Yun Zhao

Editors:

Shawn Sanders
Kevin P. Croall
Angel Cheng
Duncan Cameron

Production Artist:

Hung-Ya Lin

US Cover Design:

Yuki Chung

Production Manager:

Janice Chang

Art Director:

Yuki Chung

Marketing:

Nicole Curry

President:

Robin Kuo

English translation by
ComicsOne Corporation 2003

Publisher
ComicsOne Corp.
48531 Warm Springs Blvd., Suite 408
Fremont, CA 94539
www.ComicsOne.com

First Edition: February 2004
ISBN 1-58899-374-4

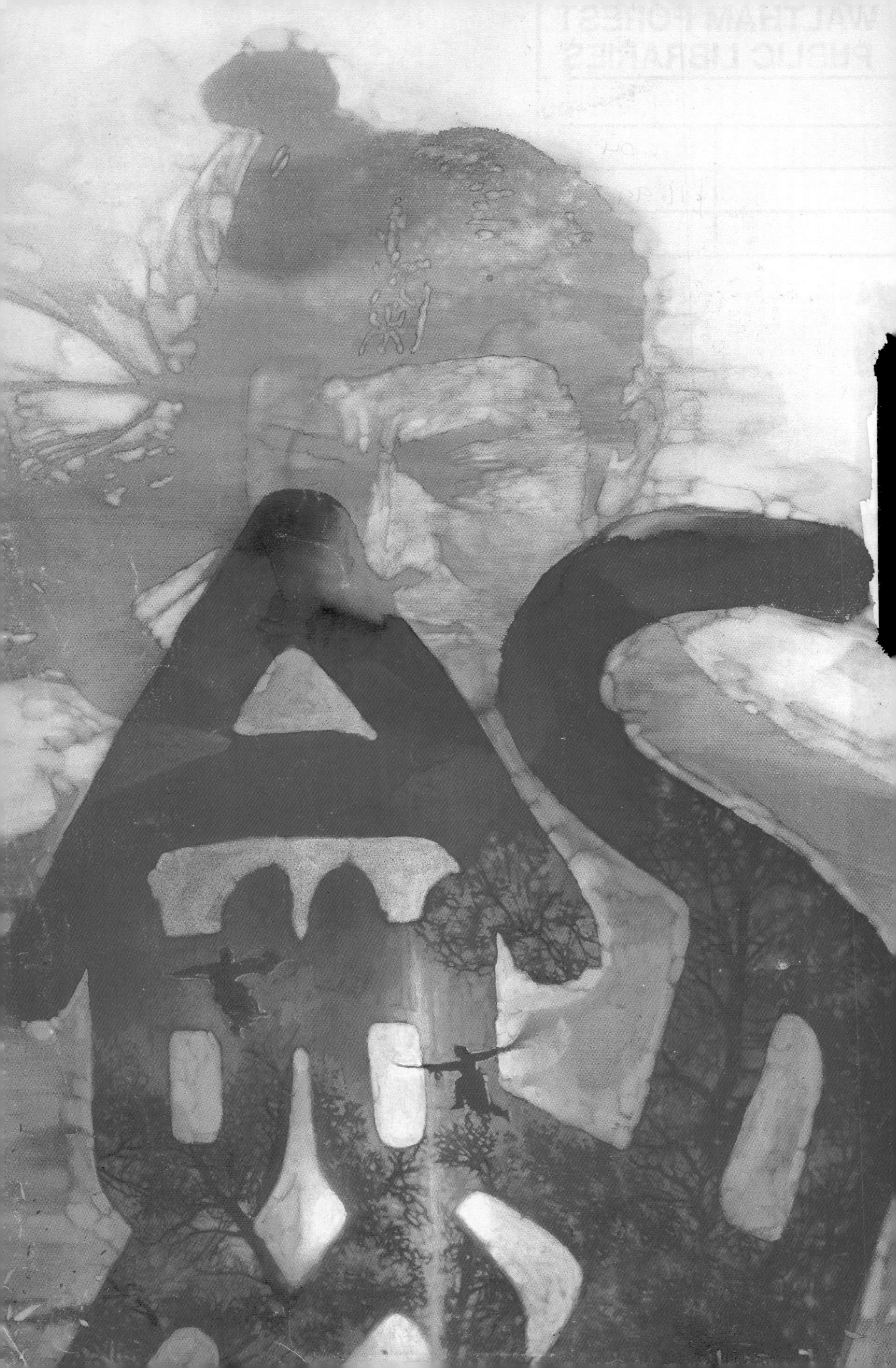

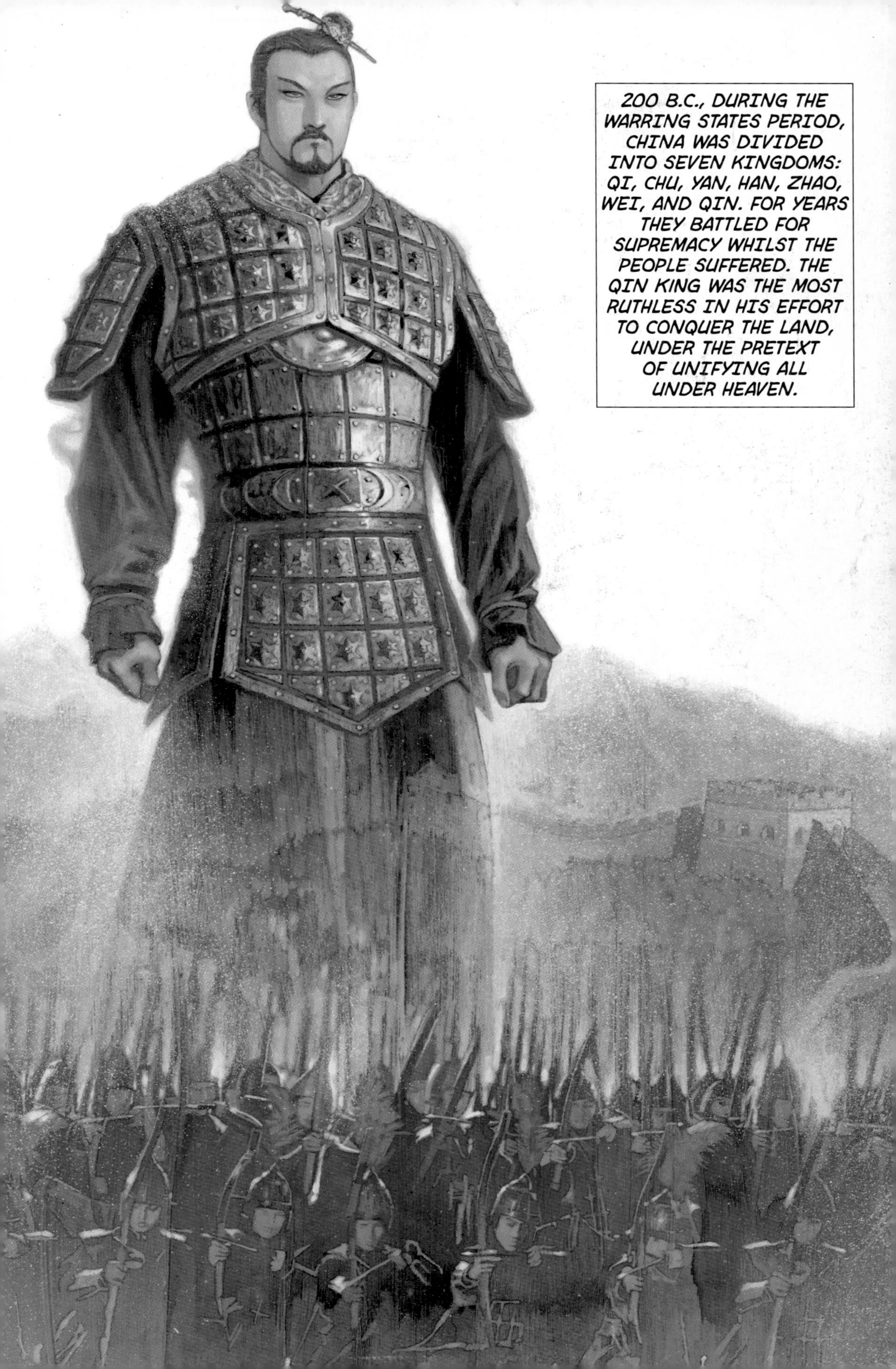
200 B.C., DURING THE WARRING STATES PERIOD, CHINA WAS DIVIDED INTO SEVEN KINGDOMS: QI, CHU, YAN, HAN, ZHAO, WEI, AND QIN. FOR YEARS THEY BATTLED FOR SUPREMACY WHILST THE PEOPLE SUFFERED. THE QIN KING WAS THE MOST RUTHLESS IN HIS EFFORT TO CONQUER THE LAND, UNDER THE PRETEXT OF UNIFYING ALL UNDER HEAVEN.

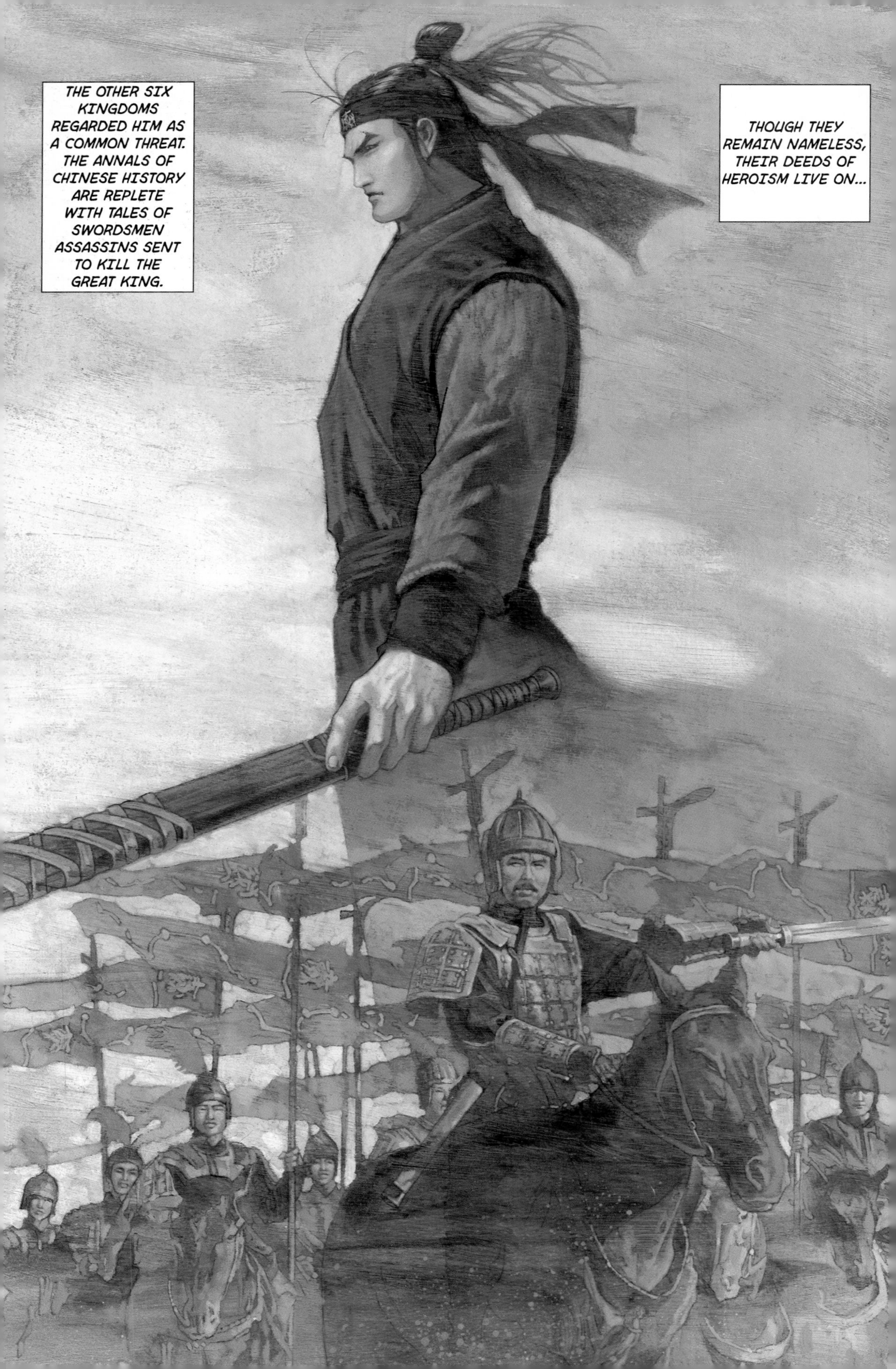
THE OTHER SIX KINGDOMS REGARDED HIM AS A COMMON THREAT. THE ANNALS OF CHINESE HISTORY ARE REPLETE WITH TALES OF SWORDSMEN ASSASSINS SENT TO KILL THE GREAT KING.
THOUGH THEY REMAIN NAMELESS, THEIR DEEDS OF HEROISM LIVE ON...

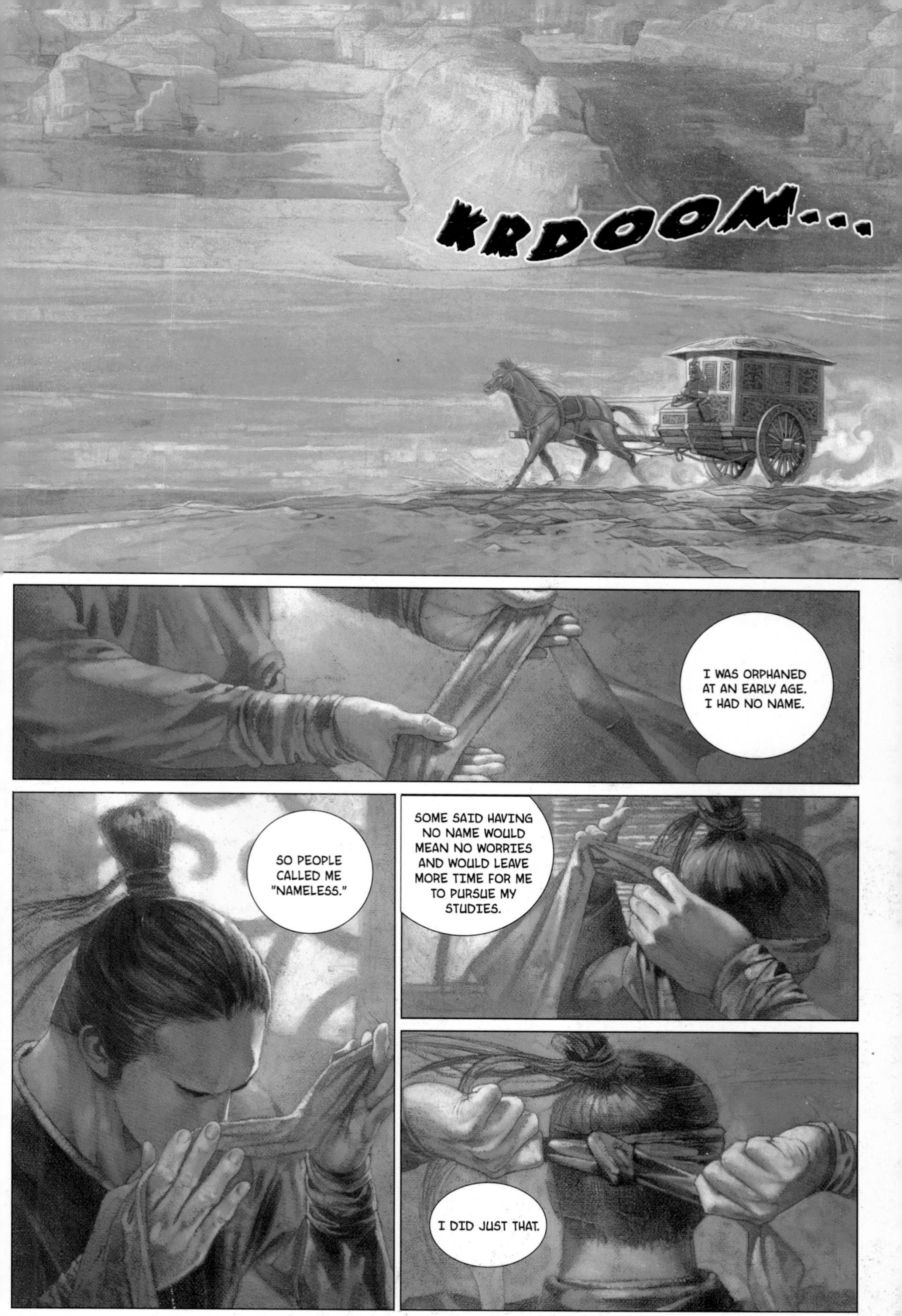
KRDOOM...
I WAS ORPHANED AT AN EARLY AGE. I HAD NO NAME.
SO PEOPLE CALLED ME "NAMELESS."
SOME SAID HAVING NO NAME WOULD MEAN NO WORRIES AND WOULD LEAVE MORE TIME FOR ME TO PURSUE MY STUDIES.
I DID JUST THAT.

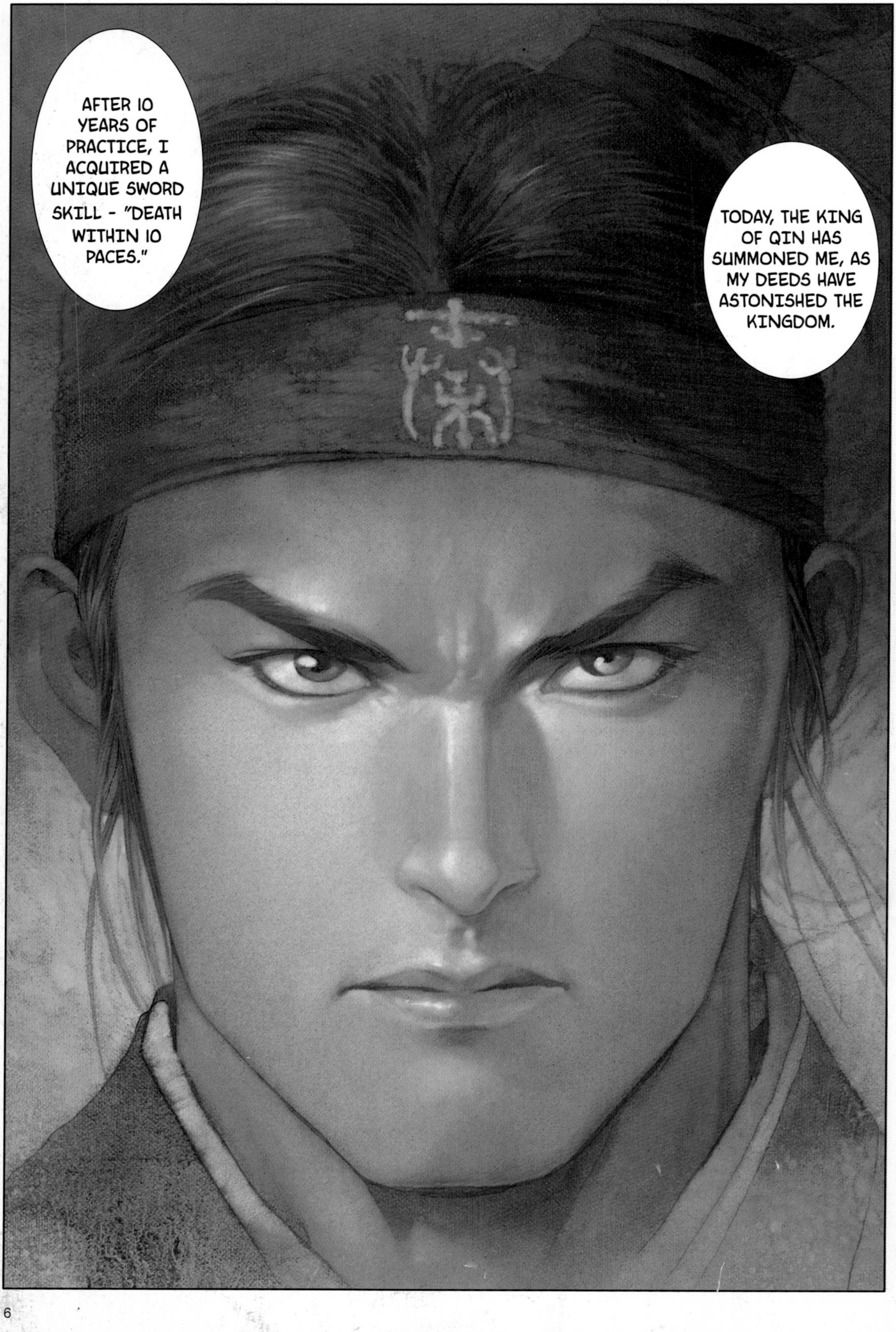
AFTER 10 YEARS OF PRACTICE, I ACQUIRED A UNIQUE SWORD SKILL - "DEATH WITHIN 10 PACES."
TODAY, THE KING OF QIN HAS SUMMONED ME, AS MY DEEDS HAVE ASTONISHED THE KINGDOM.

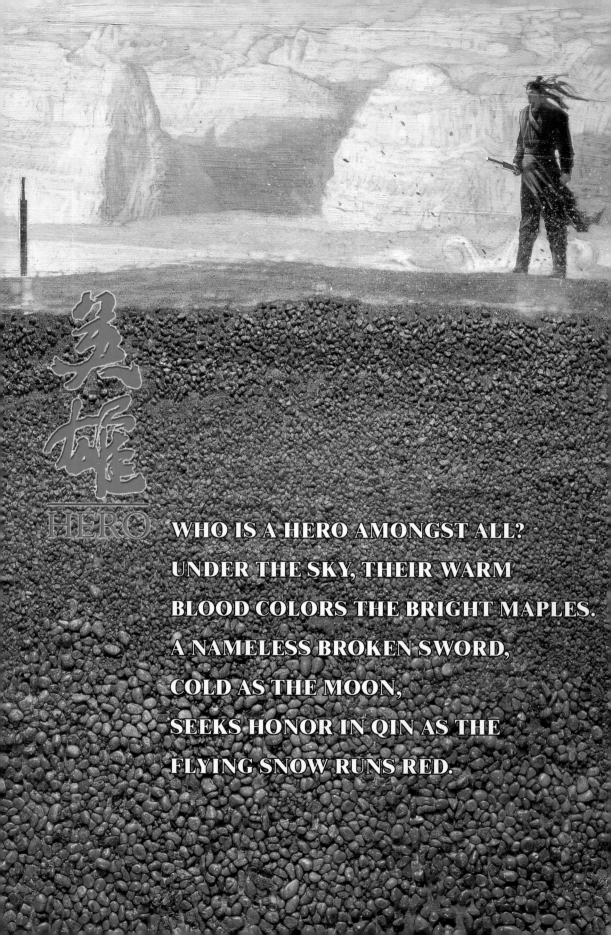

WHO IS A HERO AMONGST ALL?
UNDER THE SKY, THEIR WARM
BLOOD COLORS THE BRIGHT MAPLES.
A NAMELESS BROKEN SWORD,
COLD AS THE MOON,
SEEKS HONOR IN QIN AS THE
FLYING SNOW RUNS RED.

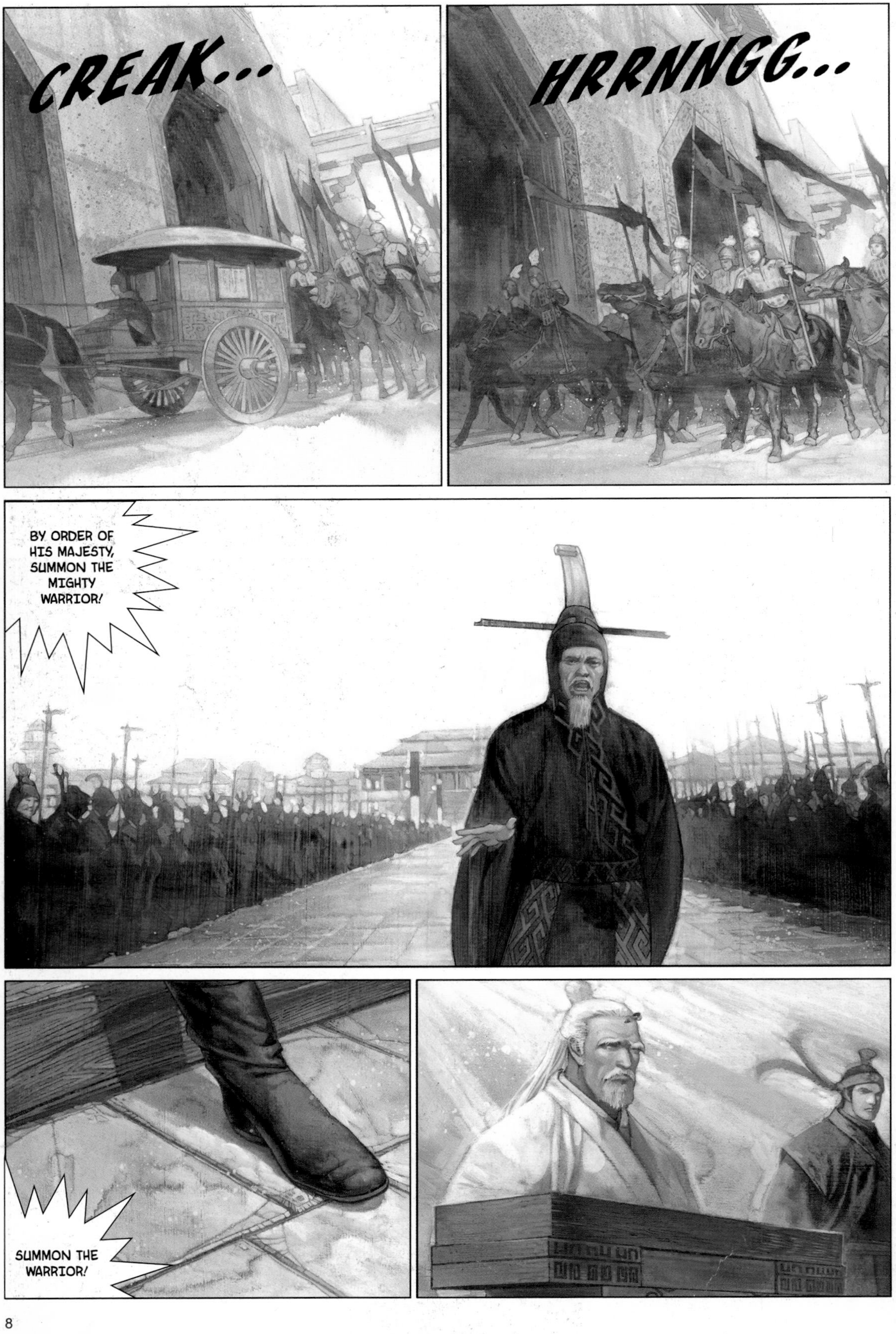
CREAK...
HRRNNGG...
BY ORDER OF HIS MAJESTY, SUMMON THE MIGHTY WARRIOR!
SUMMON THE WARRIOR!

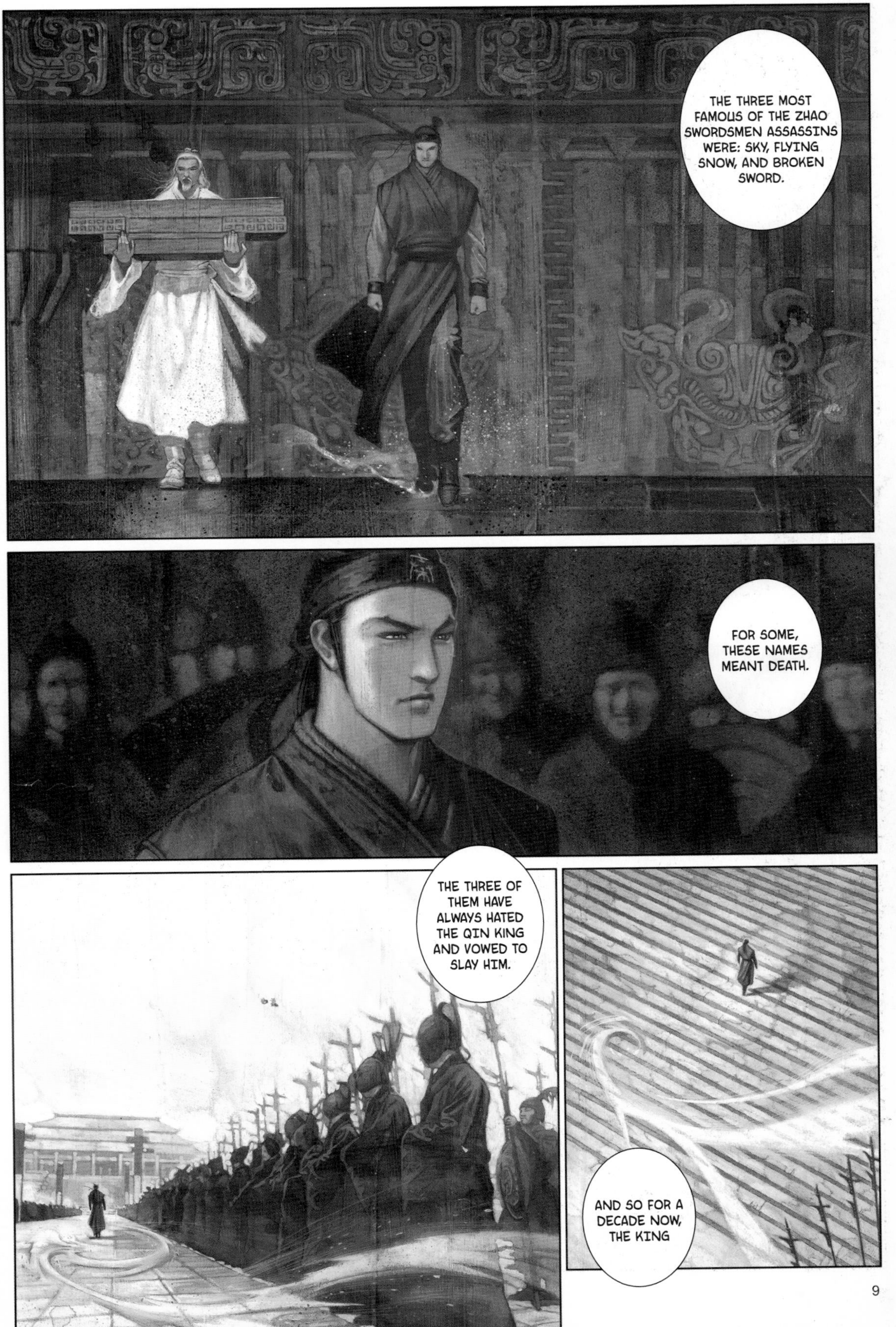
THE THREE MOST FAMOUS OF THE ZHAO SWORDSMEN ASSASSINS WERE: SKY, FLYING SNOW, AND BROKEN SWORD.
FOR SOME, THESE NAMES MEANT DEATH.
THE THREE OF THEM HAVE ALWAYS HATED THE QIN KING AND VOWED TO SLAY HIM.
AND SO FOR A DECADE NOW, THE KING

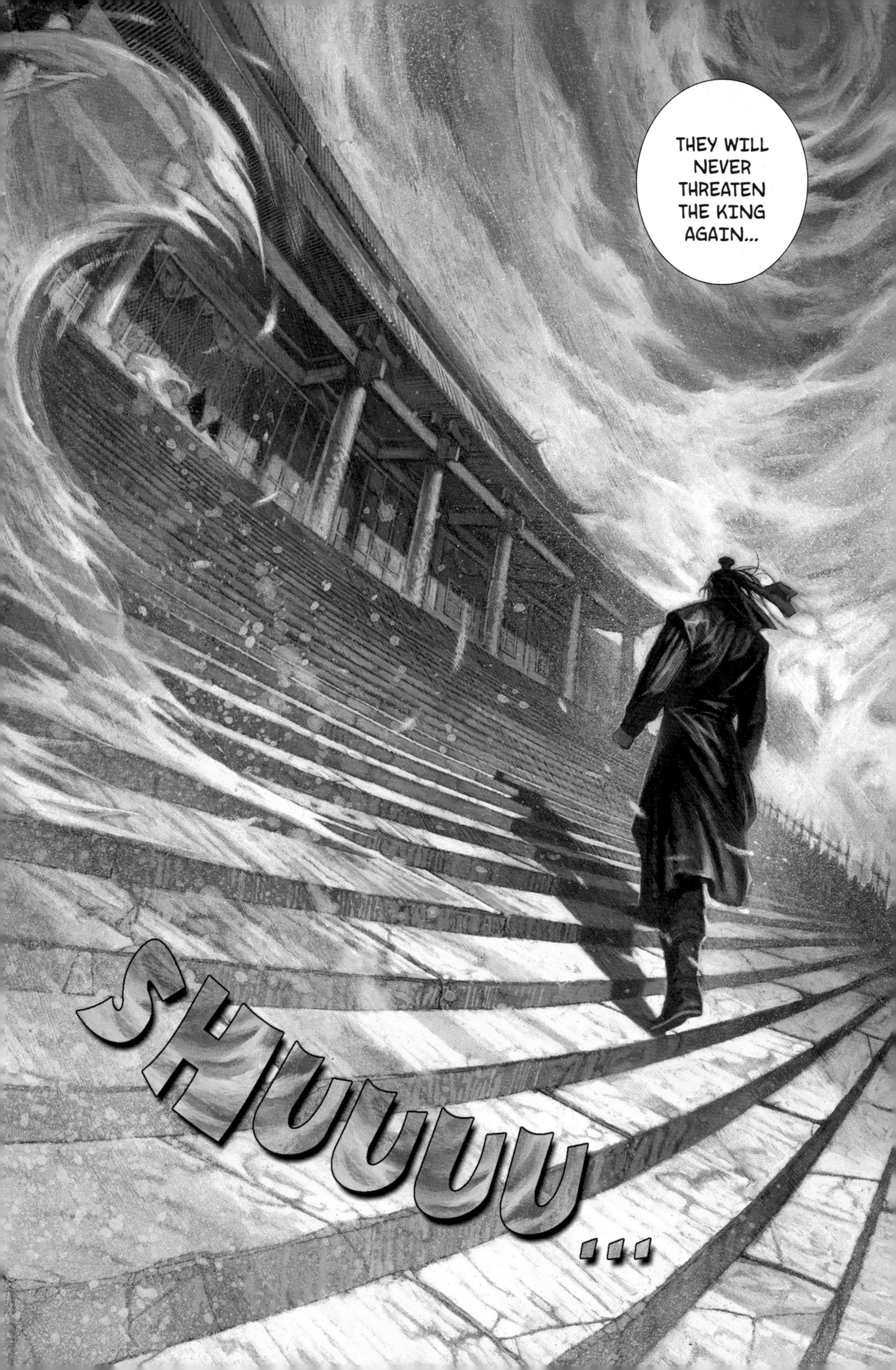
THEY WILL NEVER THREATEN THE KING AGAIN...
SHUUUUU...

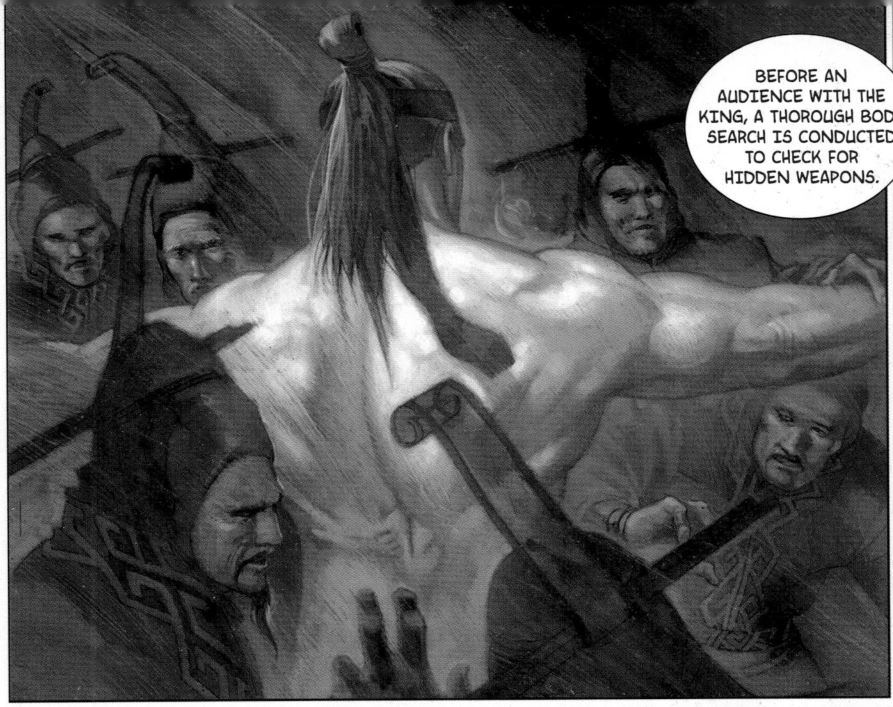
BEFORE AN AUDIENCE WITH THE KING, A THOROUGH BODY SEARCH IS CONDUCTED TO CHECK FOR HIDDEN WEAPONS.

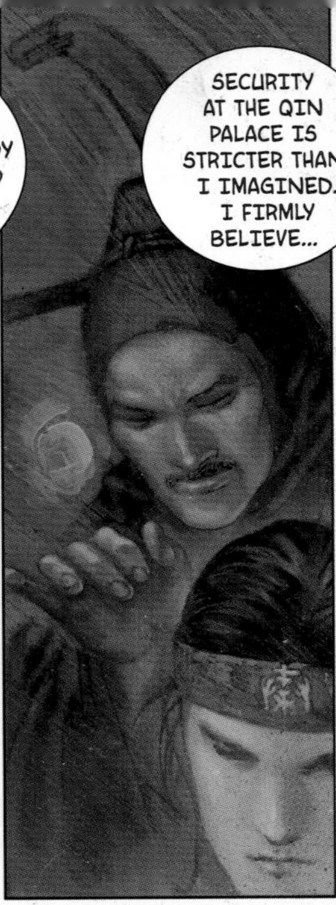
SECURITY AT THE QIN PALACE IS STRICTER THAN I IMAGINED. I FIRMLY BELIEVE...

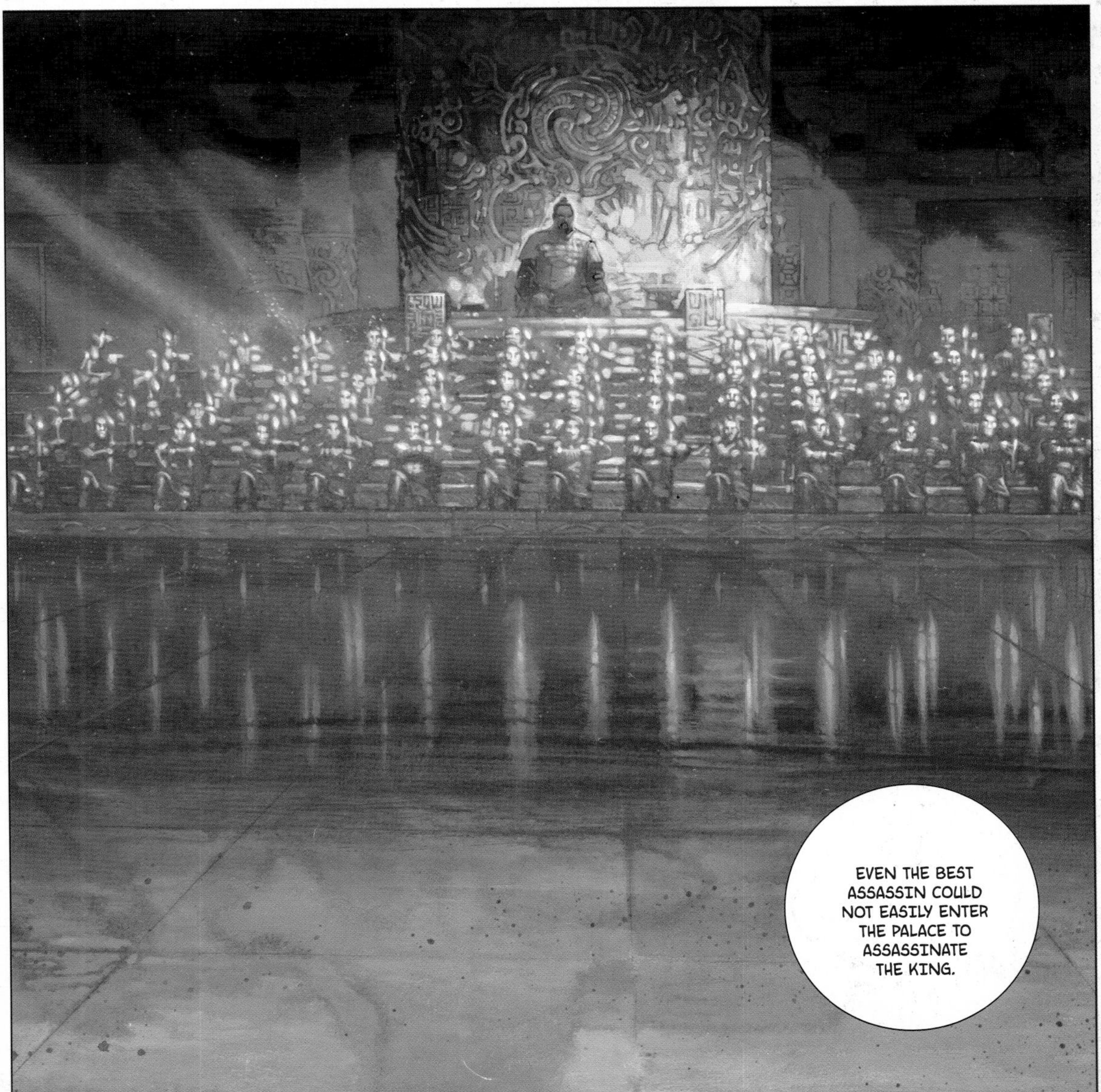
EVEN THE BEST ASSASSIN COULD NOT EASILY ENTER THE PALACE TO ASSASSINATE THE KING.

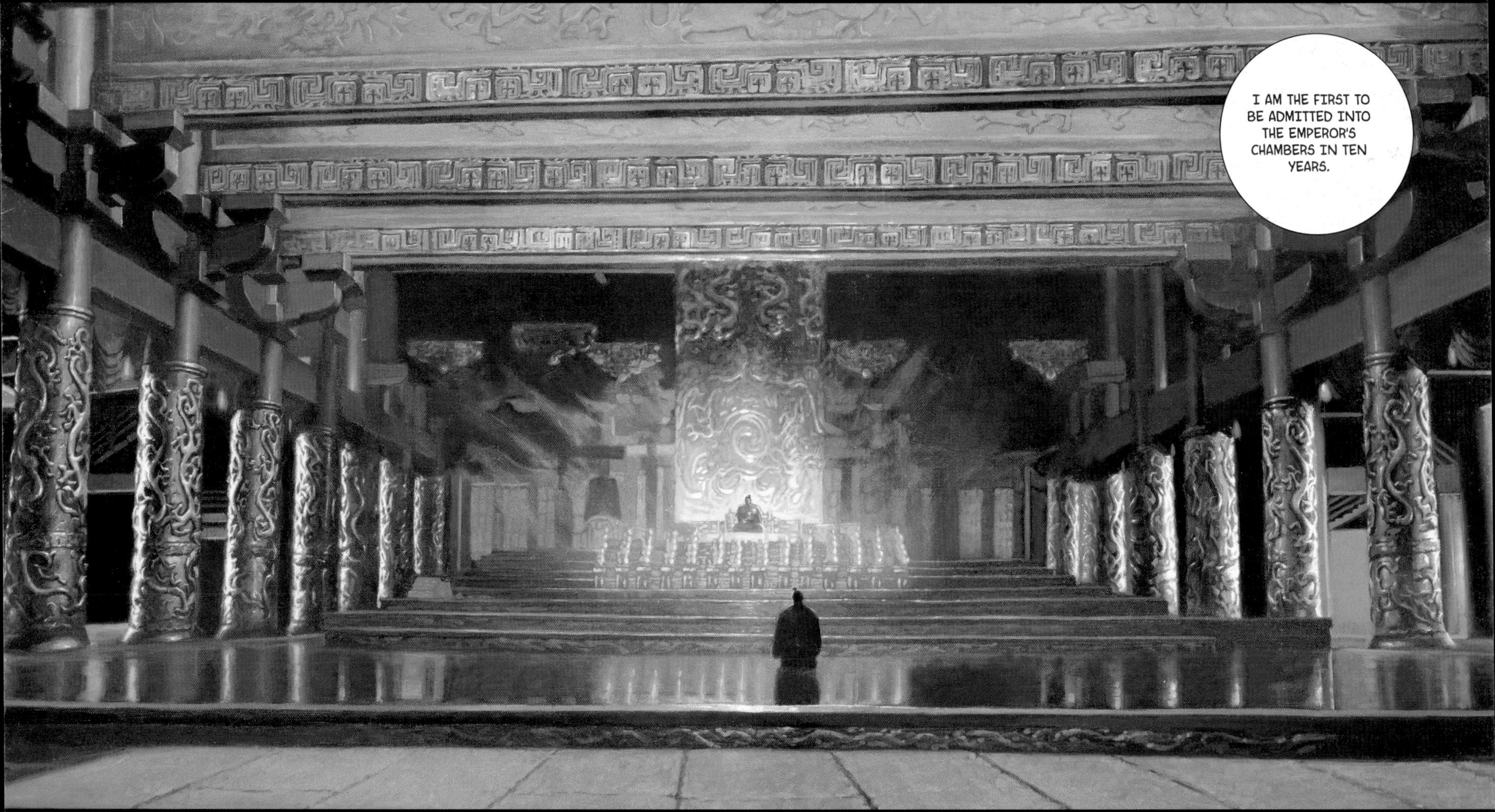
I AM THE FIRST TO BE ADMITTED INTO THE EMPEROR'S CHAMBERS IN TEN YEARS.

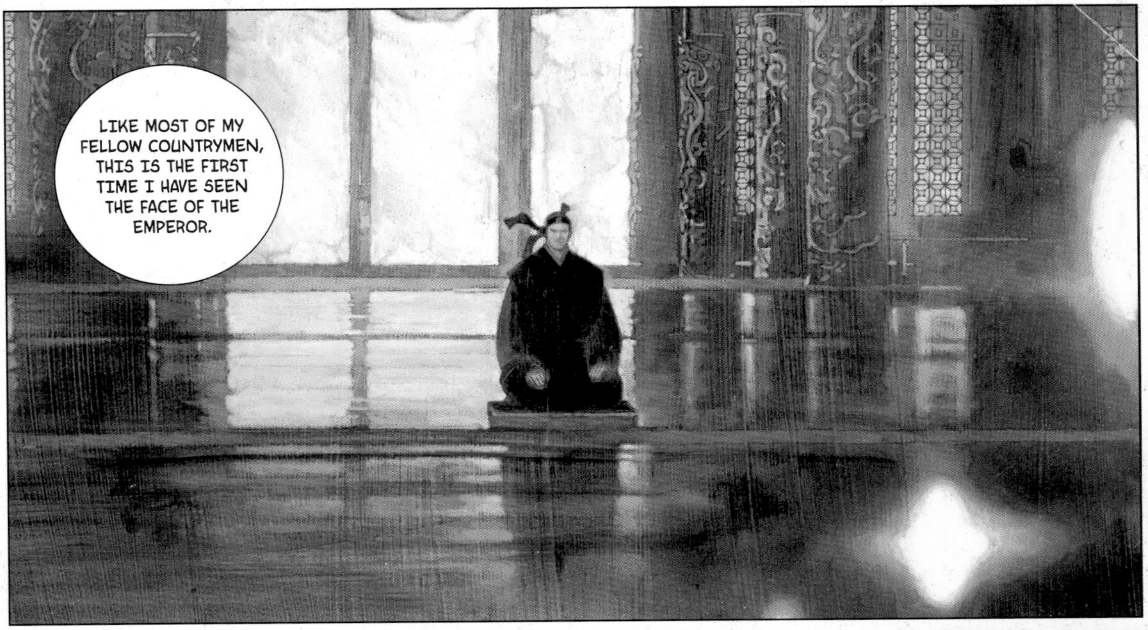
LIKE MOST OF MY FELLOW COUNTRYMEN, THIS IS THE FIRST TIME I HAVE SEEN THE FACE OF THE EMPEROR.

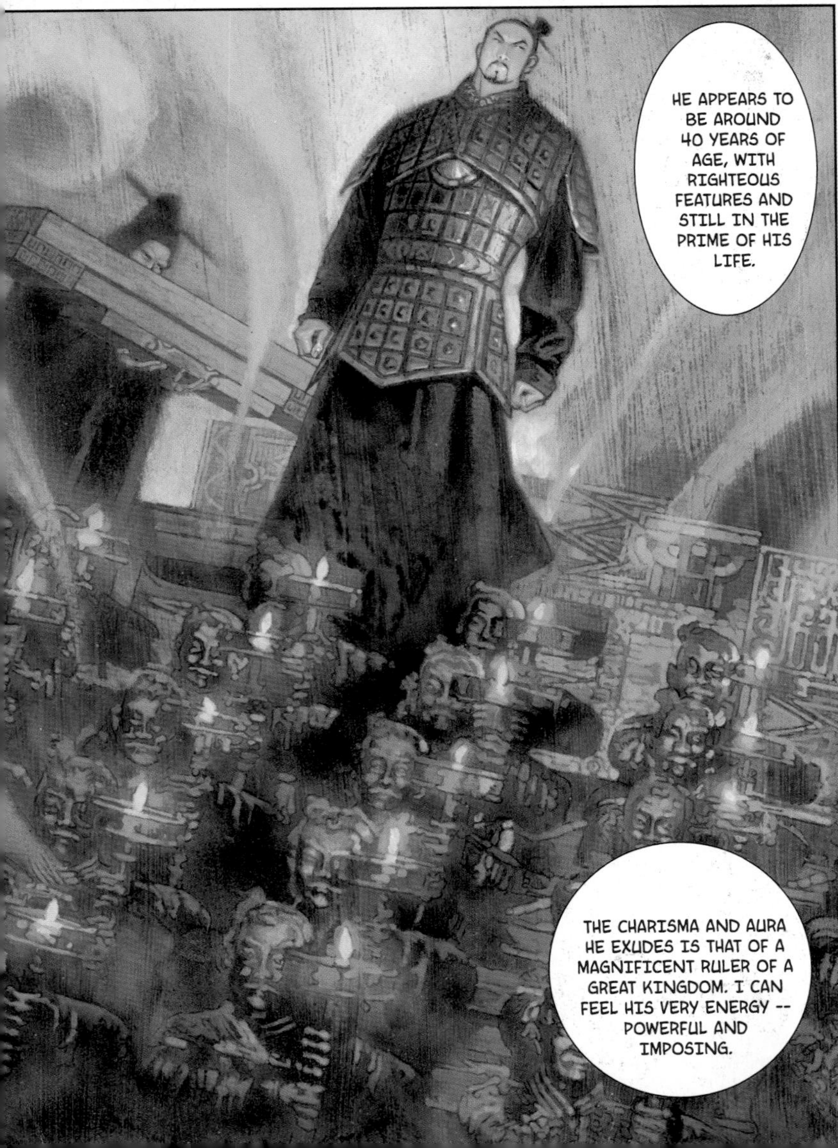
HE APPEARS TO BE AROUND 40 YEARS OF AGE, WITH RIGHTEOUS FEATURES AND STILL IN THE PRIME OF HIS LIFE.
THE CHARISMA AND AURA HE EXUDES IS THAT OF A MAGNIFICENT RULER OF A GREAT KINGDOM. I CAN FEEL HIS VERY ENERGY -- POWERFUL AND IMPOSING.

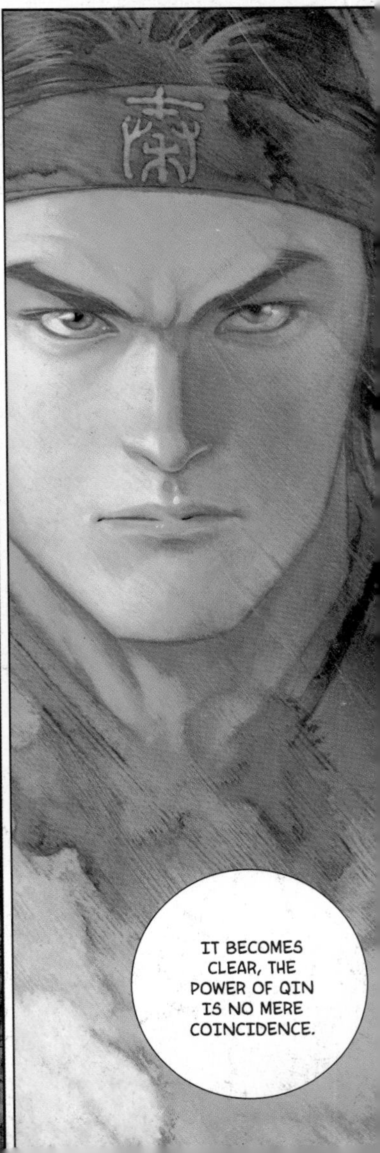
IT BECOMES CLEAR, THE POWER OF QIN IS NO MERE COINCIDENCE.

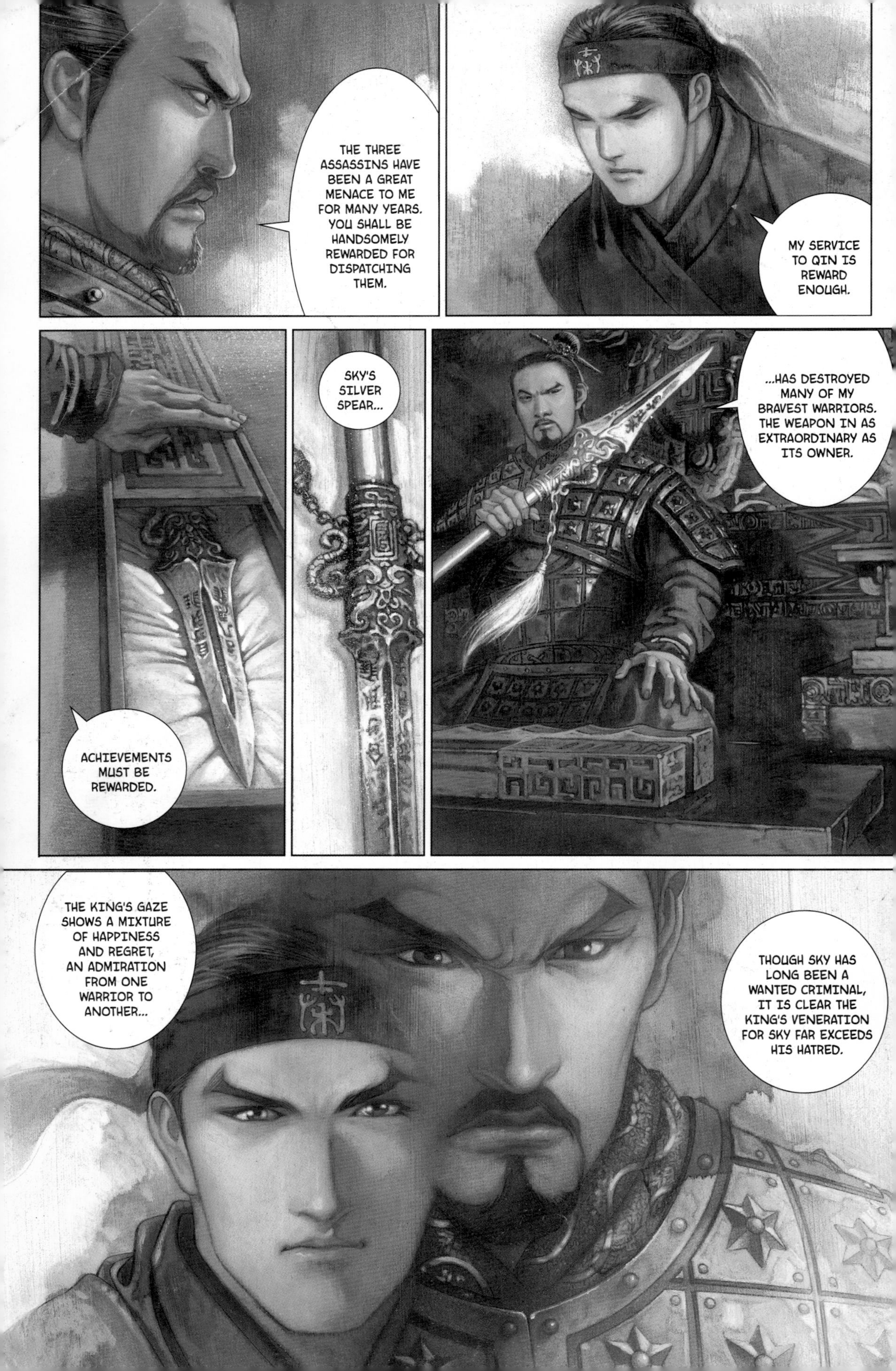
THE THREE ASSASSINS HAVE BEEN A GREAT MENACE TO ME FOR MANY YEARS. YOU SHALL BE HANDSOMELY REWARDED FOR DISPATCHING THEM.
MY SERVICE TO QIN IS REWARD ENOUGH.
ACHIEVEMENTS MUST BE REWARDED.
SKY'S SILVER SPEAR...
...HAS DESTROYED MANY OF MY BRAVEST WARRIORS. THE WEAPON IN AS EXTRAORDINARY AS ITS OWNER.
THE KING'S GAZE SHOWS A MIXTURE OF HAPPINESS AND REGRET, AN ADMIRATION FROM ONE WARRIOR TO ANOTHER...
THOUGH SKY HAS LONG BEEN A WANTED CRIMINAL, IT IS CLEAR THE KING'S VENERATION FOR SKY FAR EXCEEDS HIS HATRED.

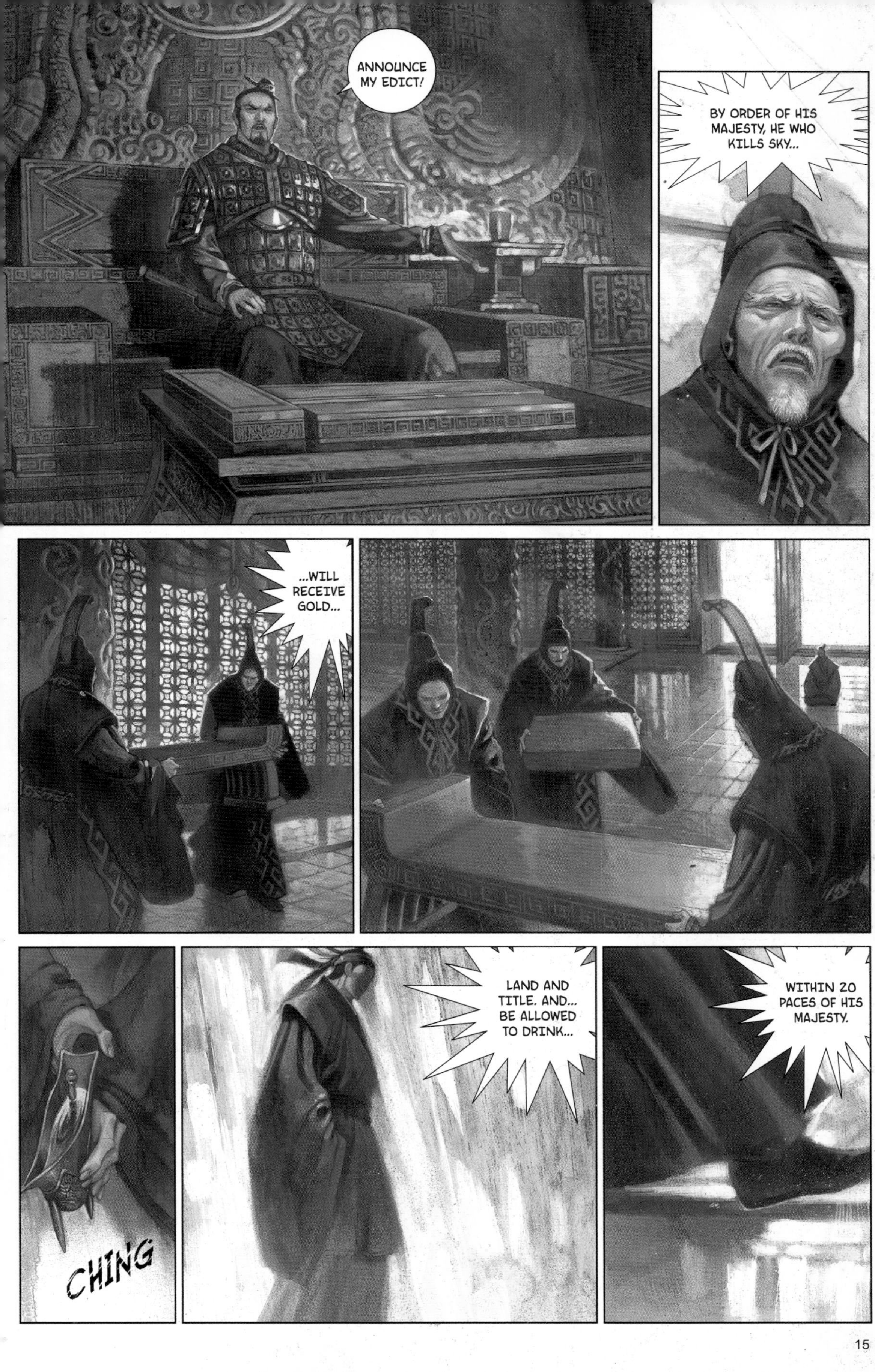
ANNOUNCE MY EDICT!
BY ORDER OF HIS MAJESTY, HE WHO KILLS SKY...
...WILL RECEIVE GOLD...
CHING
LAND AND TITLE. AND... BE ALLOWED TO DRINK...
WITHIN 20 PACES OF HIS MAJESTY.

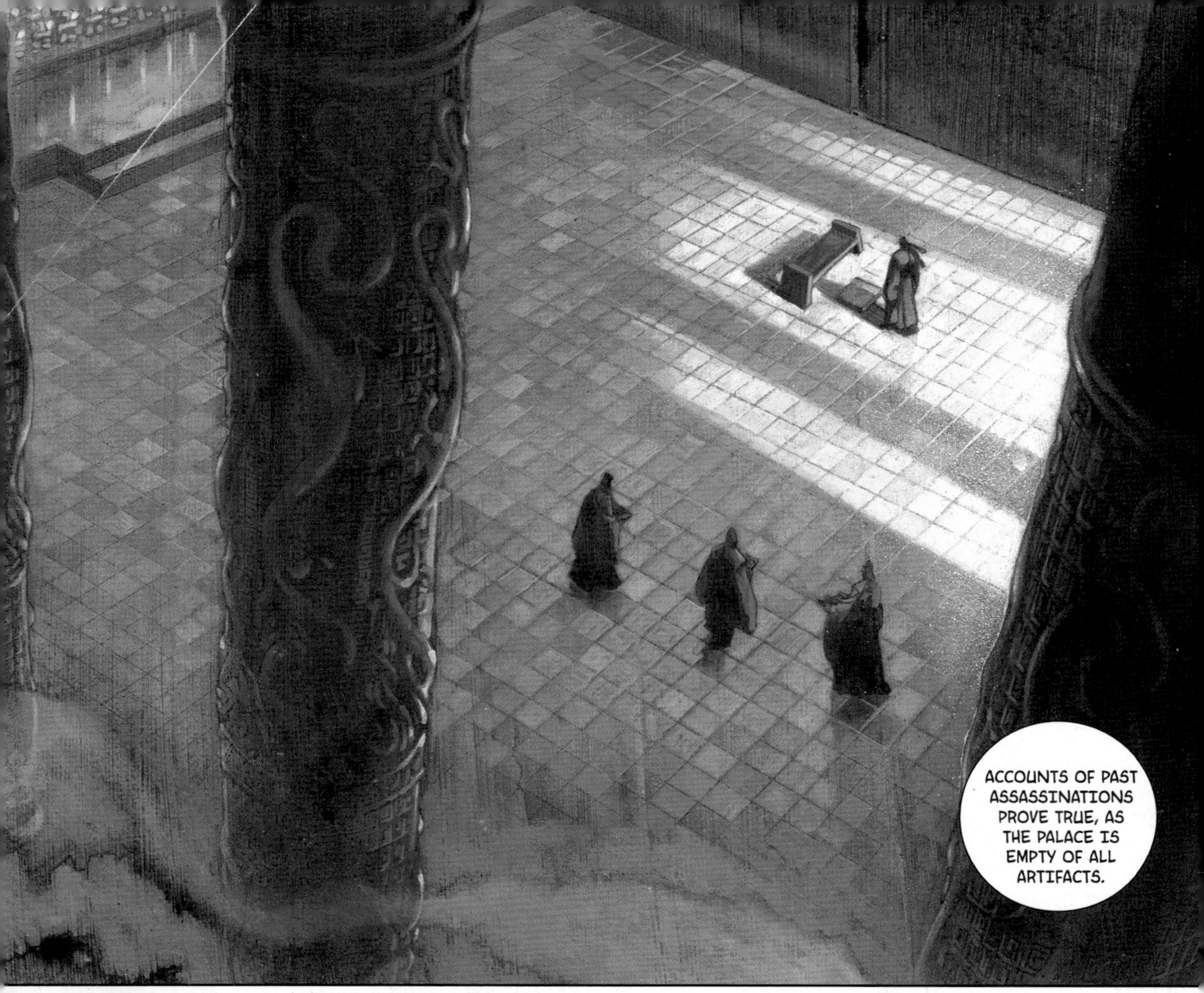
ACCOUNTS OF PAST ASSASSINATIONS PROVE TRUE, AS THE PALACE IS EMPTY OF ALL ARTIFACTS.

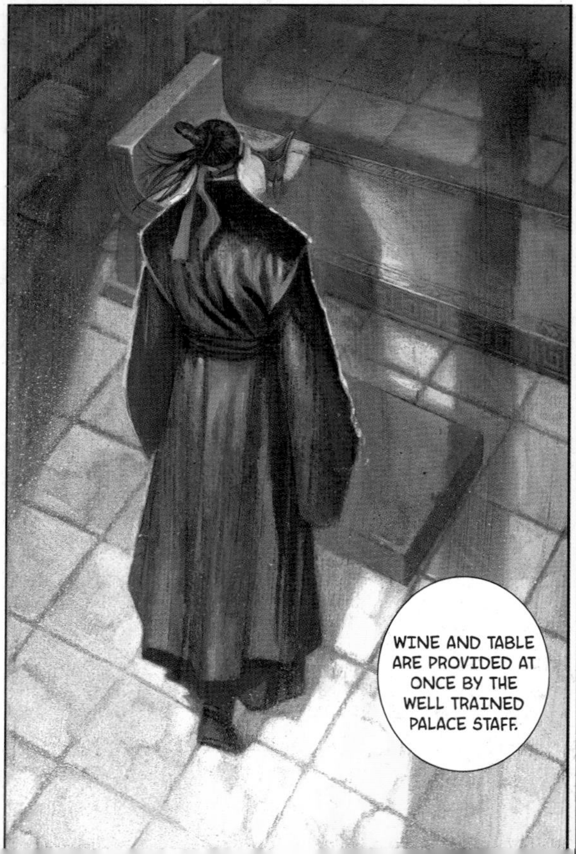
WINE AND TABLE ARE PROVIDED AT ONCE BY THE WELL TRAINED PALACE STAFF.

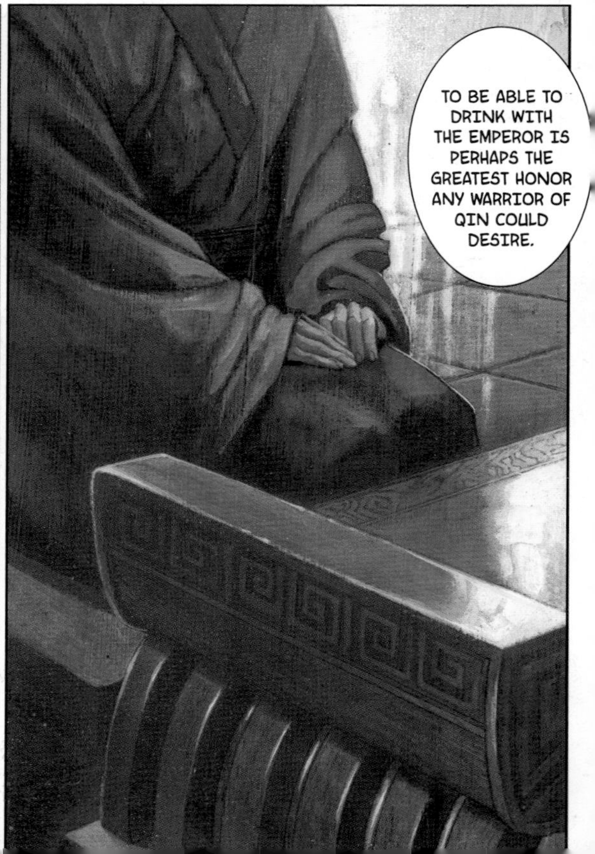
TO BE ABLE TO DRINK WITH THE EMPEROR IS PERHAPS THE GREATEST HONOR ANY WARRIOR OF QIN COULD DESIRE.

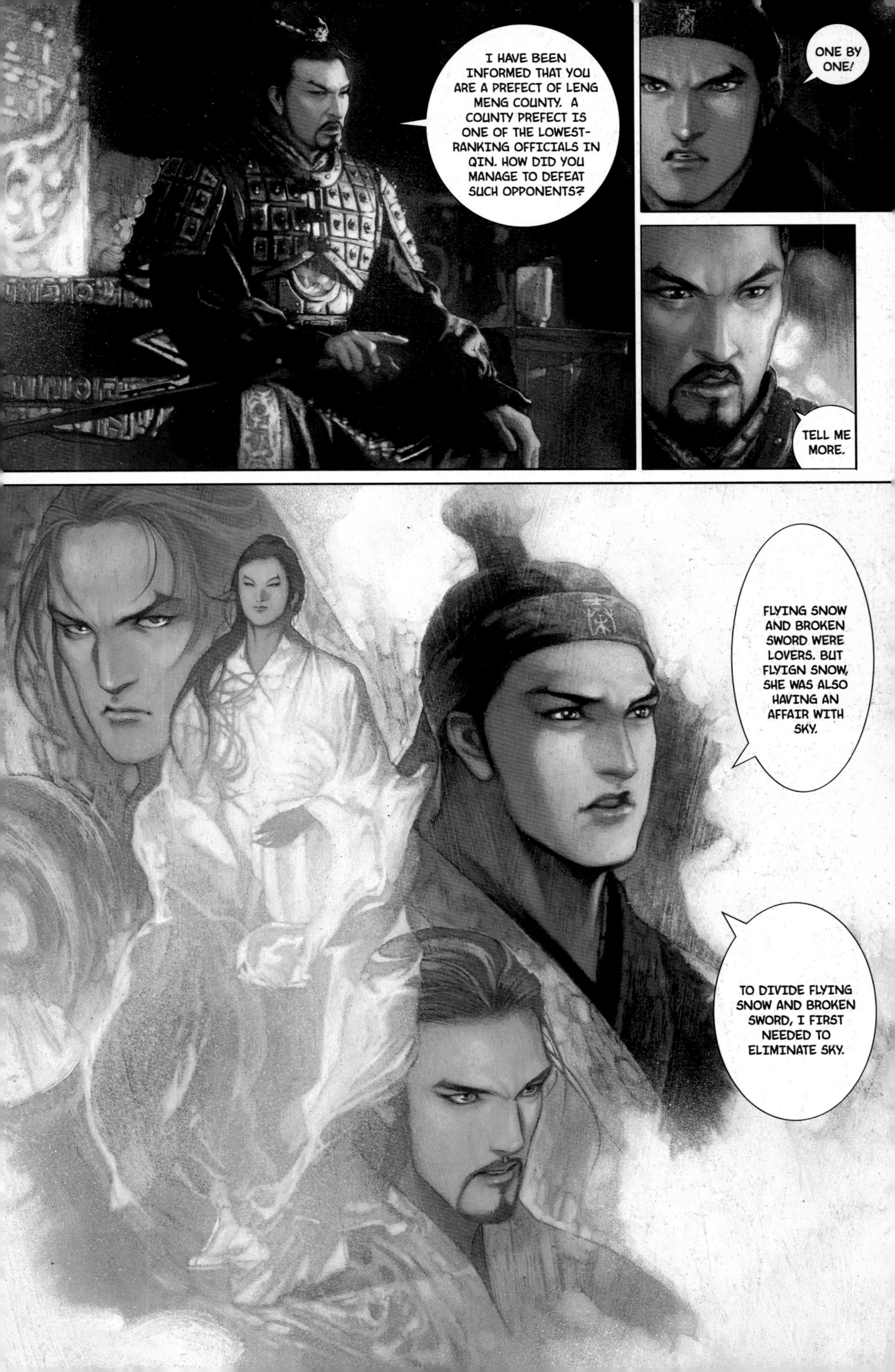
I HAVE BEEN INFORMED THAT YOU ARE A PREFECT OF LENG MENG COUNTY. A COUNTY PREFECT IS ONE OF THE LOWEST-RANKING OFFICIALS IN QIN. HOW DID YOU MANAGE TO DEFEAT SUCH OPPONENTS?
ONE BY ONE!
TELL ME MORE.
FLYING SNOW AND BROKEN SWORD WERE LOVERS. BUT FLYIGN SNOW, SHE WAS ALSO HAVING AN AFFAIR WITH SKY.
TO DIVIDE FLYING SNOW AND BROKEN SWORD, I FIRST NEEDED TO ELIMINATE SKY.

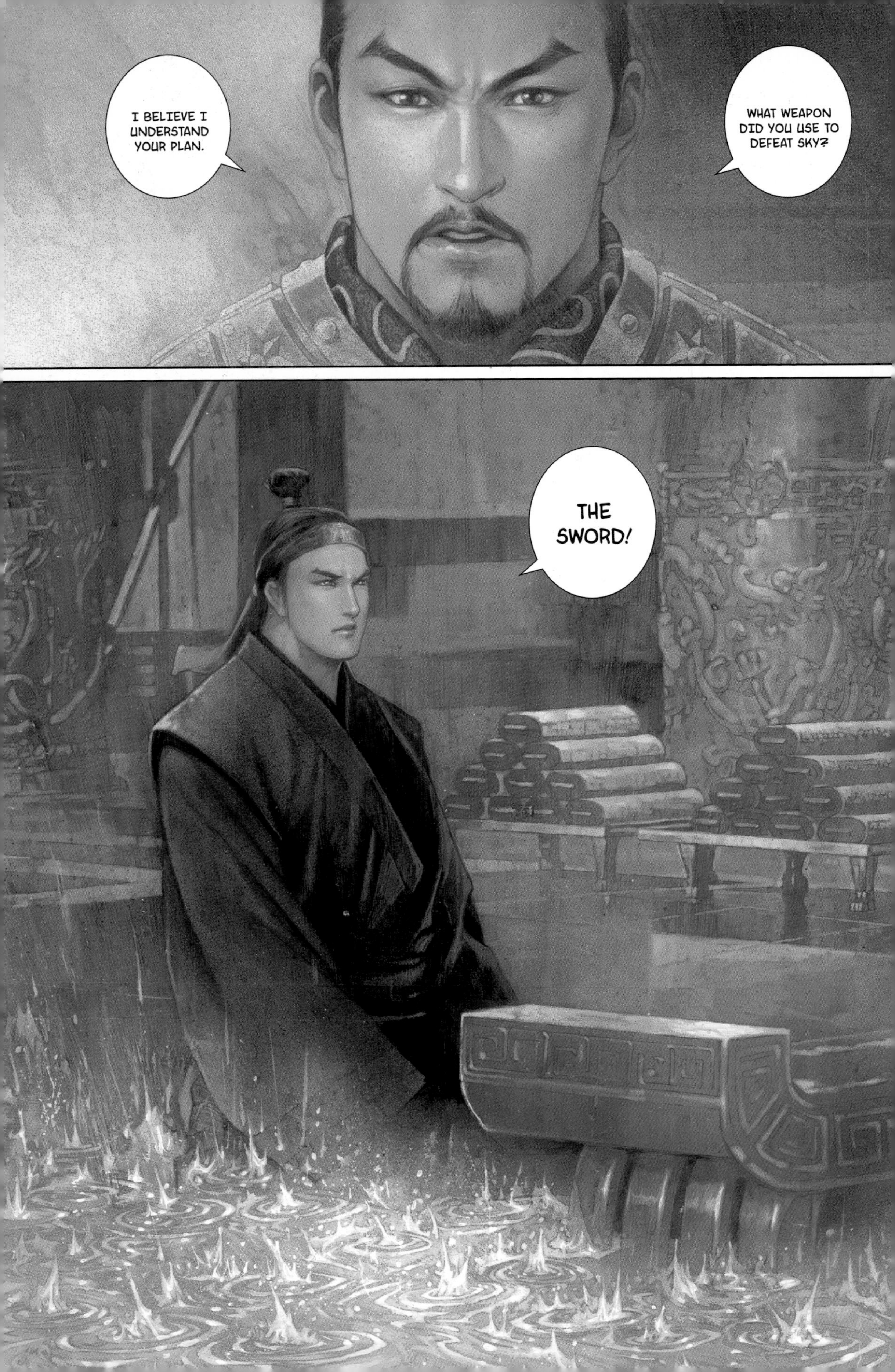
I BELIEVE I UNDERSTAND YOUR PLAN.
WHAT WEAPON DID YOU USE TO DEFEAT SKY?
THE SWORD!

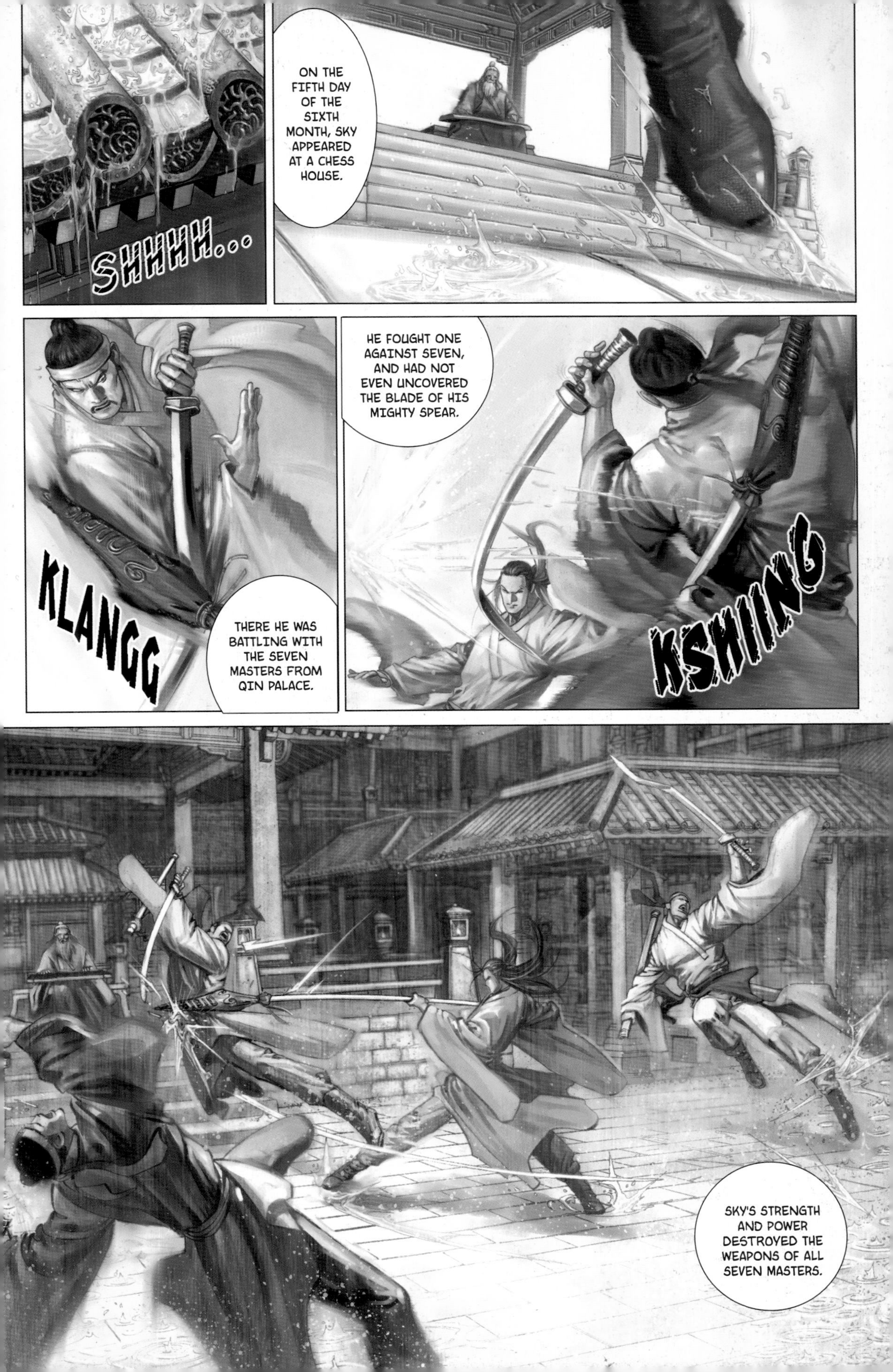

SHHHH...
ON THE FIFTH DAY OF THE SIXTH MONTH, SKY APPEARED AT A CHESS HOUSE.
KLANGG
THERE HE WAS BATTLING WITH THE SEVEN MASTERS FROM QIN PALACE.
HE FOUGHT ONE AGAINST SEVEN, AND HAD NOT EVEN UNCOVERED THE BLADE OF HIS MIGHTY SPEAR.
KSHIING
SKY'S STRENGTH AND POWER DESTROYED THE WEAPONS OF ALL SEVEN MASTERS.

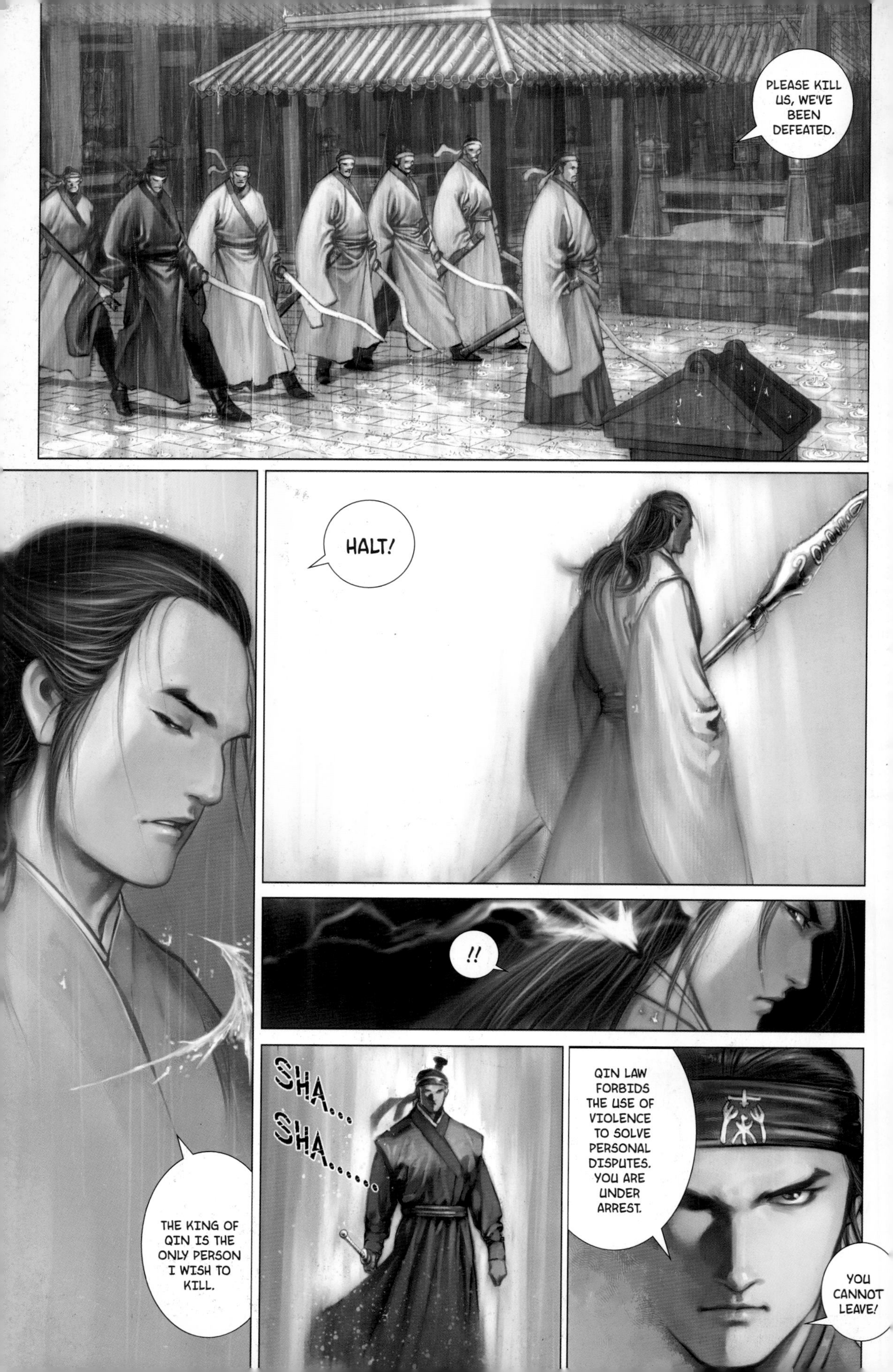
PLEASE KILL US, WE'VE BEEN DEFEATED.
HALT!
!!
THE KING OF QIN IS THE ONLY PERSON I WISH TO KILL.
SHA... SHA......
QIN LAW FORBIDS THE USE OF VIOLENCE TO SOLVE PERSONAL DISPUTES. YOU ARE UNDER ARREST.
YOU CANNOT LEAVE!

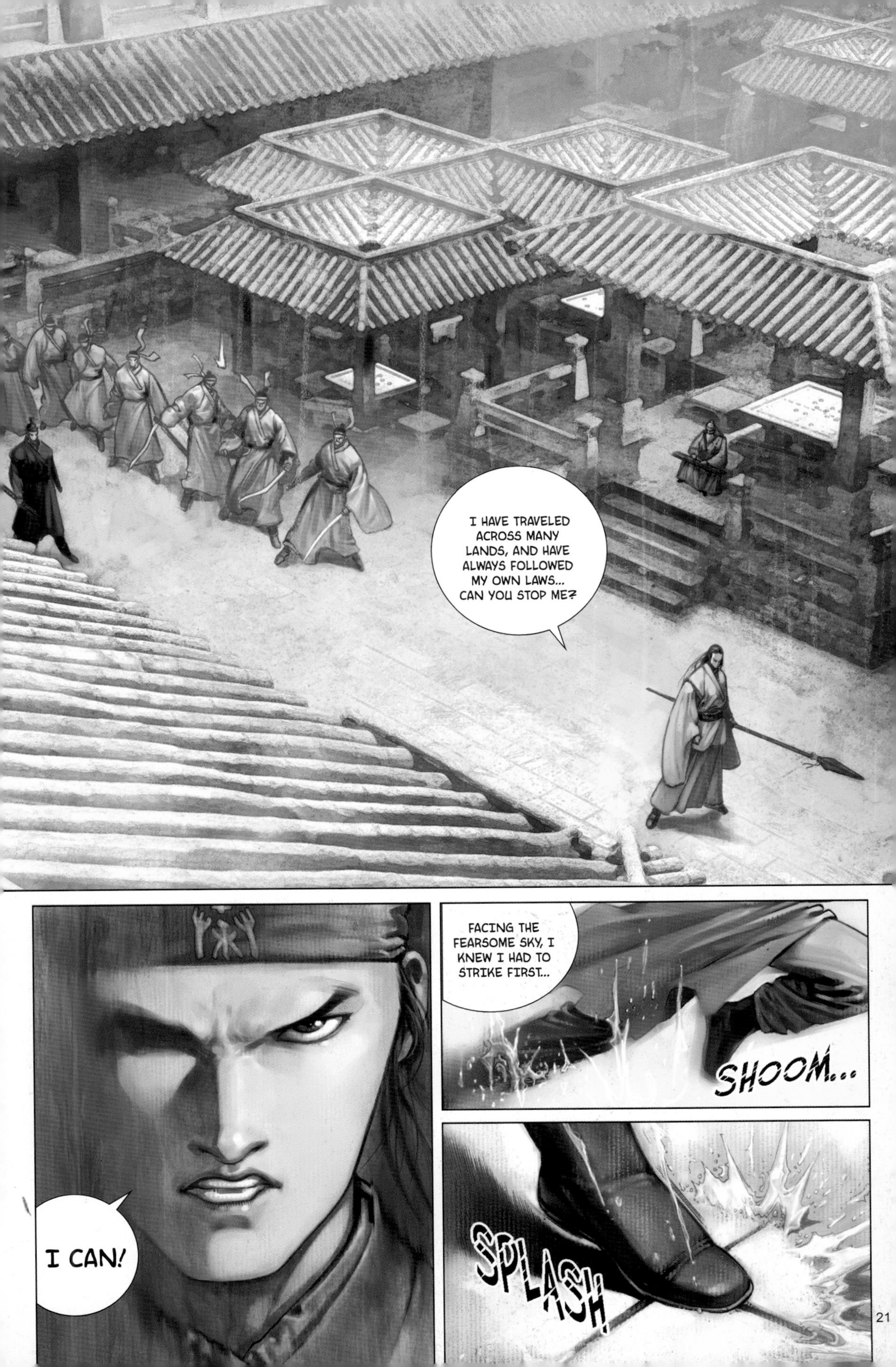
I HAVE TRAVELED ACROSS MANY LANDS, AND HAVE ALWAYS FOLLOWED MY OWN LAWS... CAN YOU STOP ME?
I CAN!
FACING THE FEARSOME SKY, I KNEW I HAD TO STRIKE FIRST...
SHOOM...
SPLASH

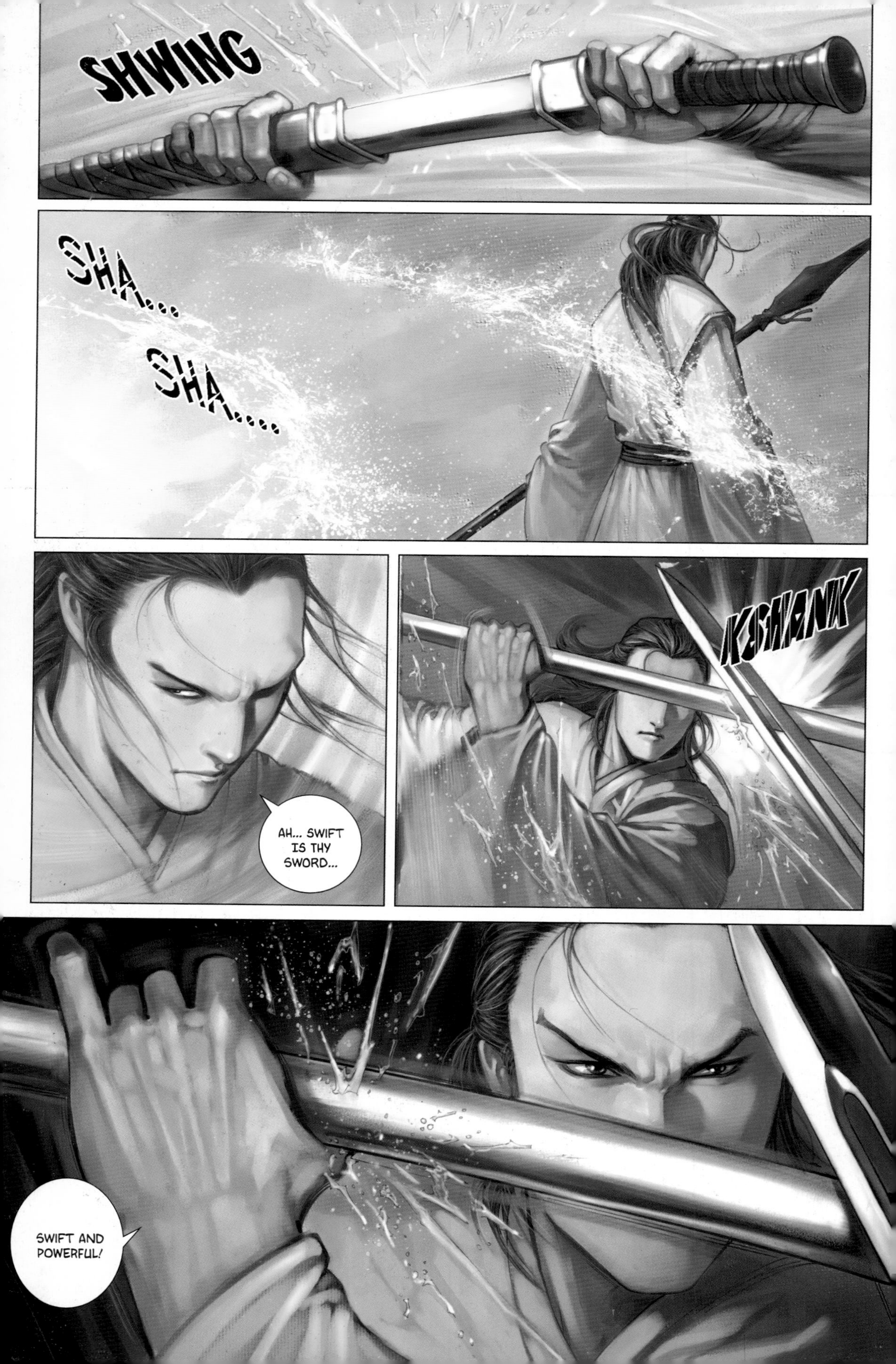
SHWING
SHA...
SHA....
AH... SWIFT IS THY SWORD...
KSHANK
SWIFT AND POWERFUL!

KSHANK

A MERE PREFECT WITH SUCH SKILLS... THE KING OF QIN KNOWS NOT WHAT HE POSSESSES.

SHMM...

SHM...

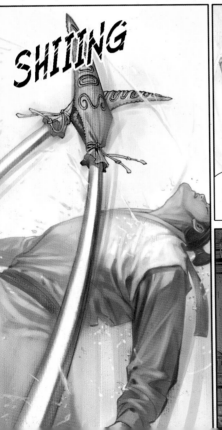

SHIIING

THANK YOU.

AH!

OLD MAN, PLEASE PLAY ONE MORE TUNE.

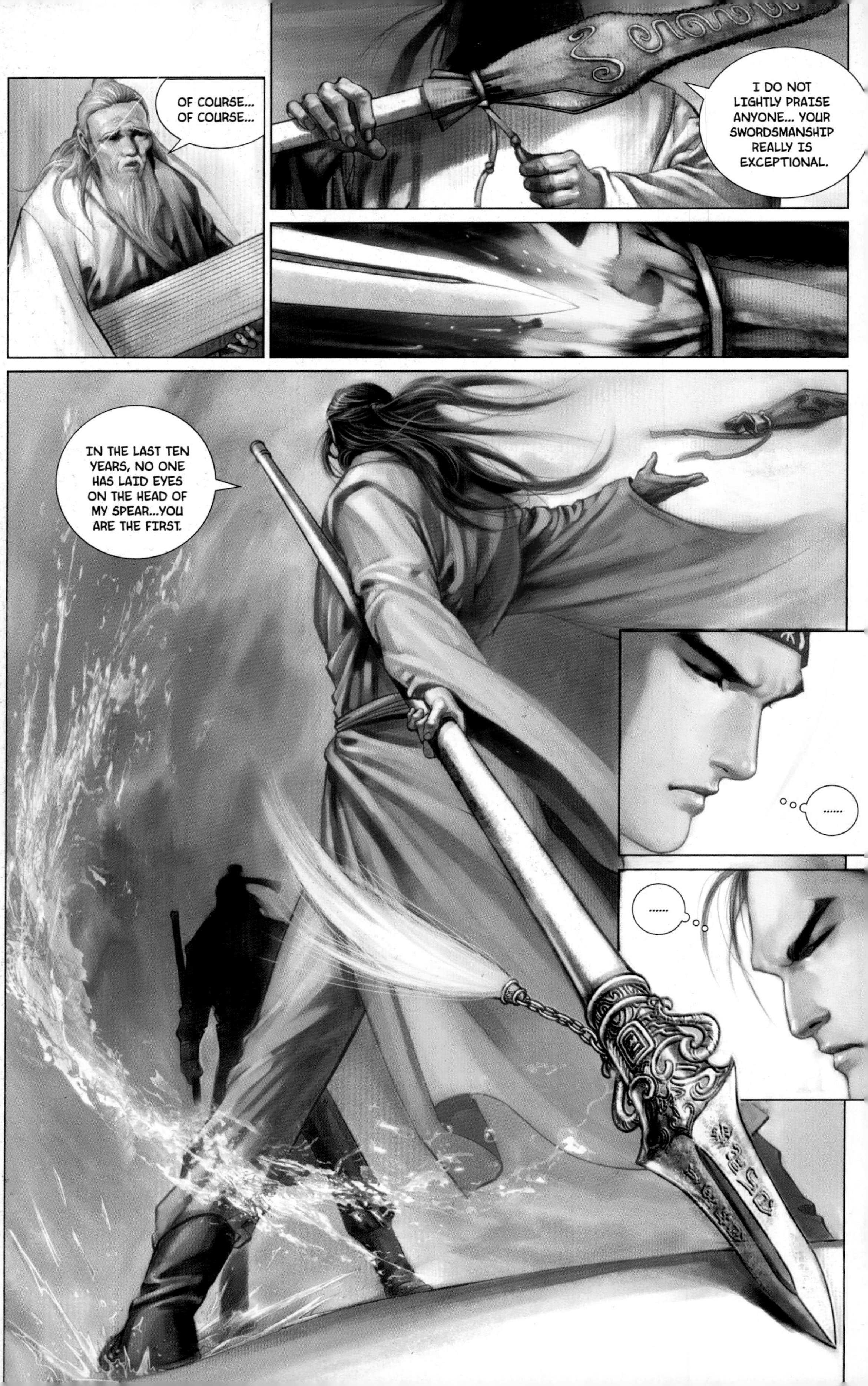
OF COURSE... OF COURSE...
I DO NOT LIGHTLY PRAISE ANYONE... YOUR SWORDSMANSHIP REALLY IS EXCEPTIONAL.
IN THE LAST TEN YEARS, NO ONE HAS LAID EYES ON THE HEAD OF MY SPEAR...YOU ARE THE FIRST.
......
......

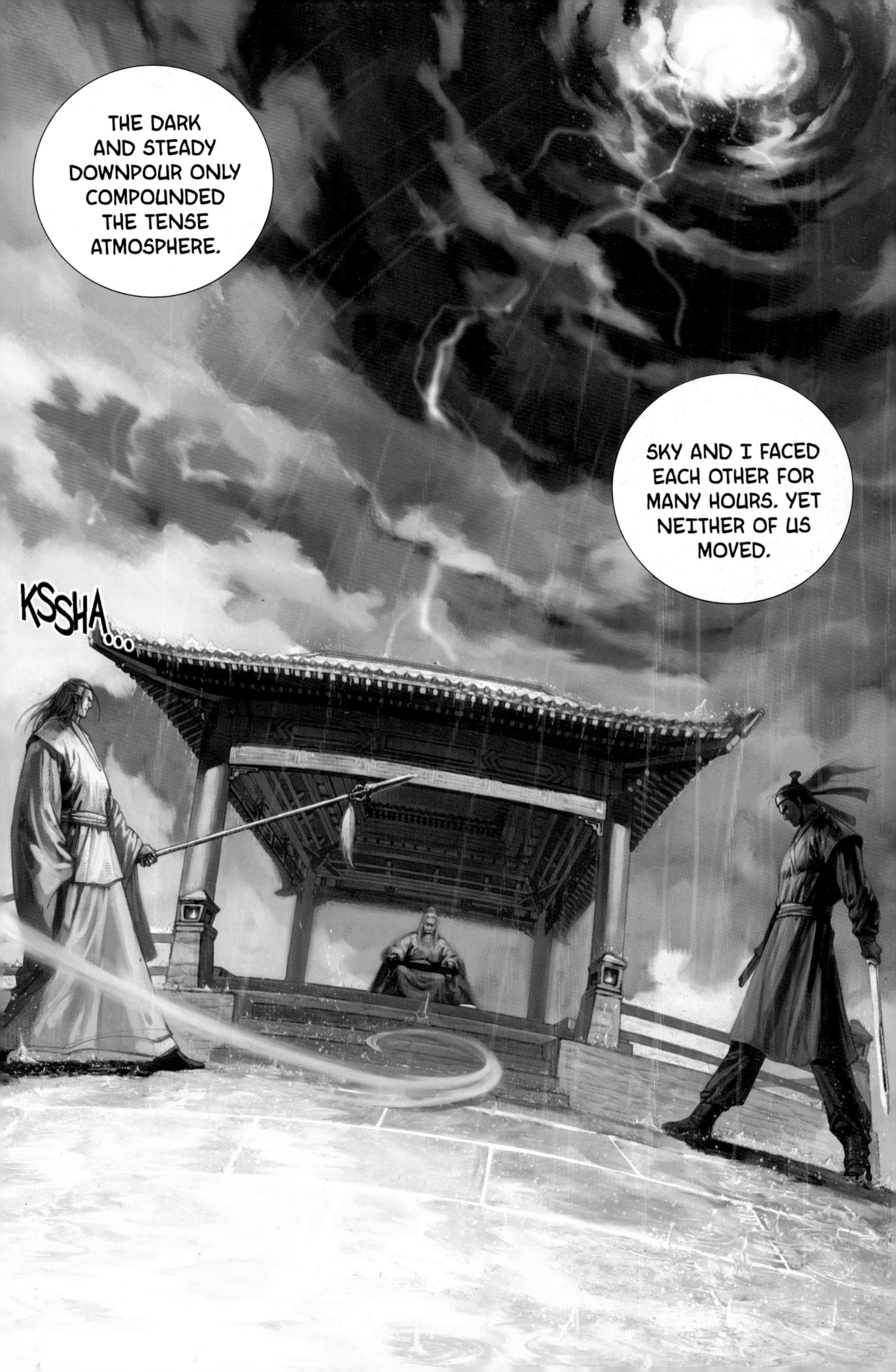
THE DARK AND STEADY DOWNPOUR ONLY COMPOUNDED THE TENSE ATMOSPHERE.
SKY AND I FACED EACH OTHER FOR MANY HOURS. YET NEITHER OF US MOVED.
KSSHA...

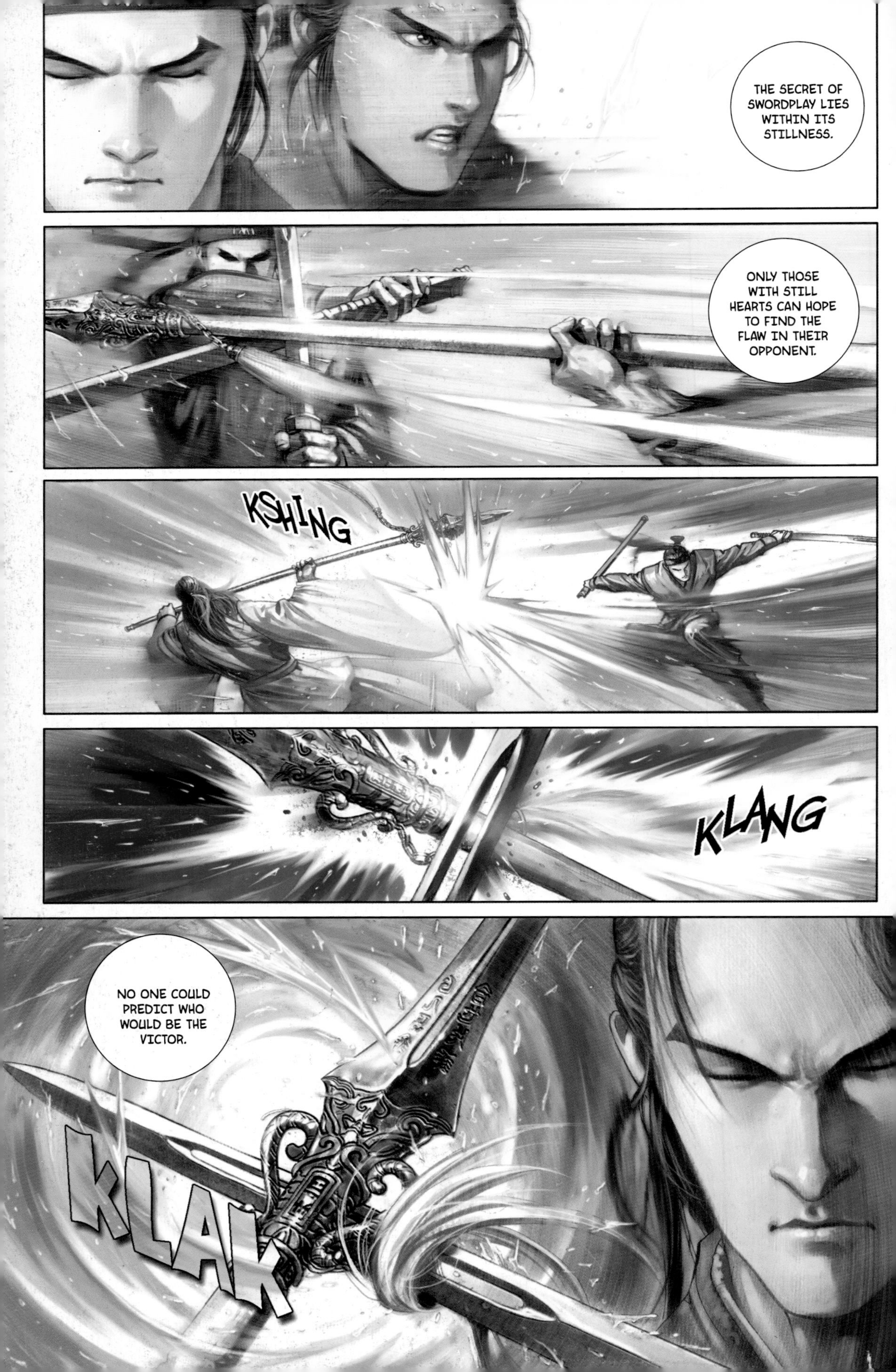
THE SECRET OF SWORDPLAY LIES WITHIN ITS STILLNESS.
ONLY THOSE WITH STILL HEARTS CAN HOPE TO FIND THE FLAW IN THEIR OPPONENT.
KSHING
KLANG
NO ONE COULD PREDICT WHO WOULD BE THE VICTOR.
KLAK

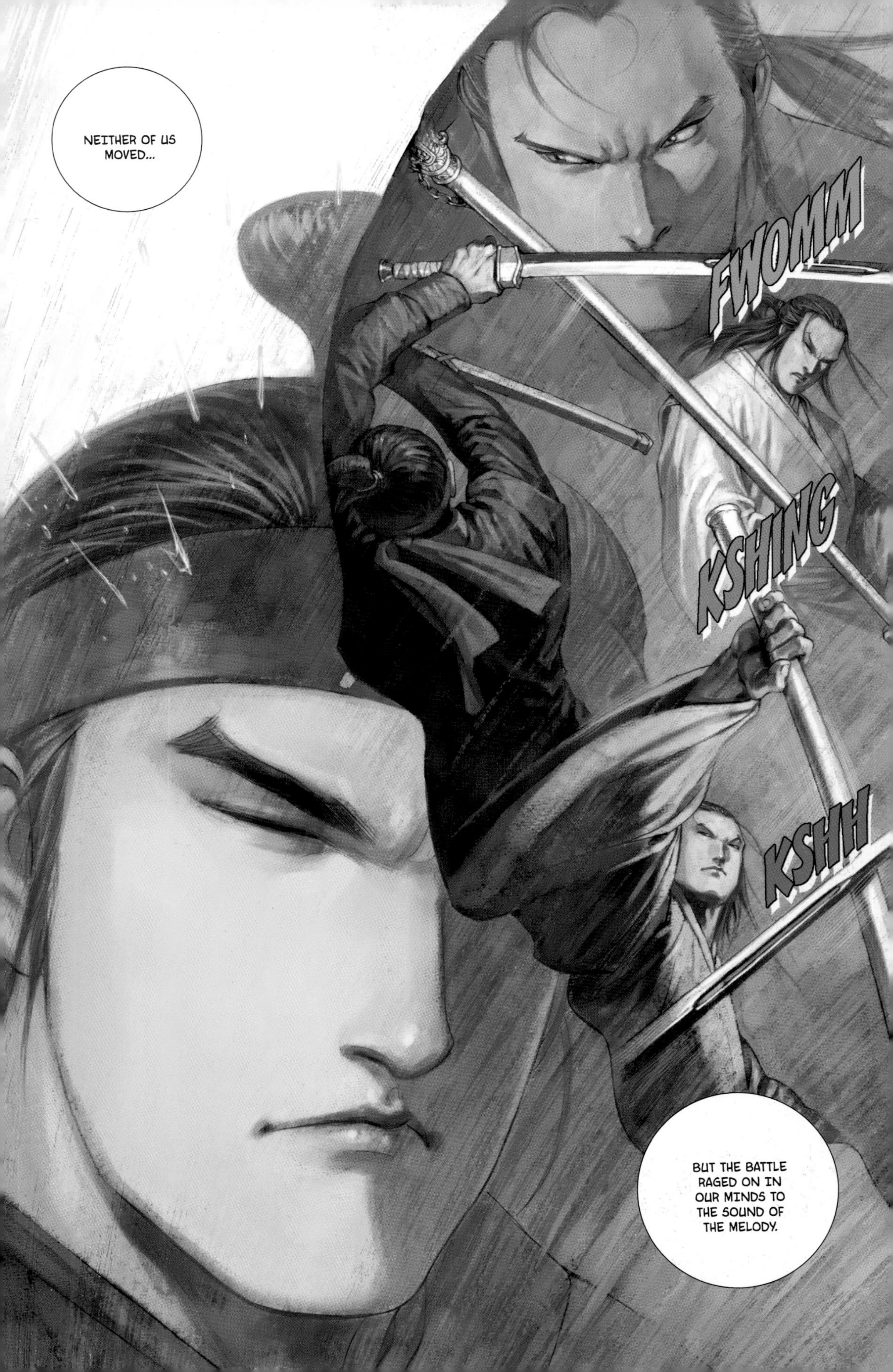
NEITHER OF US MOVED...
FWOMM
KSHING
KSHH
BUT THE BATTLE RAGED ON IN OUR MINDS TO THE SOUND OF THE MELODY.

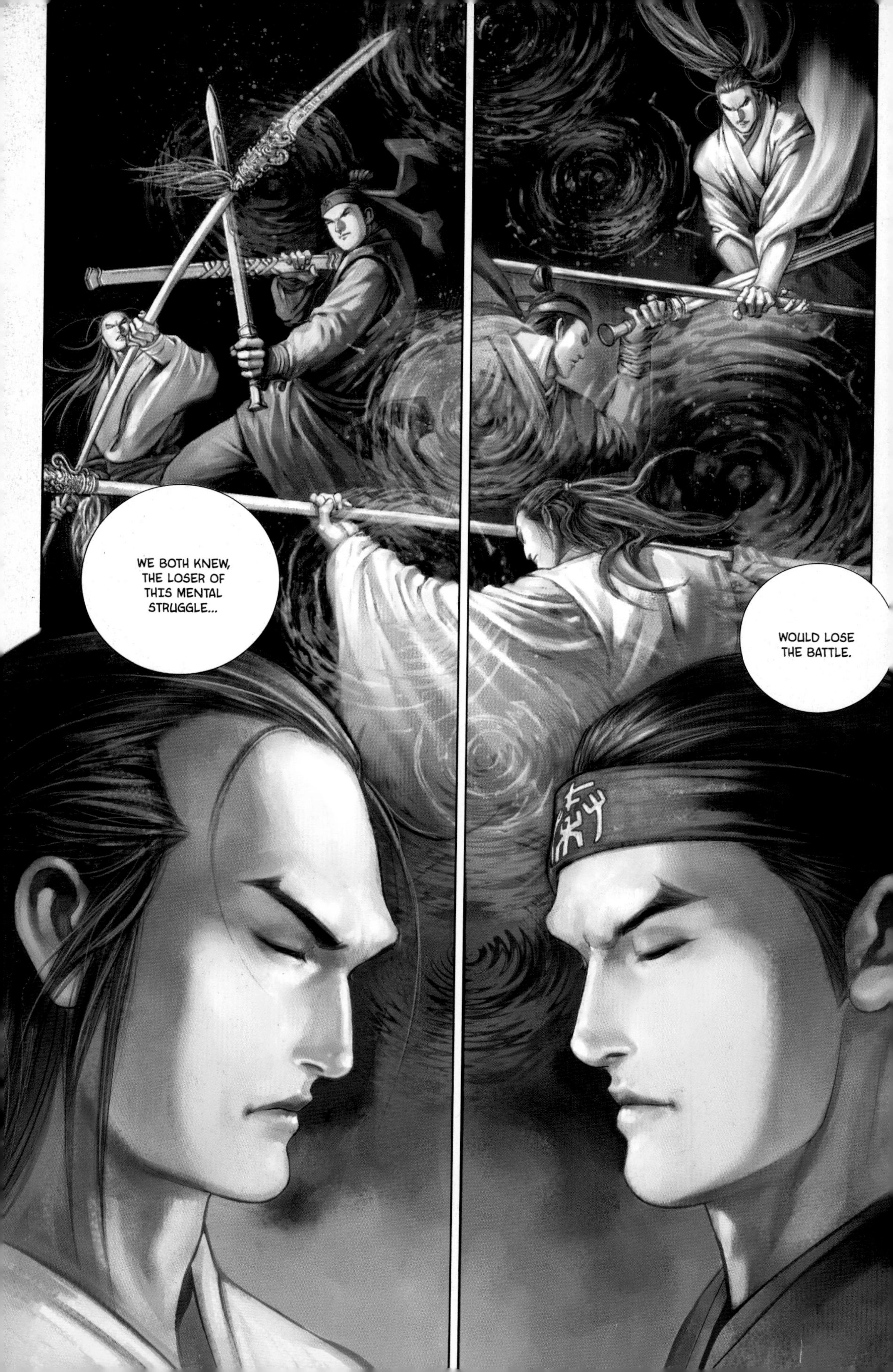
WE BOTH KNEW, THE LOSER OF THIS MENTAL STRUGGLE...
WOULD LOSE THE BATTLE.

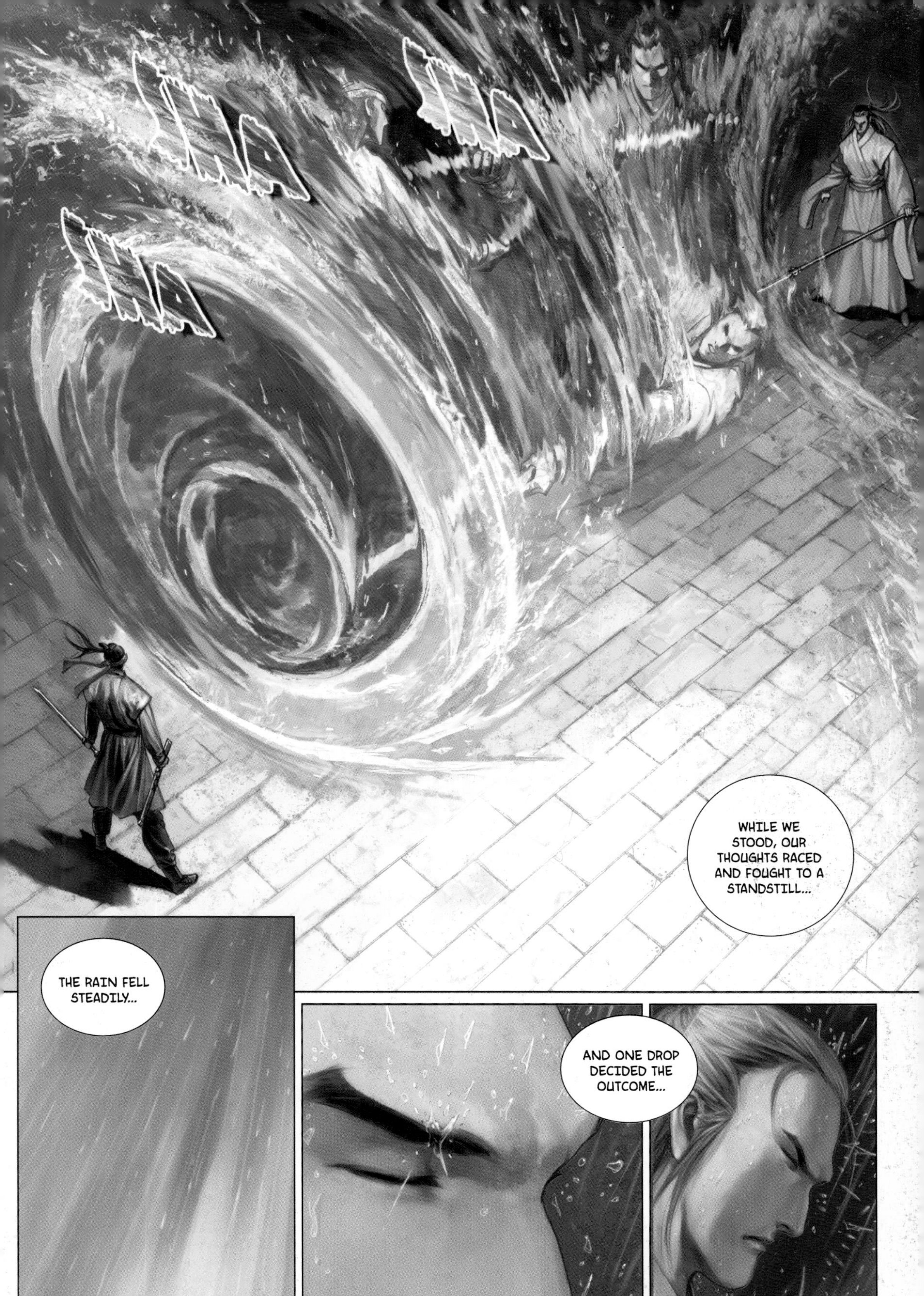
WHILE WE STOOD, OUR THOUGHTS RACED AND FOUGHT TO A STANDSTILL...
THE RAIN FELL STEADILY...
AND ONE DROP DECIDED THE OUTCOME...

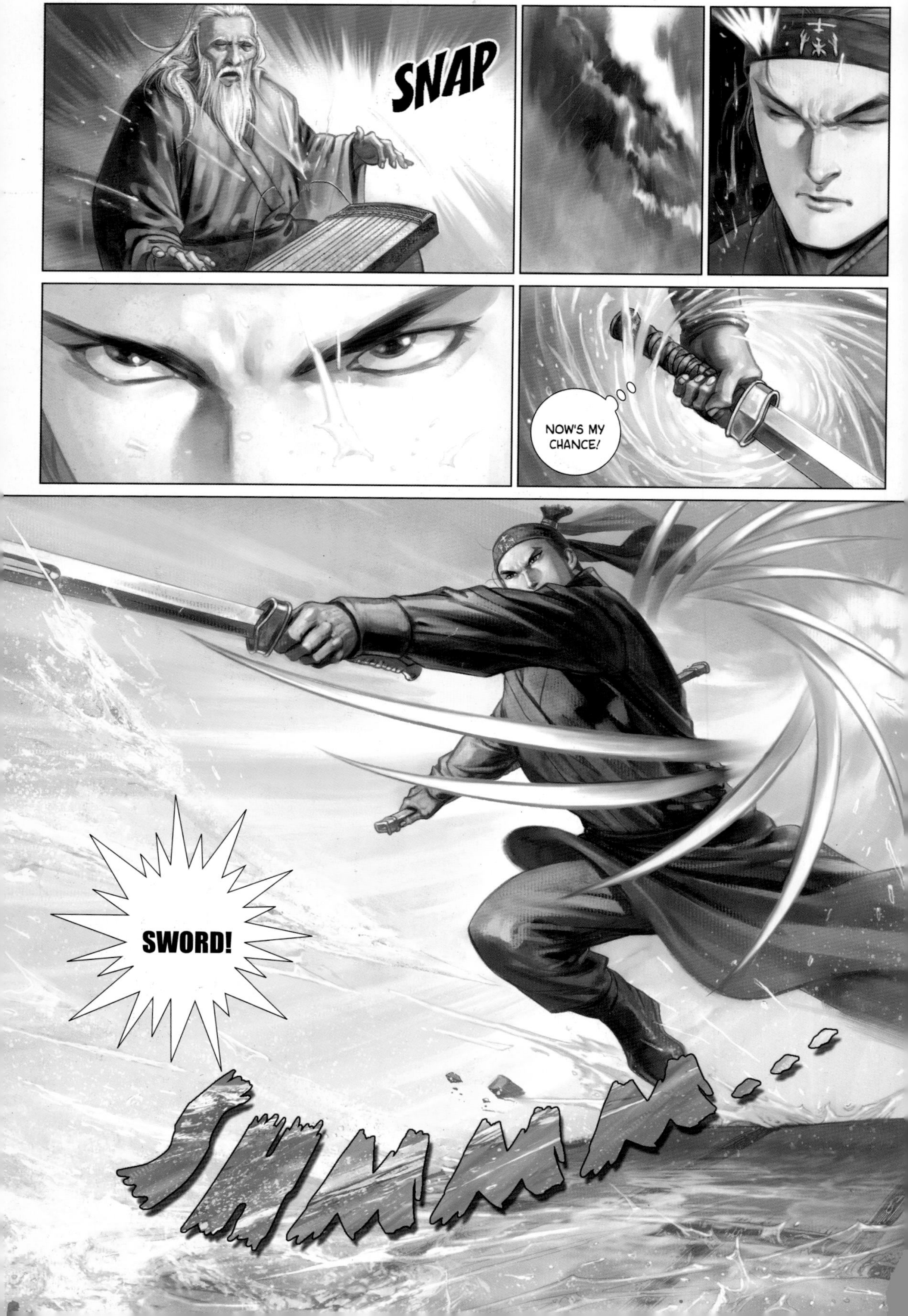
SNAP
NOW'S MY CHANCE!
SWORD!
SHMMM...

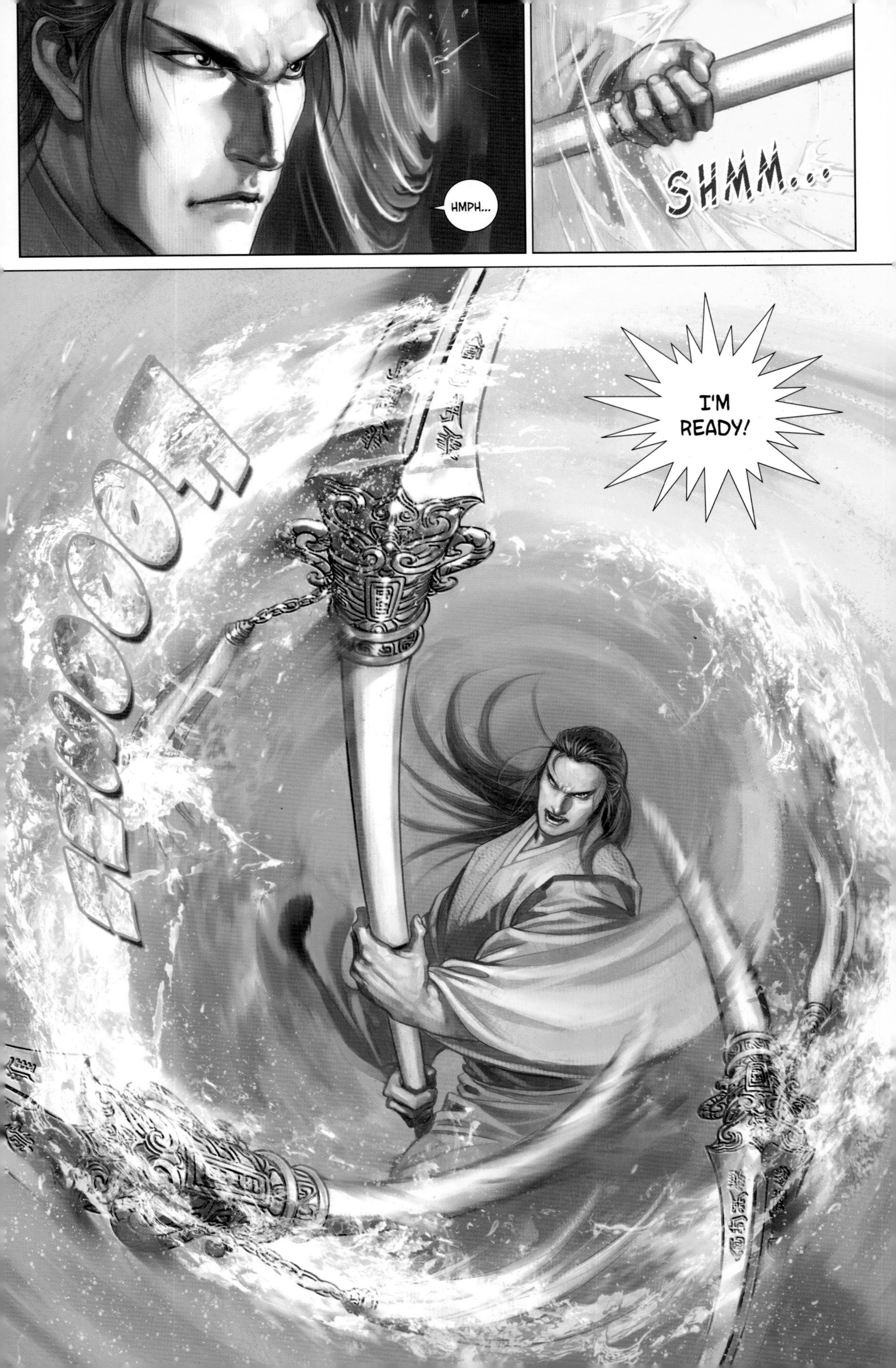
HMPH...
SHMM...
I'M READY!

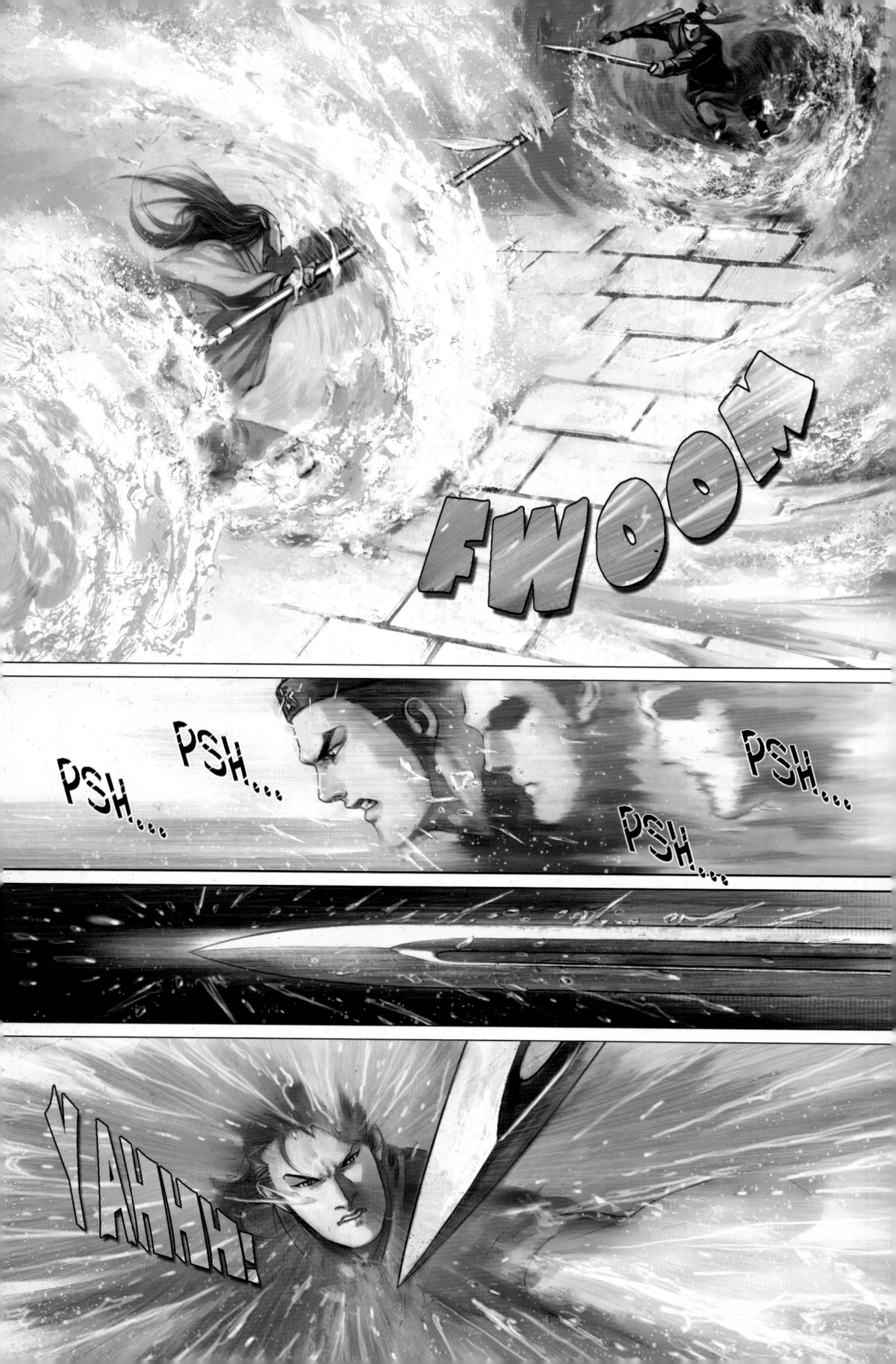
FWOOM
PSH...
PSH...
PSH...
PSH...
YAHHH!

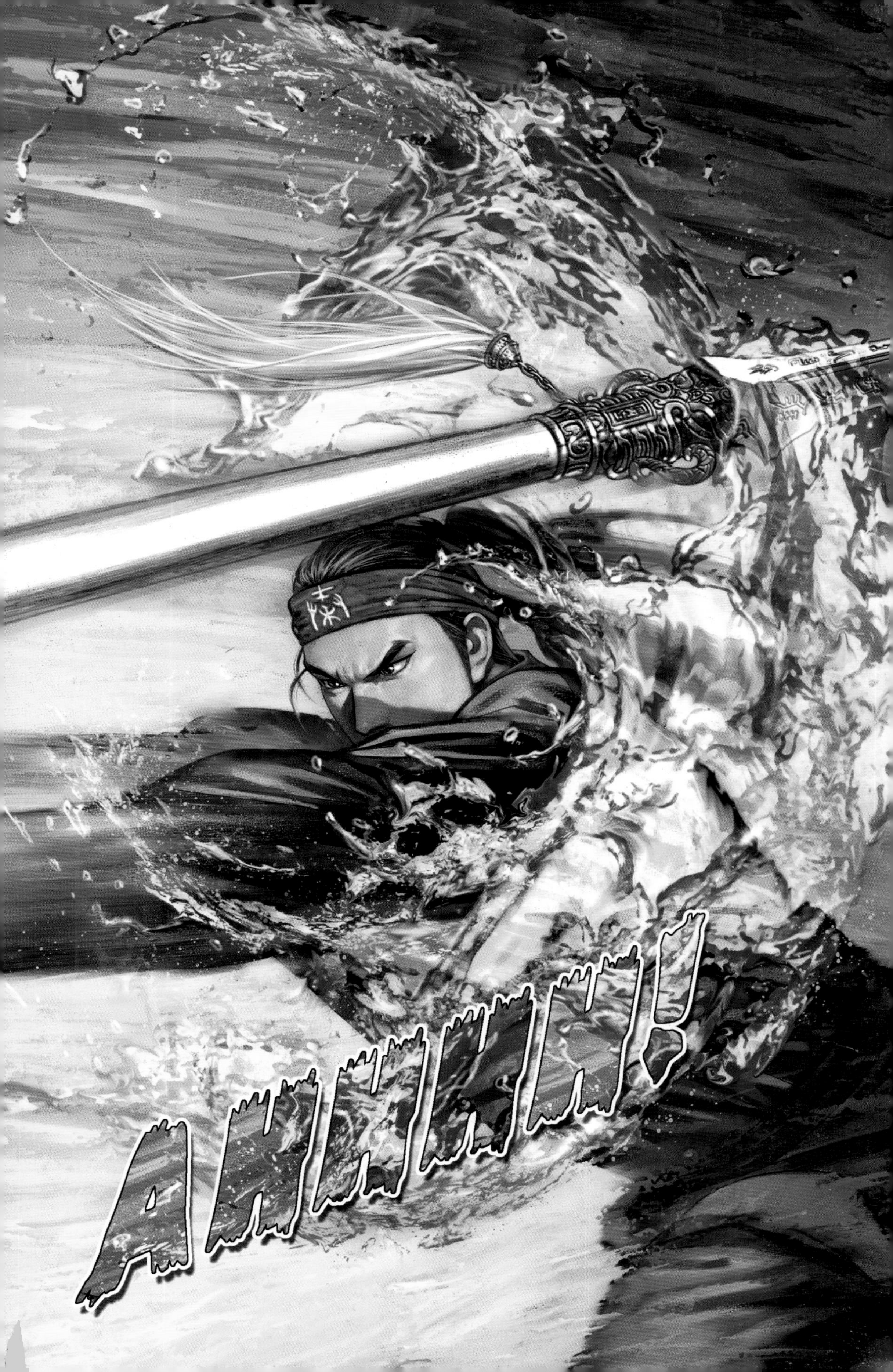
AHHHH!

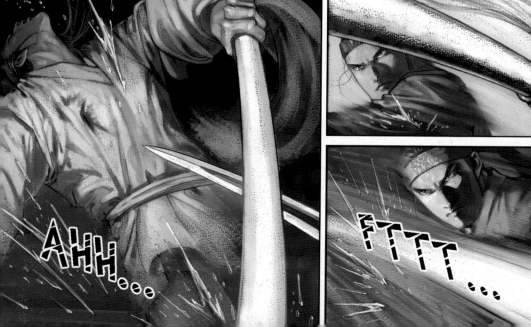

AHH...

FTTT...

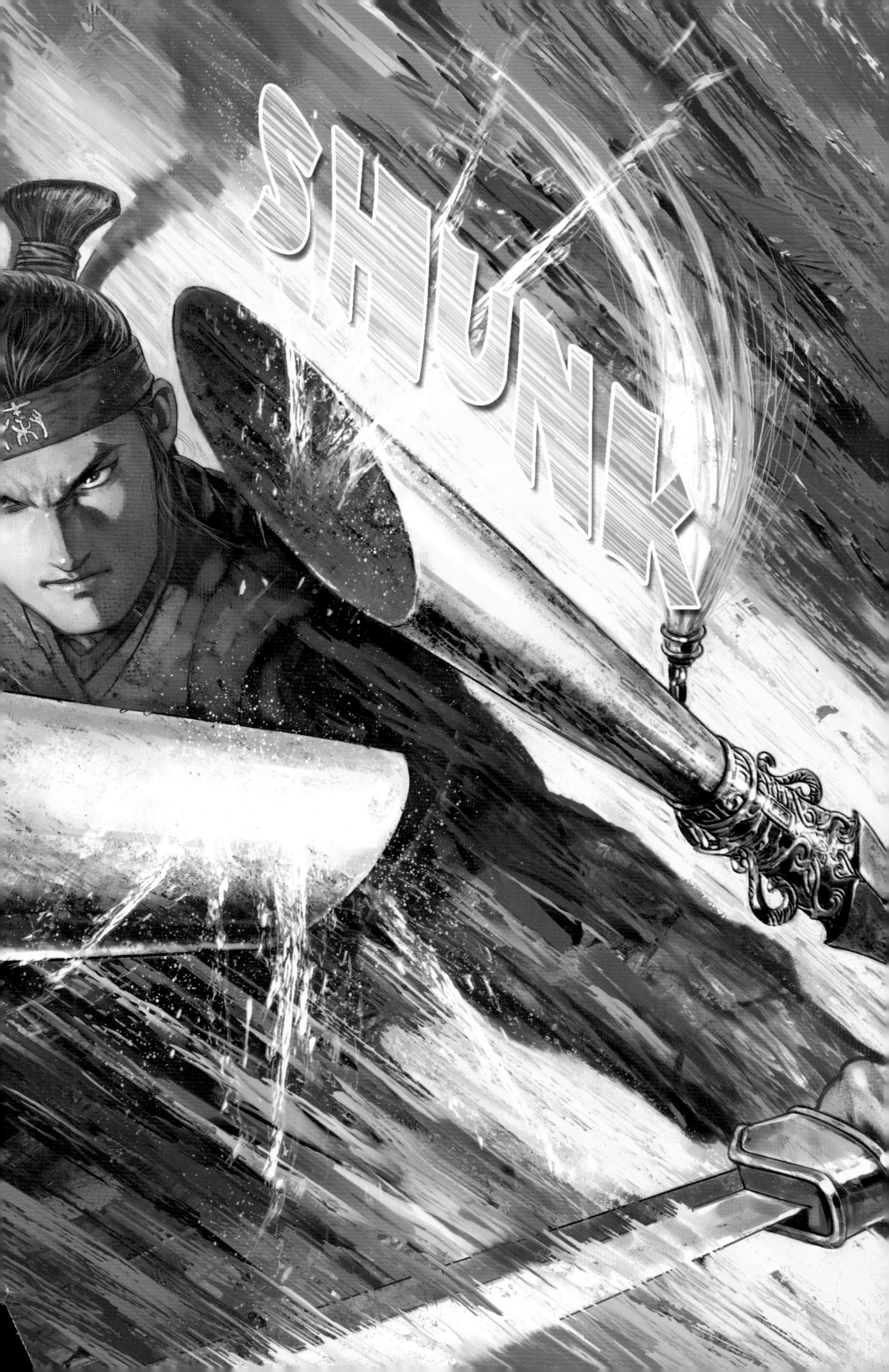
SHUNK

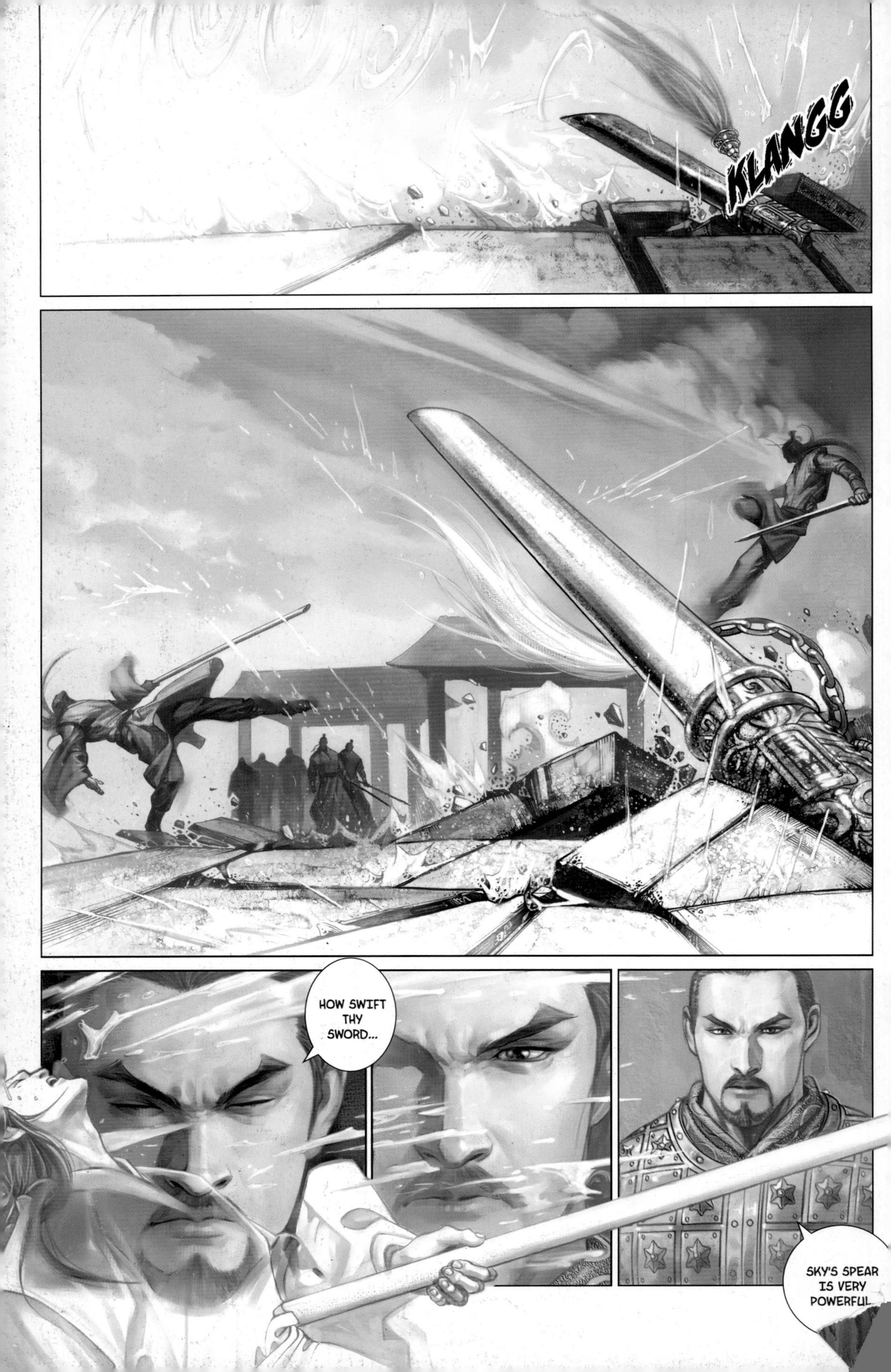
KLANGG
HOW SWIFT THY SWORD...
SKY'S SPEAR IS VERY POWERFUL

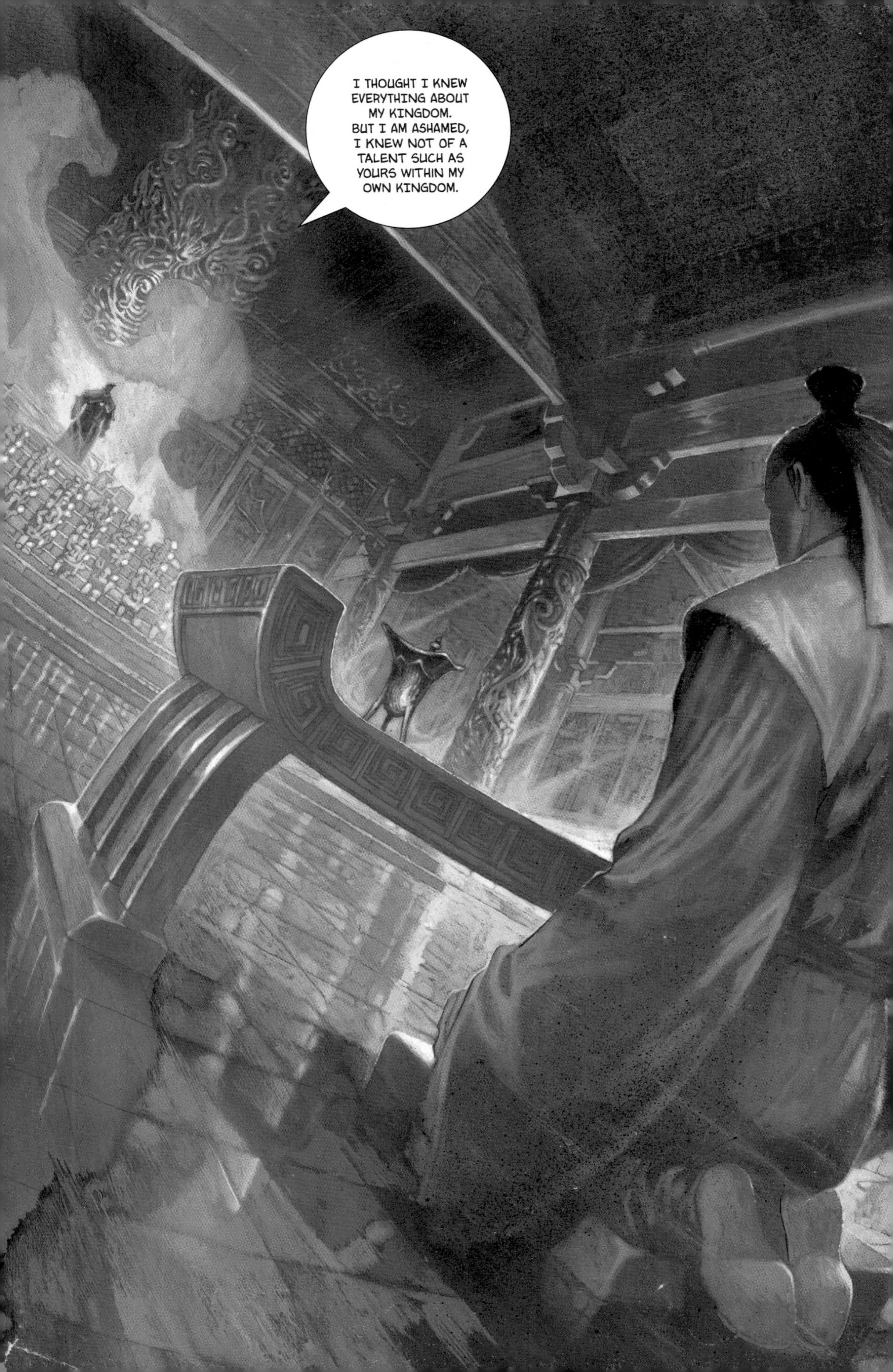
I THOUGHT I KNEW EVERYTHING ABOUT MY KINGDOM. BUT I AM ASHAMED, I KNEW NOT OF A TALENT SUCH AS YOURS WITHIN MY OWN KINGDOM.

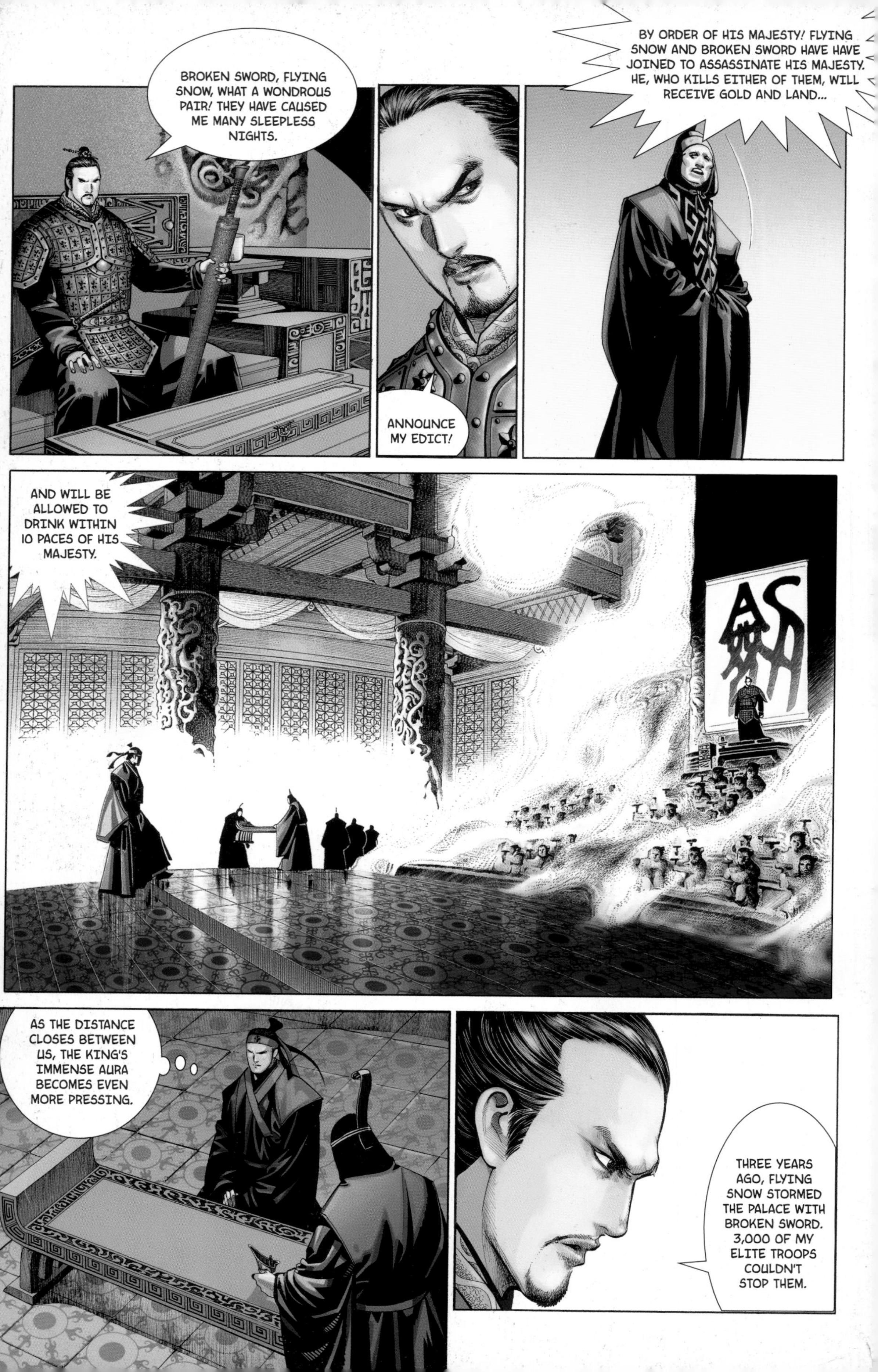
BROKEN SWORD, FLYING SNOW, WHAT A WONDROUS PAIR! THEY HAVE CAUSED ME MANY SLEEPLESS NIGHTS.
ANNOUNCE MY EDICT!
BY ORDER OF HIS MAJESTY! FLYING SNOW AND BROKEN SWORD HAVE HAVE JOINED TO ASSASSINATE HIS MAJESTY. HE, WHO KILLS EITHER OF THEM, WILL RECEIVE GOLD AND LAND...
AND WILL BE ALLOWED TO DRINK WITHIN 10 PACES OF HIS MAJESTY.
AS THE DISTANCE CLOSES BETWEEN US, THE KING'S IMMENSE AURA BECOMES EVEN MORE PRESSING.
THREE YEARS AGO, FLYING SNOW STORMED THE PALACE WITH BROKEN SWORD. 3,000 OF MY ELITE TROOPS COULDN'T STOP THEM.

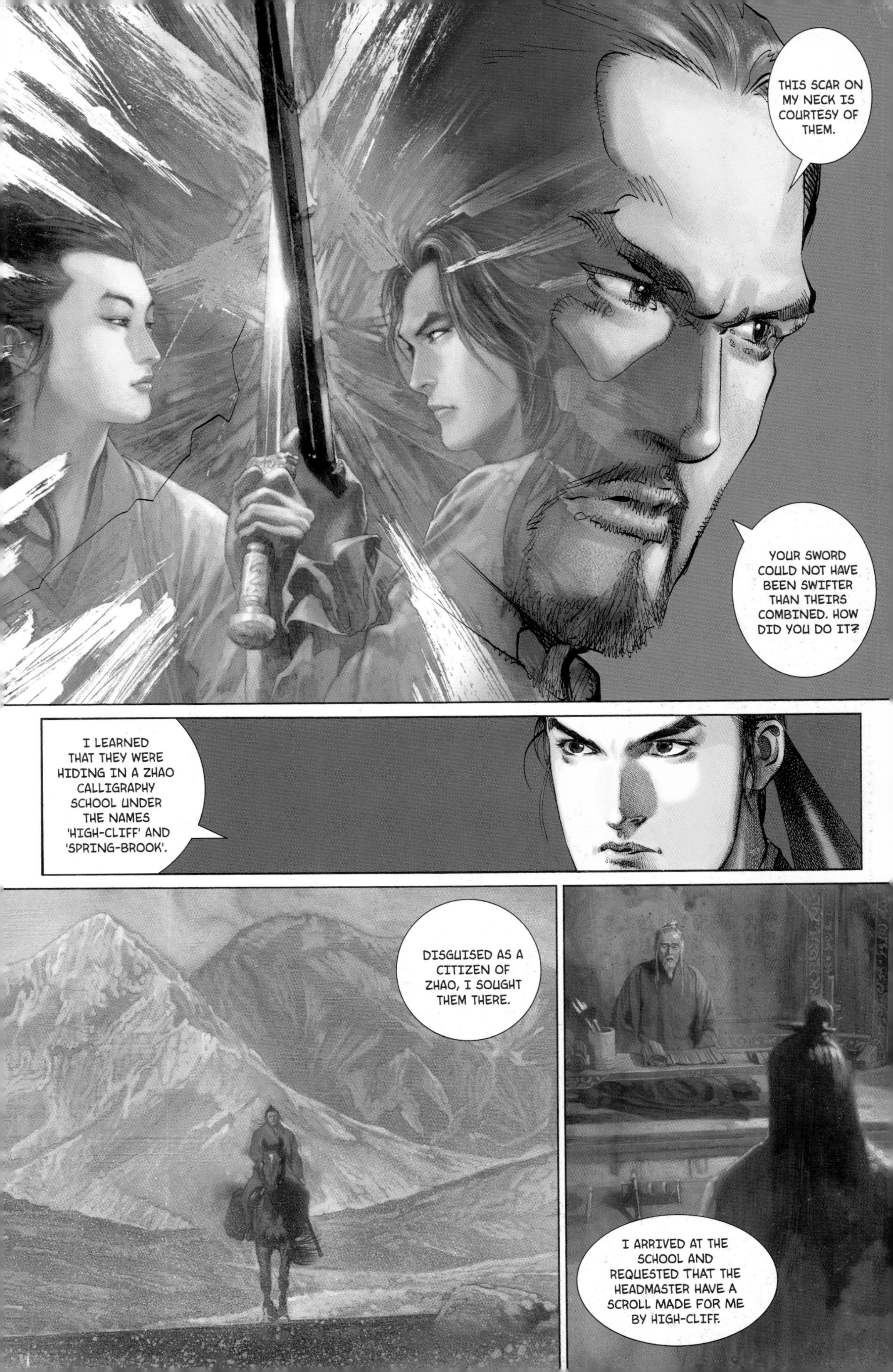
THIS SCAR ON MY NECK IS COURTESY OF THEM.
YOUR SWORD COULD NOT HAVE BEEN SWIFTER THAN THEIRS COMBINED. HOW DID YOU DO IT?
I LEARNED THAT THEY WERE HIDING IN A ZHAO CALLIGRAPHY SCHOOL UNDER THE NAMES 'HIGH-CLIFF' AND 'SPRING-BROOK'.
DISGUISED AS A CITIZEN OF ZHAO, I SOUGHT THEM THERE.
I ARRIVED AT THE SCHOOL AND REQUESTED THAT THE HEADMASTER HAVE A SCROLL MADE FOR ME BY HIGH-CLIFF.

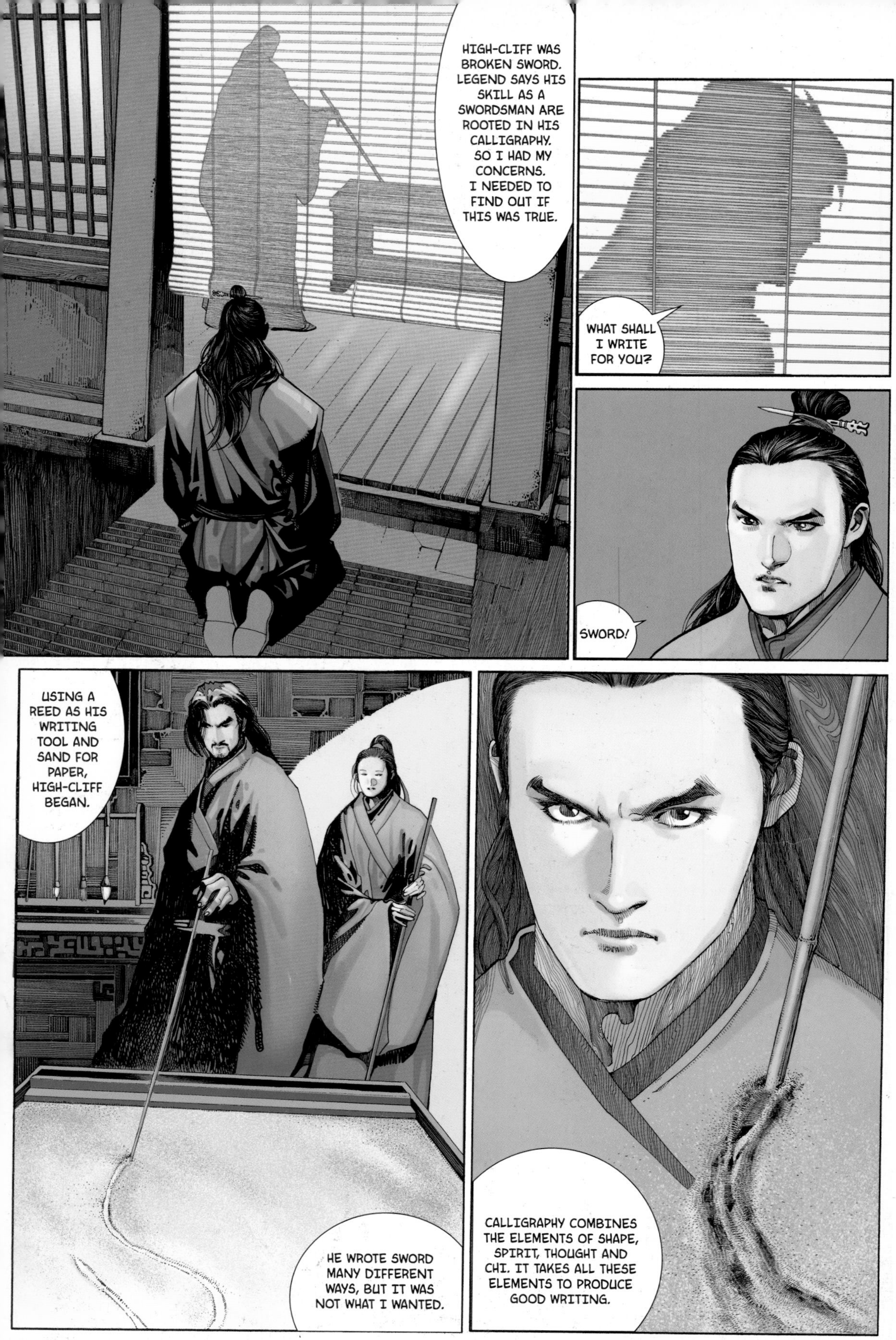
HIGH-CLIFF WAS BROKEN SWORD. LEGEND SAYS HIS SKILL AS A SWORDSMAN ARE ROOTED IN HIS CALLIGRAPHY. SO I HAD MY CONCERNS. I NEEDED TO FIND OUT IF THIS WAS TRUE.
WHAT SHALL I WRITE FOR YOU?
SWORD!
USING A REED AS HIS WRITING TOOL AND SAND FOR PAPER, HIGH-CLIFF BEGAN.
HE WROTE SWORD MANY DIFFERENT WAYS, BUT IT WAS NOT WHAT I WANTED.
CALLIGRAPHY COMBINES THE ELEMENTS OF SHAPE, SPIRIT, THOUGHT AND CHI. IT TAKES ALL THESE ELEMENTS TO PRODUCE GOOD WRITING.

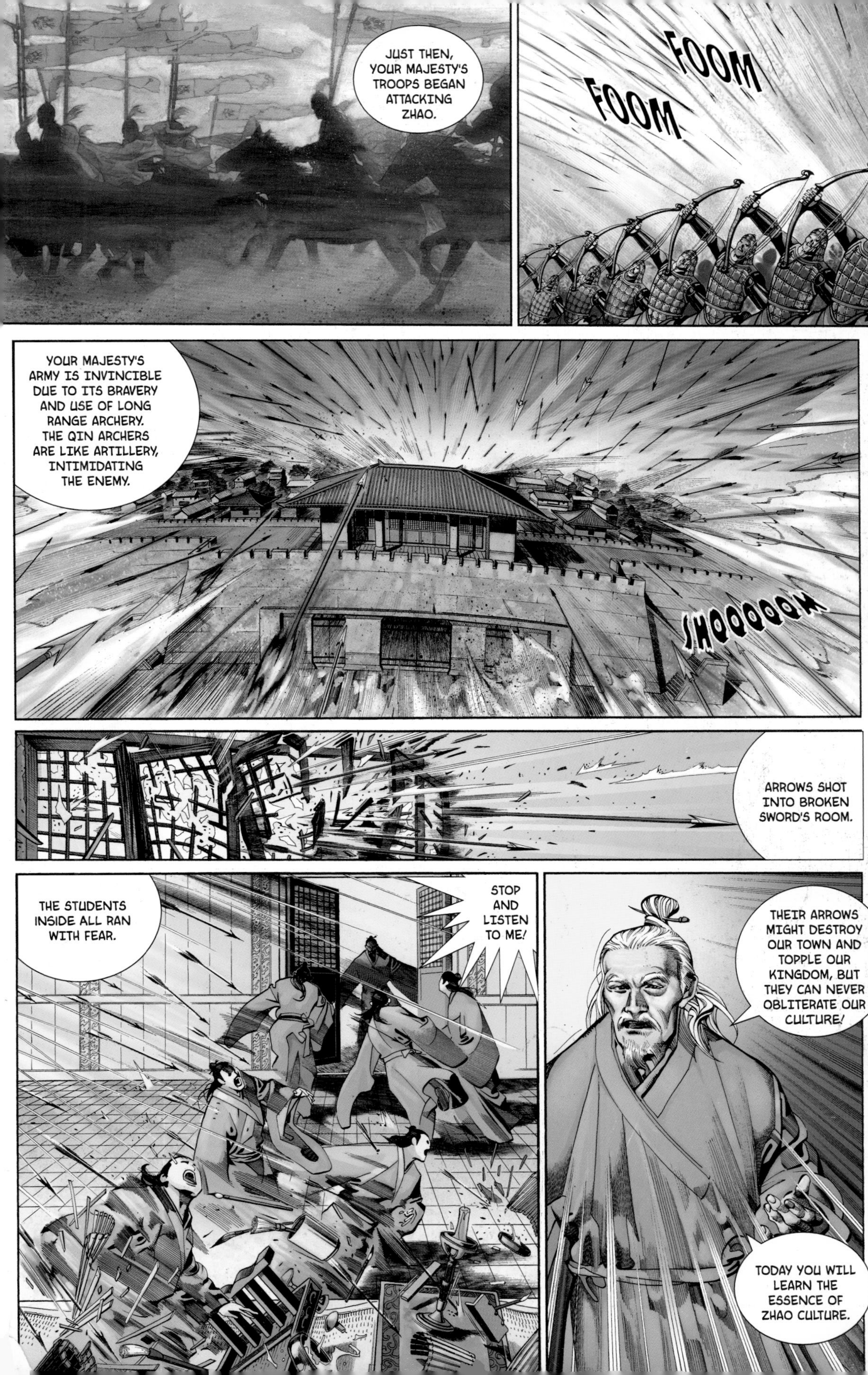
JUST THEN, YOUR MAJESTY'S TROOPS BEGAN ATTACKING ZHAO.
FOOM
FOOM
YOUR MAJESTY'S ARMY IS INVINCIBLE DUE TO ITS BRAVERY AND USE OF LONG RANGE ARCHERY. THE QIN ARCHERS ARE LIKE ARTILLERY, INTIMIDATING THE ENEMY.
SHOOOOOM
ARROWS SHOT INTO BROKEN SWORD'S ROOM.
THE STUDENTS INSIDE ALL RAN WITH FEAR.
STOP AND LISTEN TO ME!
THEIR ARROWS MIGHT DESTROY OUR TOWN AND TOPPLE OUR KINGDOM, BUT THEY CAN NEVER OBLITERATE OUR CULTURE!
TODAY YOU WILL LEARN THE ESSENCE OF ZHAO CULTURE.

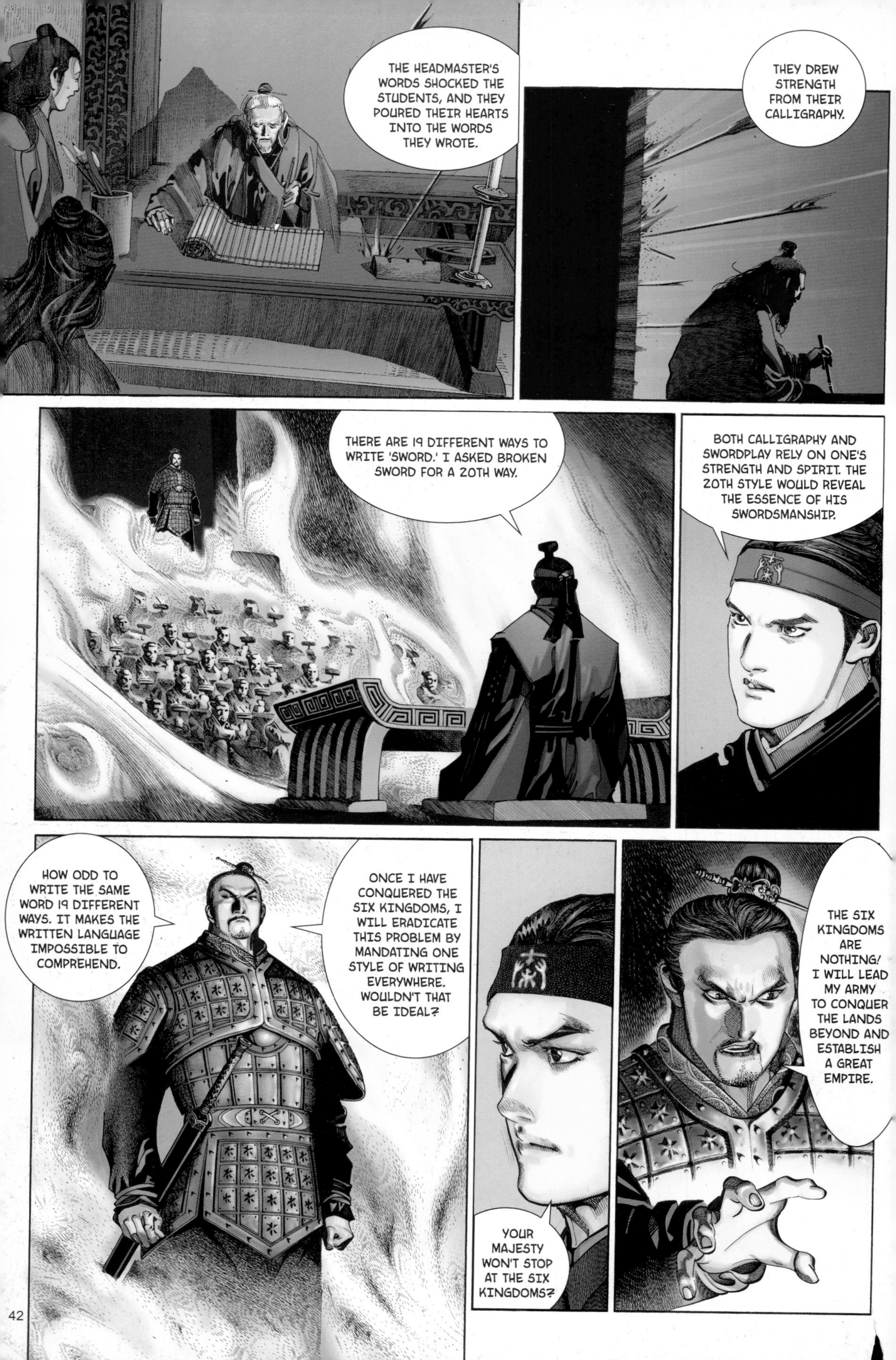
THE HEADMASTER'S WORDS SHOCKED THE STUDENTS, AND THEY POURED THEIR HEARTS INTO THE WORDS THEY WROTE.
THEY DREW STRENGTH FROM THEIR CALLIGRAPHY.
THERE ARE 19 DIFFERENT WAYS TO WRITE 'SWORD.' I ASKED BROKEN SWORD FOR A 20TH WAY.
BOTH CALLIGRAPHY AND SWORDPLAY RELY ON ONE'S STRENGTH AND SPIRIT. THE 20TH STYLE WOULD REVEAL THE ESSENCE OF HIS SWORDSMANSHIP.
HOW ODD TO WRITE THE SAME WORD 19 DIFFERENT WAYS. IT MAKES THE WRITTEN LANGUAGE IMPOSSIBLE TO COMPREHEND.
ONCE I HAVE CONQUERED THE SIX KINGDOMS, I WILL ERADICATE THIS PROBLEM BY MANDATING ONE STYLE OF WRITING EVERYWHERE. WOULDN'T THAT BE IDEAL?
YOUR MAJESTY WON'T STOP AT THE SIX KINGDOMS?
THE SIX KINGDOMS ARE NOTHING! I WILL LEAD MY ARMY TO CONQUER THE LANDS BEYOND AND ESTABLISH A GREAT EMPIRE.

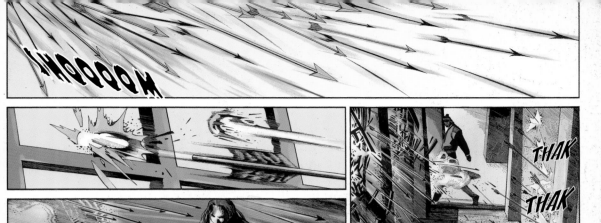

VHOOOOM

SHUNK

THAK

THAK

THAK

THAK

I HAD TO STOP THE RAINING ARROWS.

A SKIRT OF BRIGHT RED FLEW PAST ME LIKE THE WIND.

I KNEW THEN THAT IT WAS FLYING SNOW.

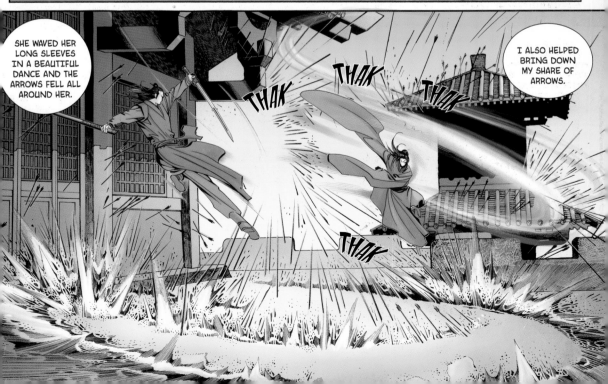

SHE WAVED HER LONG SLEEVES IN A BEAUTIFUL DANCE AND THE ARROWS FELL ALL AROUND HER.

THAK

THAK

THAK

THAK

THAK

I ALSO HELPED BRING DOWN MY SHARE OF ARROWS.

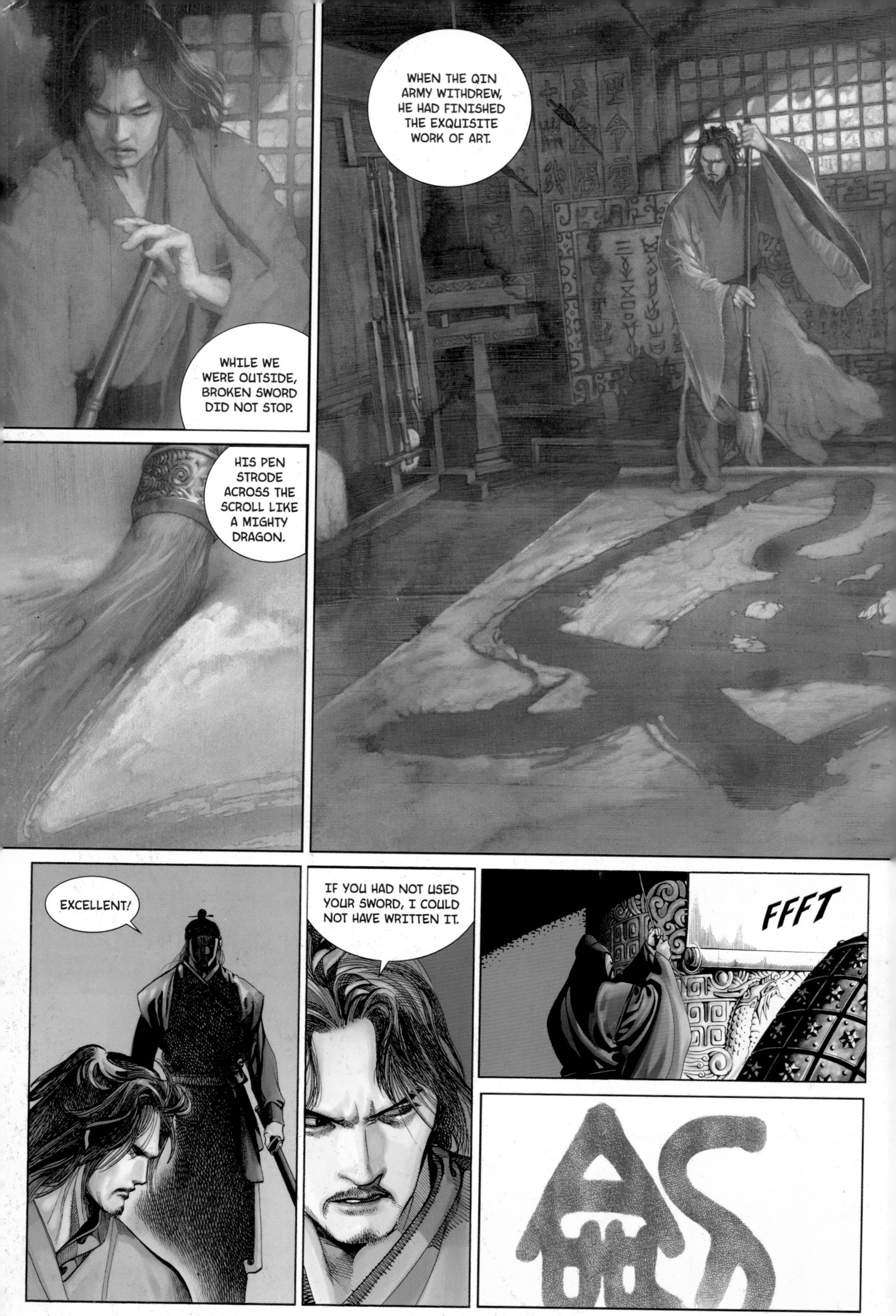
WHILE WE WERE OUTSIDE, BROKEN SWORD DID NOT STOP.
HIS PEN STRODE ACROSS THE SCROLL LIKE A MIGHTY DRAGON.
WHEN THE QIN ARMY WITHDREW, HE HAD FINISHED THE EXQUISITE WORK OF ART.
EXCELLENT!
IF YOU HAD NOT USED YOUR SWORD, I COULD NOT HAVE WRITTEN IT.
FFFT

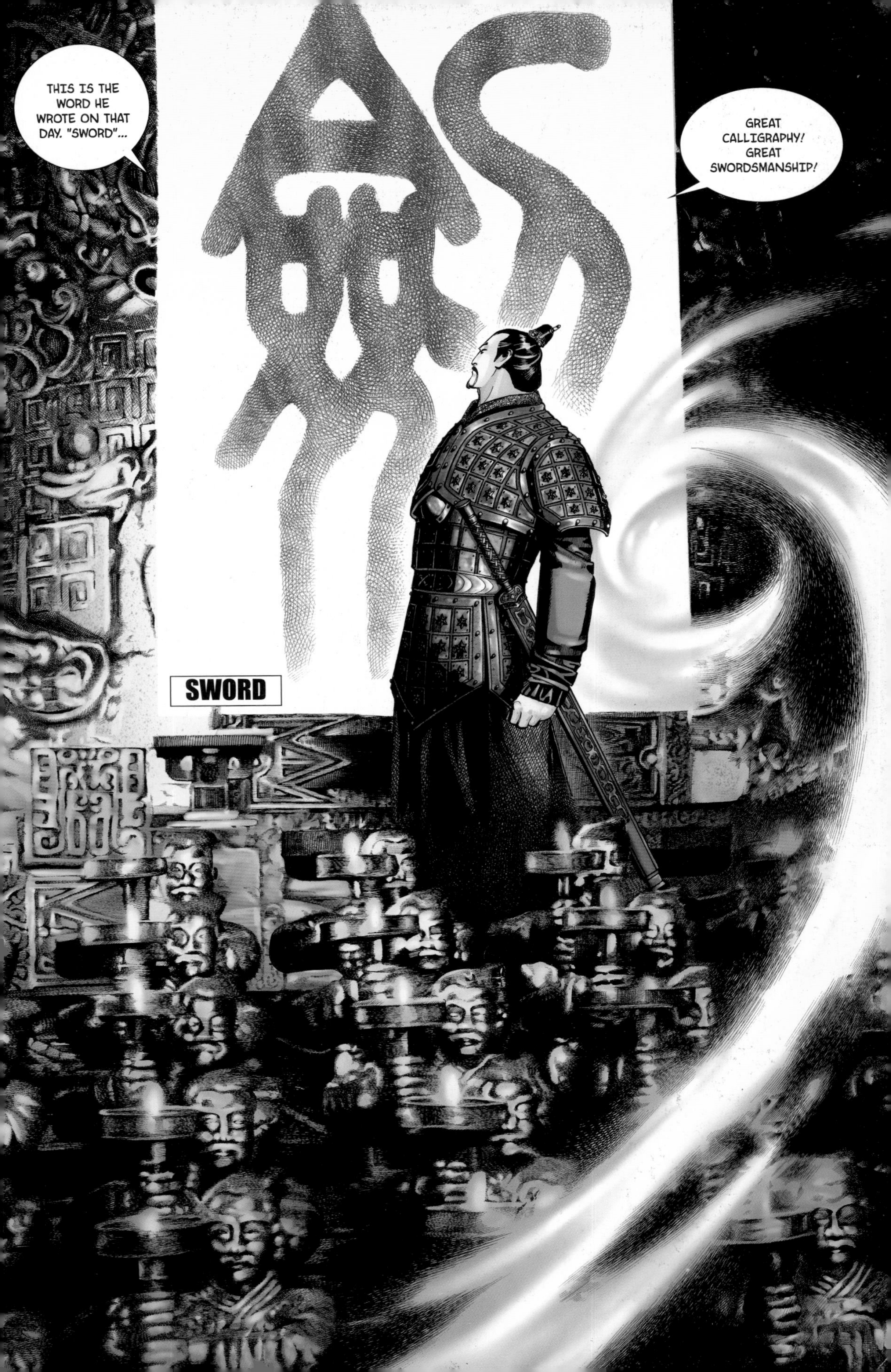
THIS IS THE WORD HE WROTE ON THAT DAY. "SWORD"...
GREAT CALLIGRAPHY! GREAT SWORDSMANSHIP!
SWORD

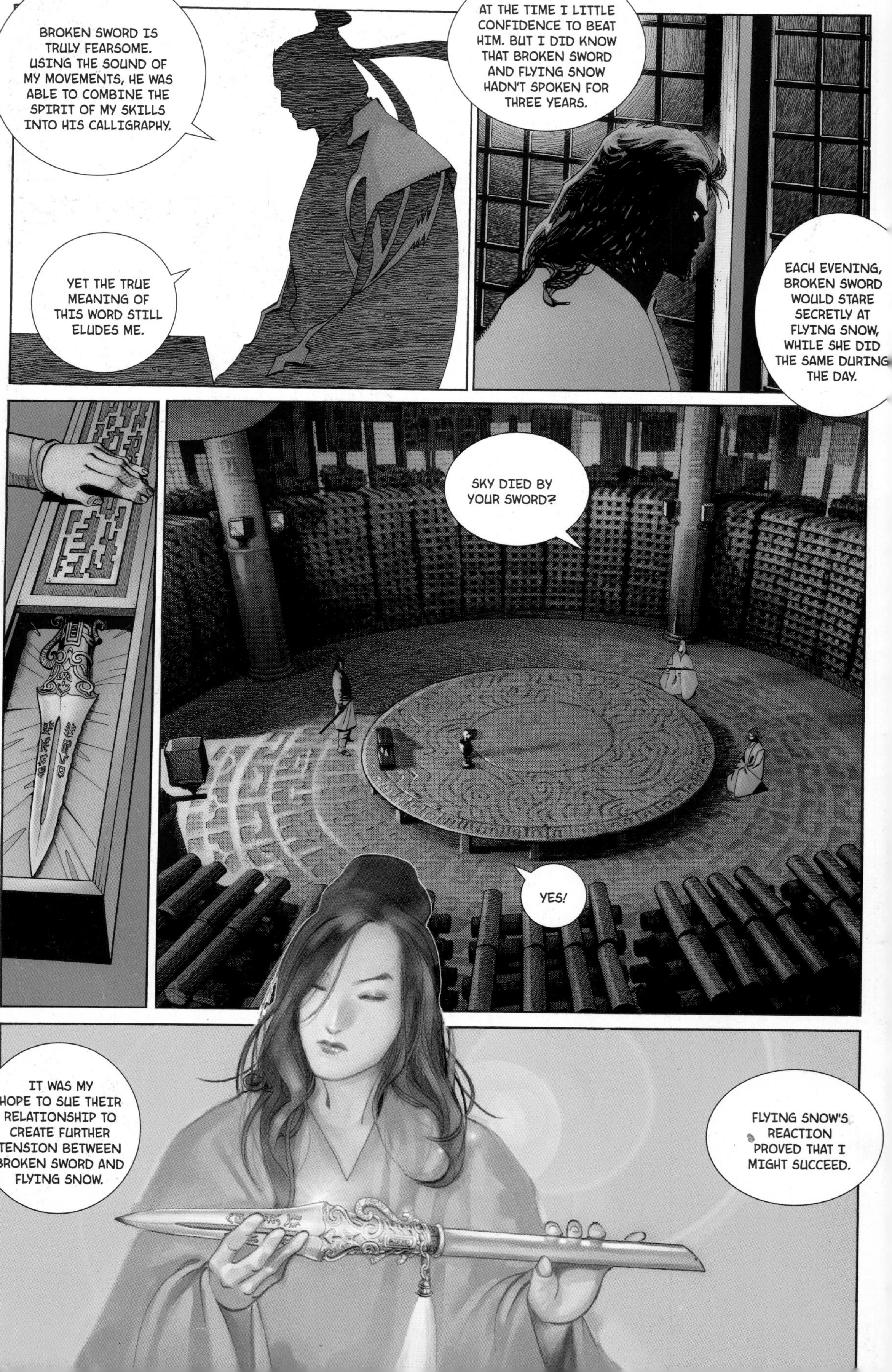
BROKEN SWORD IS TRULY FEARSOME. USING THE SOUND OF MY MOVEMENTS, HE WAS ABLE TO COMBINE THE SPIRIT OF MY SKILLS INTO HIS CALLIGRAPHY.
YET THE TRUE MEANING OF THIS WORD STILL ELUDES ME.
AT THE TIME I LITTLE CONFIDENCE TO BEAT HIM. BUT I DID KNOW THAT BROKEN SWORD AND FLYING SNOW HADN'T SPOKEN FOR THREE YEARS.
EACH EVENING, BROKEN SWORD WOULD STARE SECRETLY AT FLYING SNOW, WHILE SHE DID THE SAME DURING THE DAY.
SKY DIED BY YOUR SWORD?
YES!
IT WAS MY HOPE TO SUE THEIR RELATIONSHIP TO CREATE FURTHER TENSION BETWEEN BROKEN SWORD AND FLYING SNOW.
FLYING SNOW'S REACTION PROVED THAT I MIGHT SUCCEED.

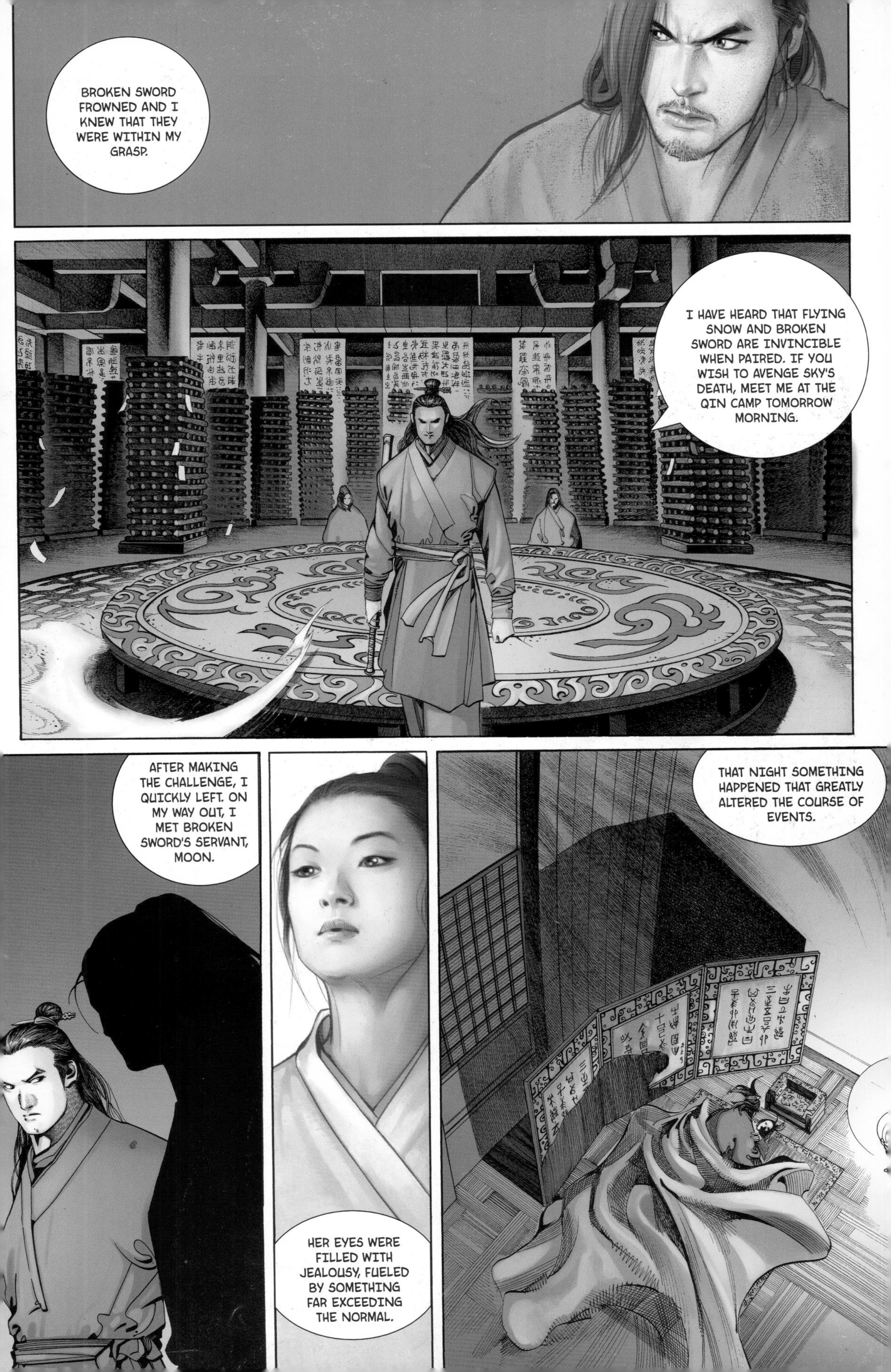
BROKEN SWORD FROWNED AND I KNEW THAT THEY WERE WITHIN MY GRASP.
I HAVE HEARD THAT FLYING SNOW AND BROKEN SWORD ARE INVINCIBLE WHEN PAIRED. IF YOU WISH TO AVENGE SKY'S DEATH, MEET ME AT THE QIN CAMP TOMORROW MORNING.
AFTER MAKING THE CHALLENGE, I QUICKLY LEFT. ON MY WAY OUT, I MET BROKEN SWORD'S SERVANT, MOON.
HER EYES WERE FILLED WITH JEALOUSY, FUELED BY SOMETHING FAR EXCEEDING THE NORMAL.
THAT NIGHT SOMETHING HAPPENED THAT GREATLY ALTERED THE COURSE OF EVENTS.

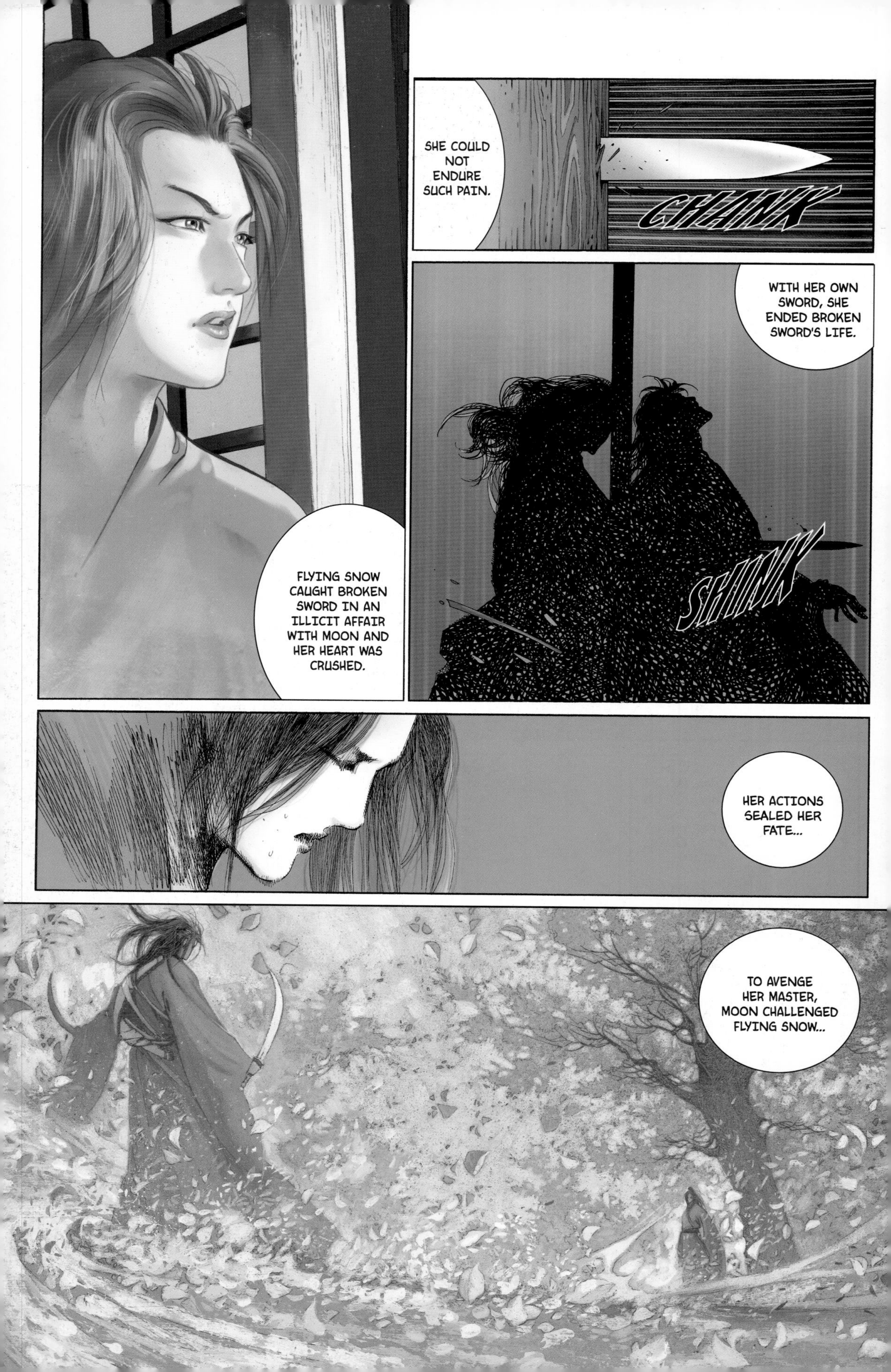
SHE COULD NOT ENDURE SUCH PAIN.
CHANK
WITH HER OWN SWORD, SHE ENDED BROKEN SWORD'S LIFE.
FLYING SNOW CAUGHT BROKEN SWORD IN AN ILLICIT AFFAIR WITH MOON AND HER HEART WAS CRUSHED.
SHINK
HER ACTIONS SEALED HER FATE...
TO AVENGE HER MASTER, MOON CHALLENGED FLYING SNOW...

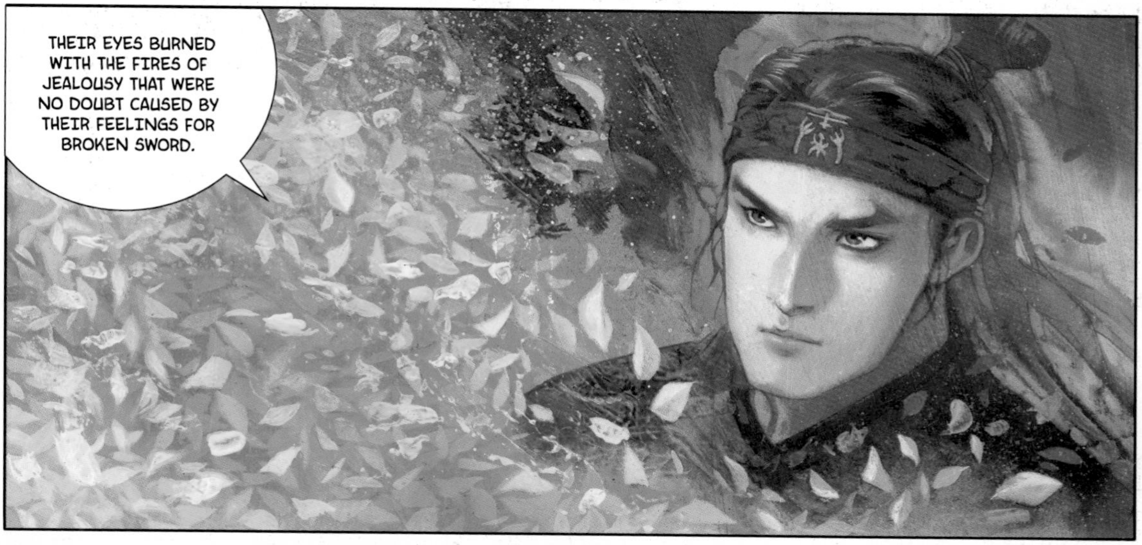
THEIR EYES BURNED WITH THE FIRES OF JEALOUSY THAT WERE NO DOUBT CAUSED BY THEIR FEELINGS FOR BROKEN SWORD.

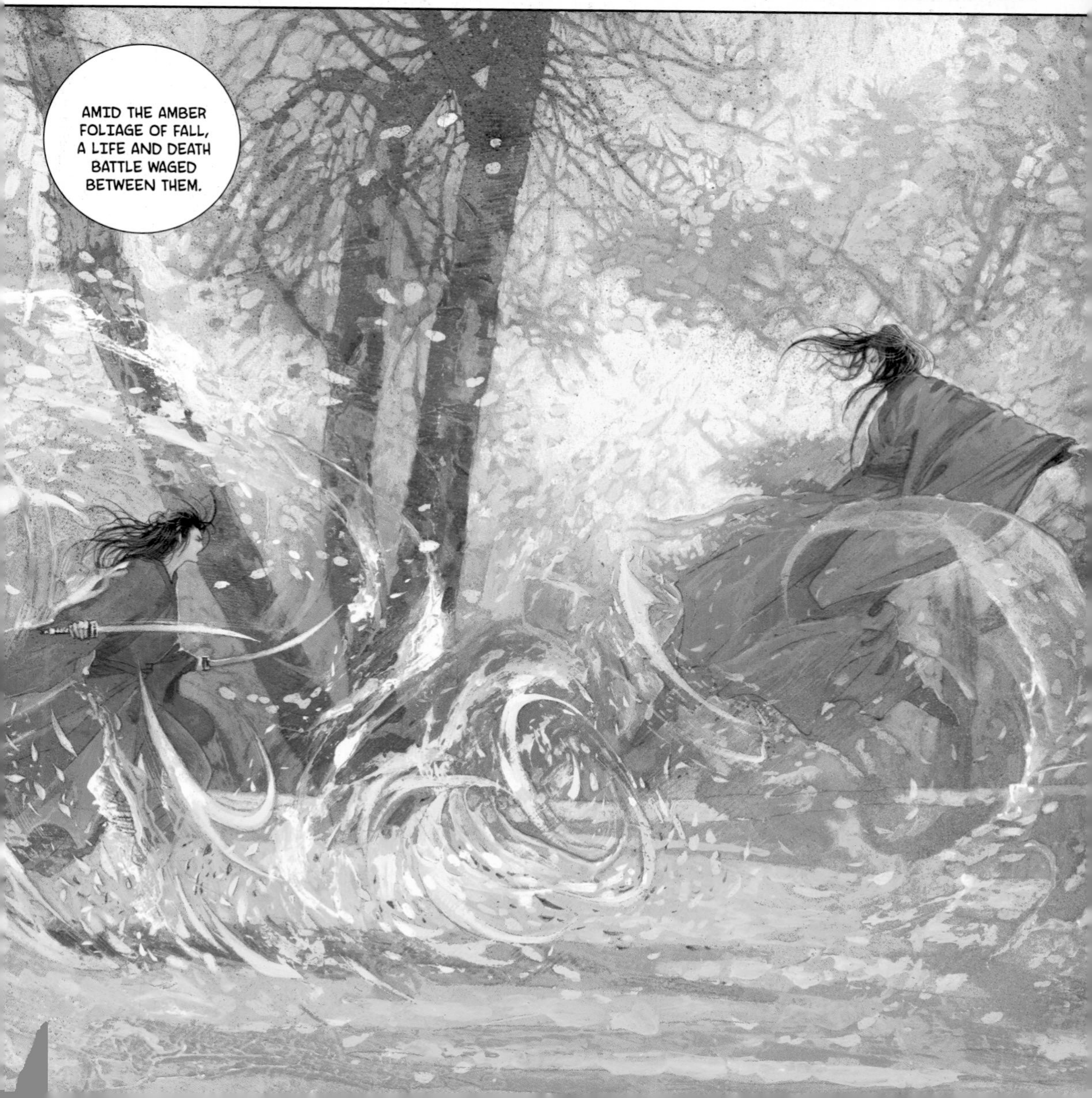
AMID THE AMBER FOLIAGE OF FALL, A LIFE AND DEATH BATTLE WAGED BETWEEN THEM.

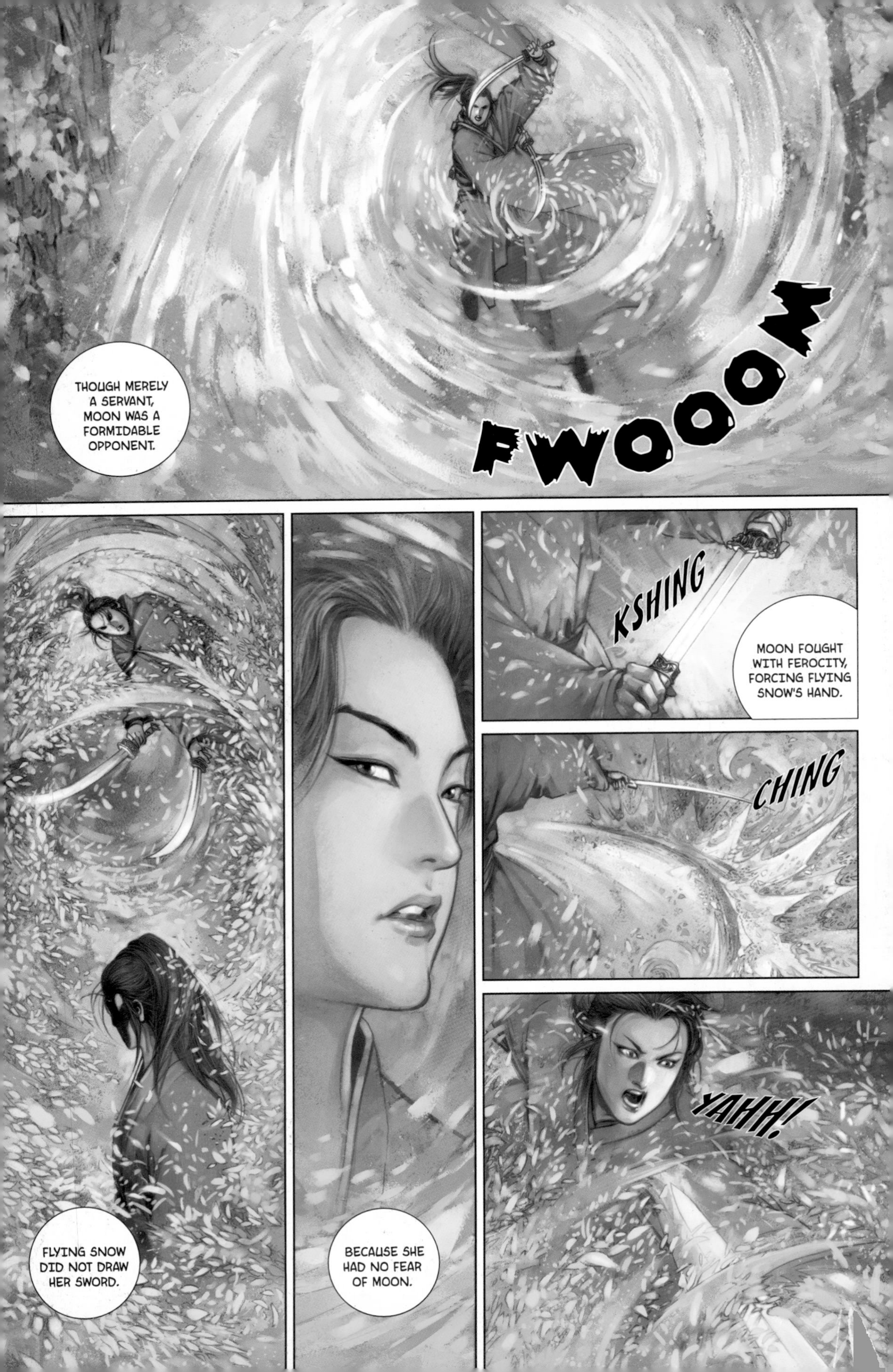
THOUGH MERELY A SERVANT, MOON WAS A FORMIDABLE OPPONENT.
FWOOOM
FLYING SNOW DID NOT DRAW HER SWORD.
BECAUSE SHE HAD NO FEAR OF MOON.
KSHING
MOON FOUGHT WITH FEROCITY, FORCING FLYING SNOW'S HAND.
CHING
YAHH!

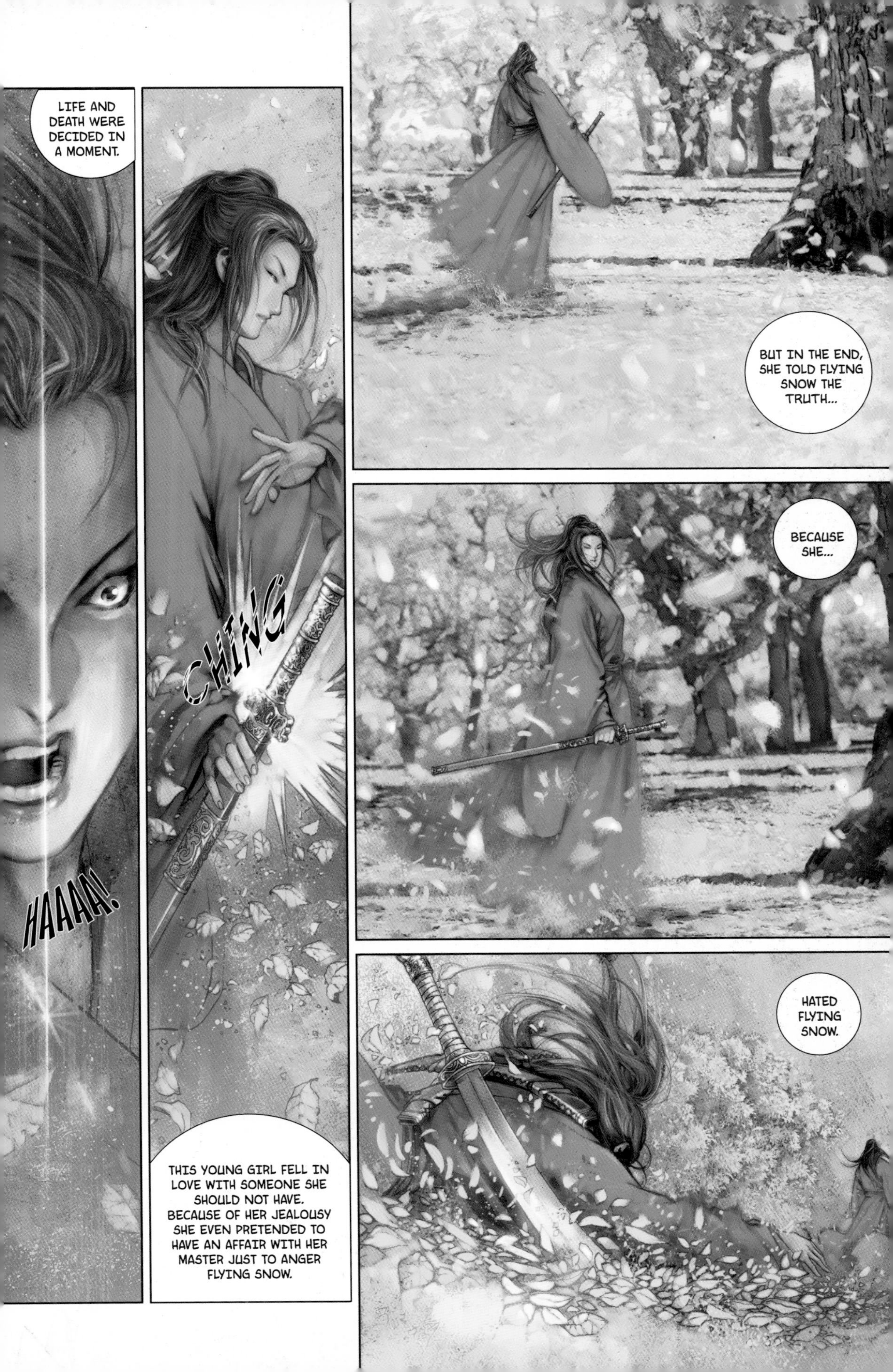
LIFE AND DEATH WERE DECIDED IN A MOMENT.
HAAAA!
CHING
THIS YOUNG GIRL FELL IN LOVE WITH SOMEONE SHE SHOULD NOT HAVE. BECAUSE OF HER JEALOUSY SHE EVEN PRETENDED TO HAVE AN AFFAIR WITH HER MASTER JUST TO ANGER FLYING SNOW.
BUT IN THE END, SHE TOLD FLYING SNOW THE TRUTH...
BECAUSE SHE...
HATED FLYING SNOW.

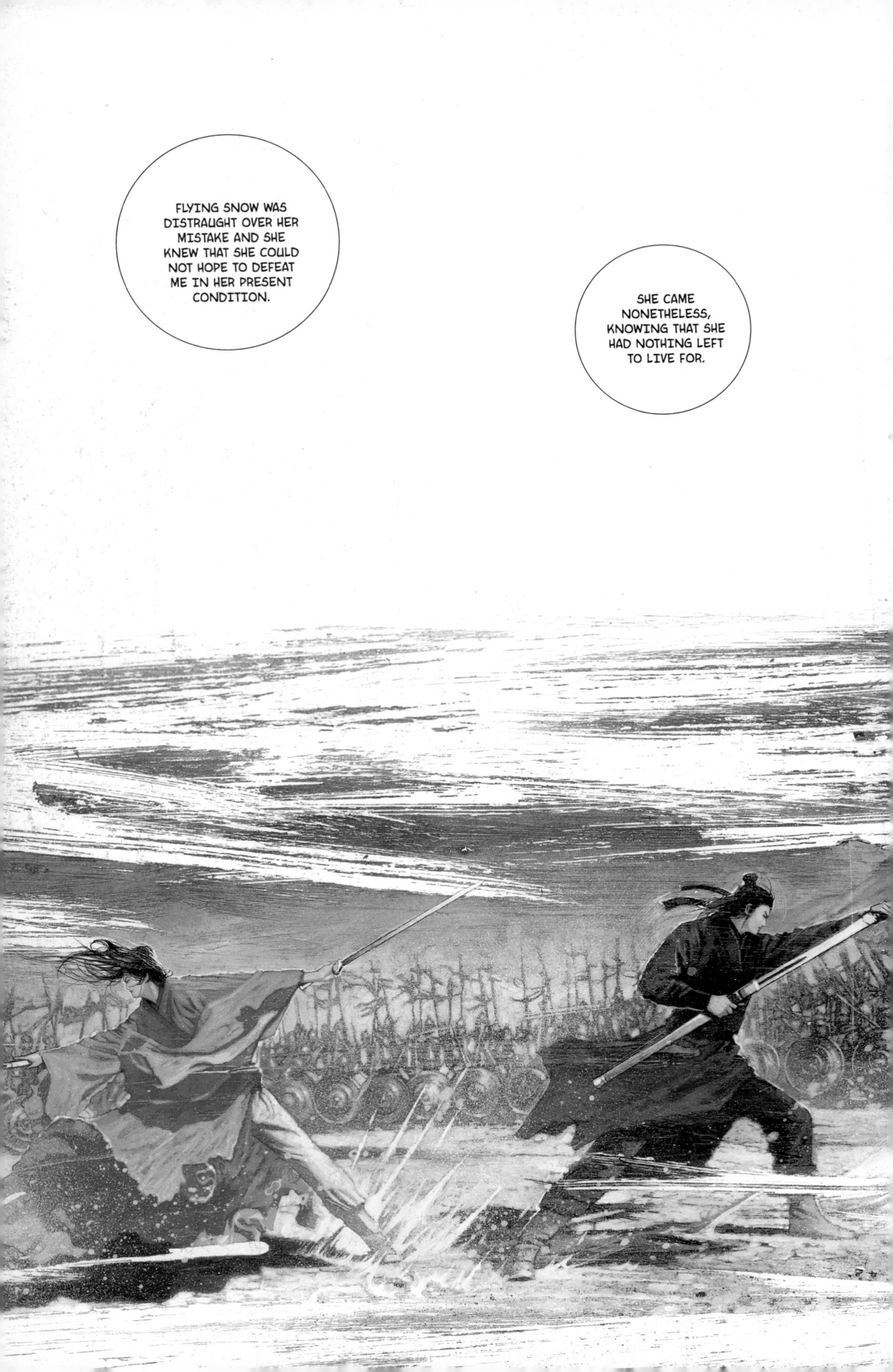
FLYING SNOW WAS DISTRAUGHT OVER HER MISTAKE AND SHE KNEW THAT SHE COULD NOT HOPE TO DEFEAT ME IN HER PRESENT CONDITION.
SHE CAME NONETHELESS, KNOWING THAT SHE HAD NOTHING LEFT TO LIVE FOR.

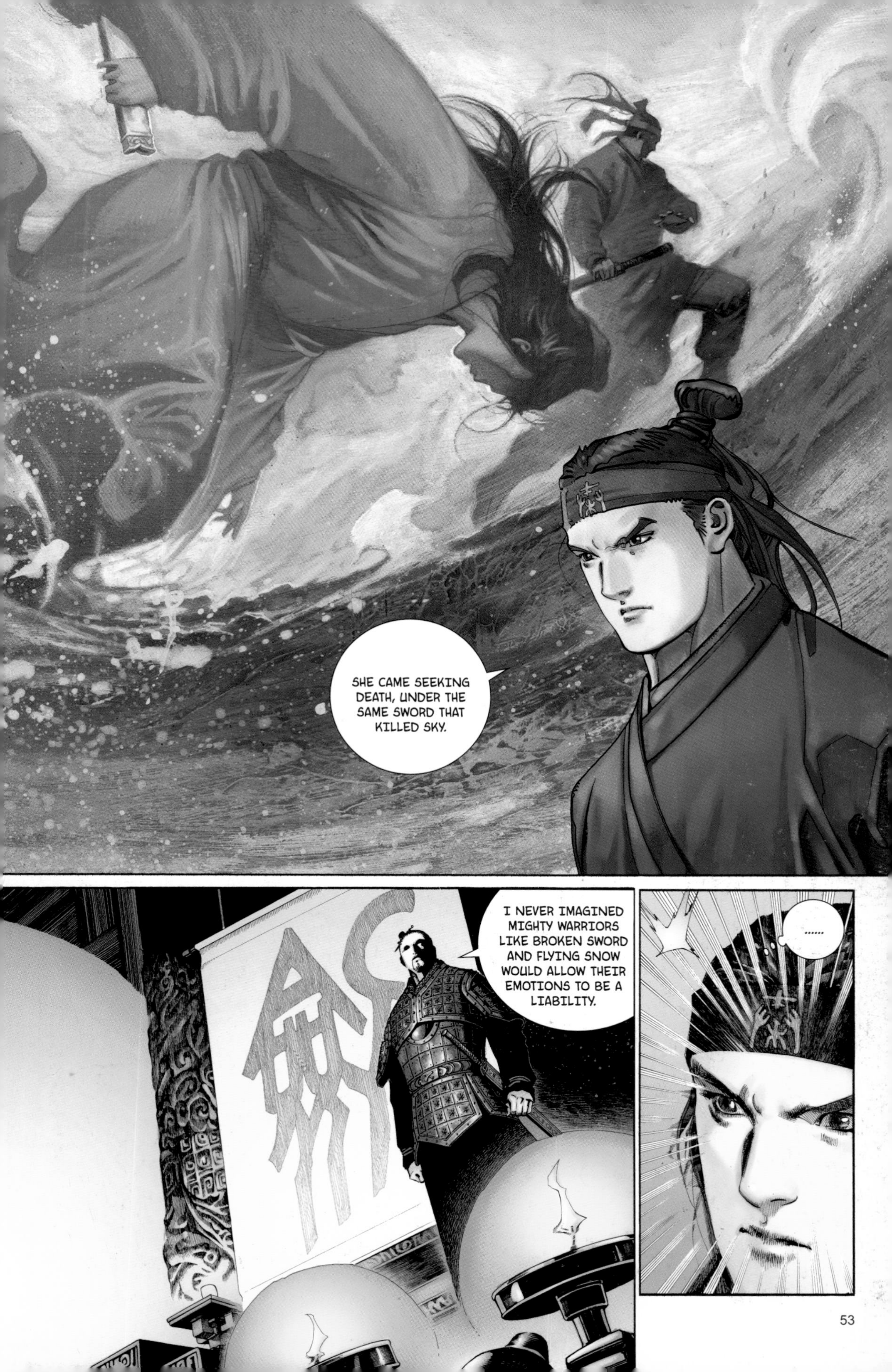

SHE CAME SEEKING DEATH, UNDER THE SAME SWORD THAT KILLED SKY.
I NEVER IMAGINED MIGHTY WARRIORS LIKE BROKEN SWORD AND FLYING SNOW WOULD ALLOW THEIR EMOTIONS TO BE A LIABILITY.
......

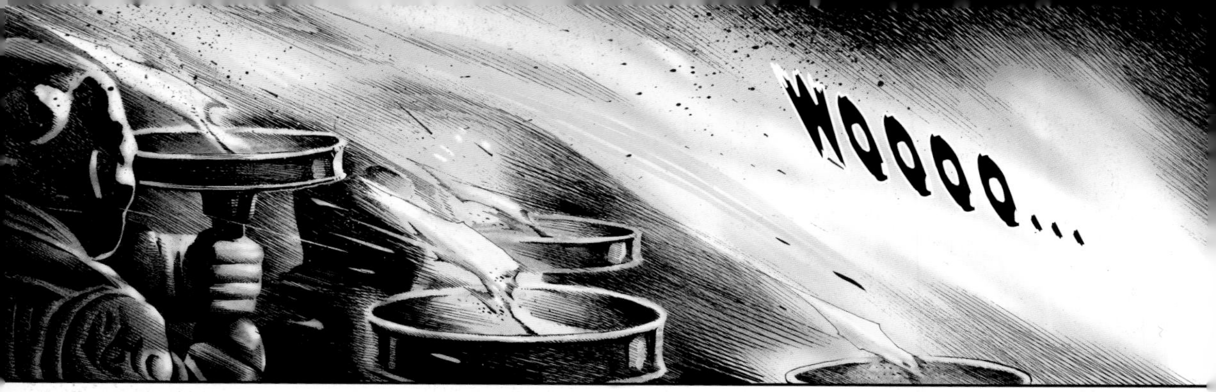
WOOOO...

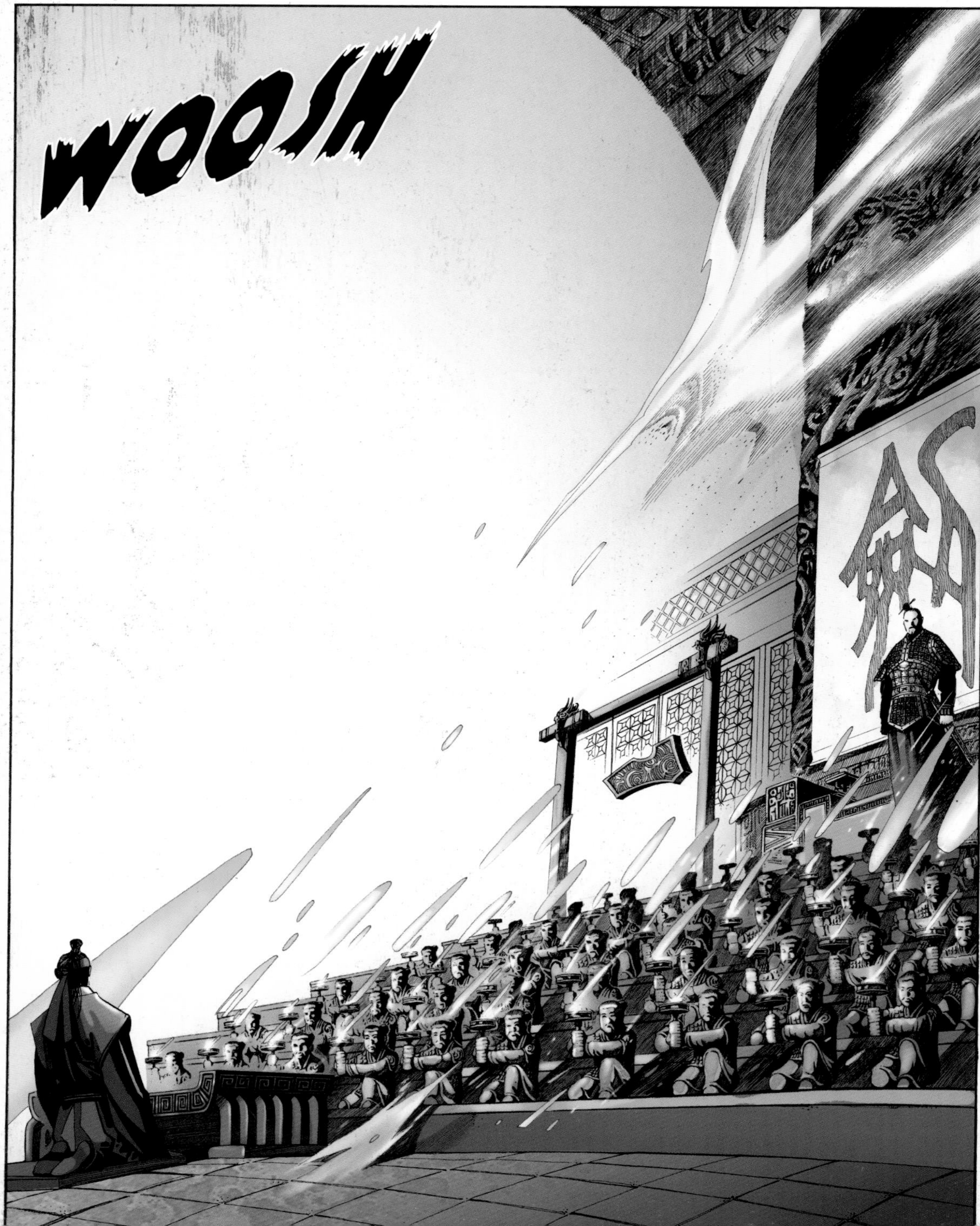
WOOSH

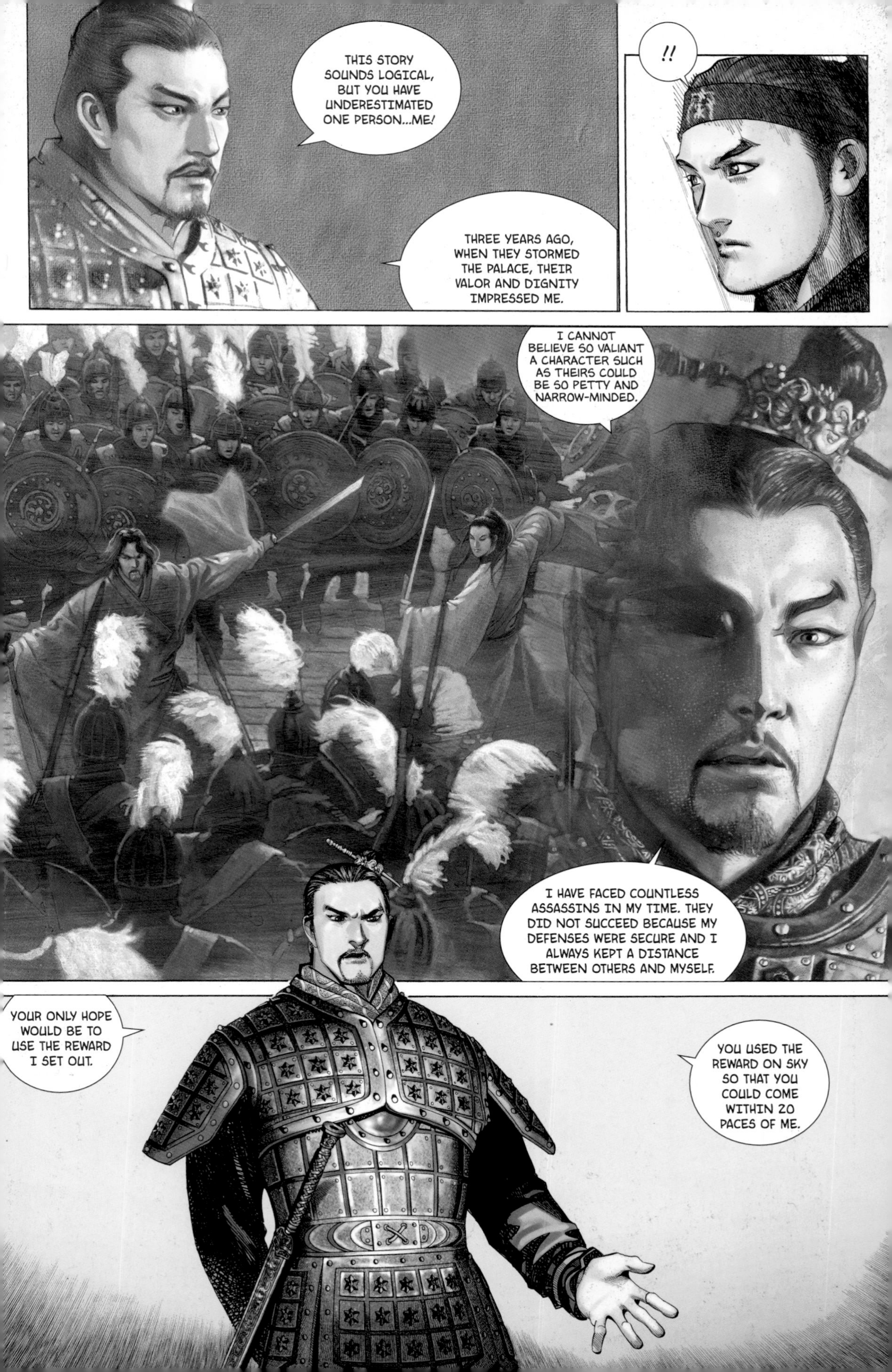
THIS STORY SOUNDS LOGICAL, BUT YOU HAVE UNDERESTIMATED ONE PERSON...ME!
!!
THREE YEARS AGO, WHEN THEY STORMED THE PALACE, THEIR VALOR AND DIGNITY IMPRESSED ME.
I CANNOT BELIEVE SO VALIANT A CHARACTER SUCH AS THEIRS COULD BE SO PETTY AND NARROW-MINDED.
I HAVE FACED COUNTLESS ASSASSINS IN MY TIME. THEY DID NOT SUCCEED BECAUSE MY DEFENSES WERE SECURE AND I ALWAYS KEPT A DISTANCE BETWEEN OTHERS AND MYSELF.
YOUR ONLY HOPE WOULD BE TO USE THE REWARD I SET OUT.
YOU USED THE REWARD ON SKY SO THAT YOU COULD COME WITHIN 20 PACES OF ME.

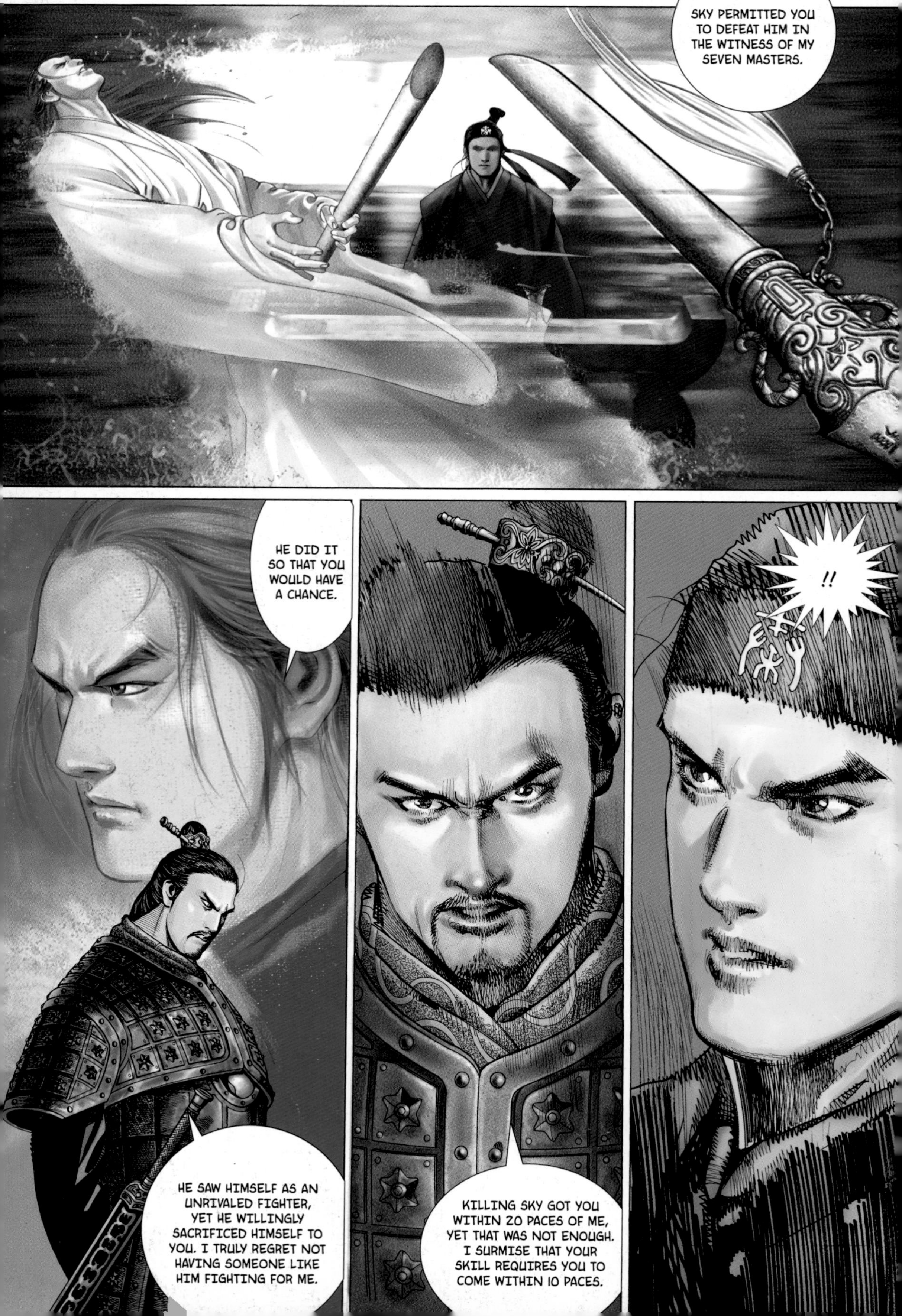
SKY PERMITTED YOU TO DEFEAT HIM IN THE WITNESS OF MY SEVEN MASTERS.
HE DID IT SO THAT YOU WOULD HAVE A CHANCE.
HE SAW HIMSELF AS AN UNRIVALED FIGHTER, YET HE WILLINGLY SACRIFICED HIMSELF TO YOU. I TRULY REGRET NOT HAVING SOMEONE LIKE HIM FIGHTING FOR ME.
KILLING SKY GOT YOU WITHIN 20 PACES OF ME, YET THAT WAS NOT ENOUGH. I SURMISE THAT YOUR SKILL REQUIRES YOU TO COME WITHIN 10 PACES.
!!

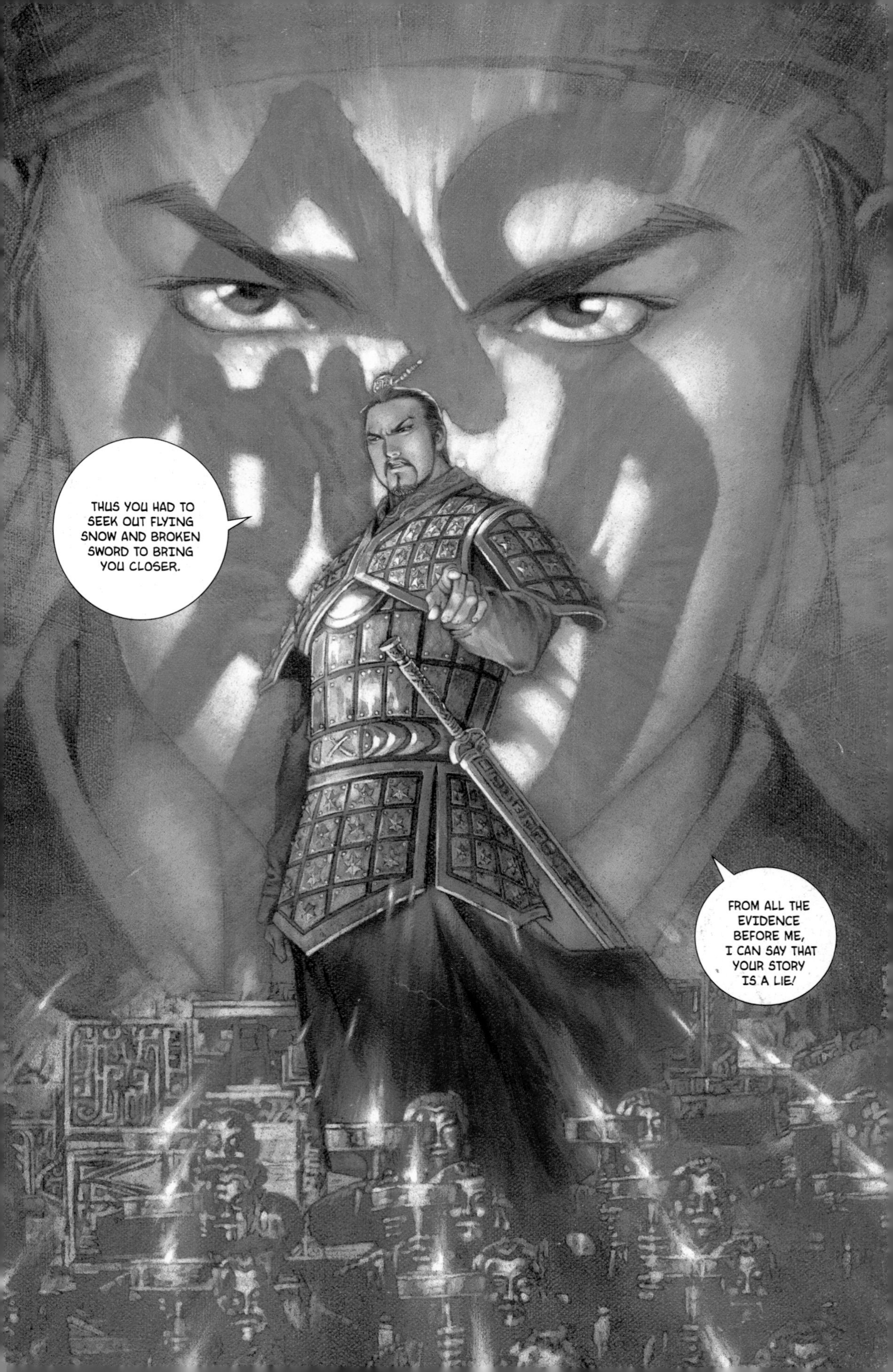
THUS YOU HAD TO SEEK OUT FLYING SNOW AND BROKEN SWORD TO BRING YOU CLOSER.
FROM ALL THE EVIDENCE BEFORE ME, I CAN SAY THAT YOUR STORY IS A LIE!

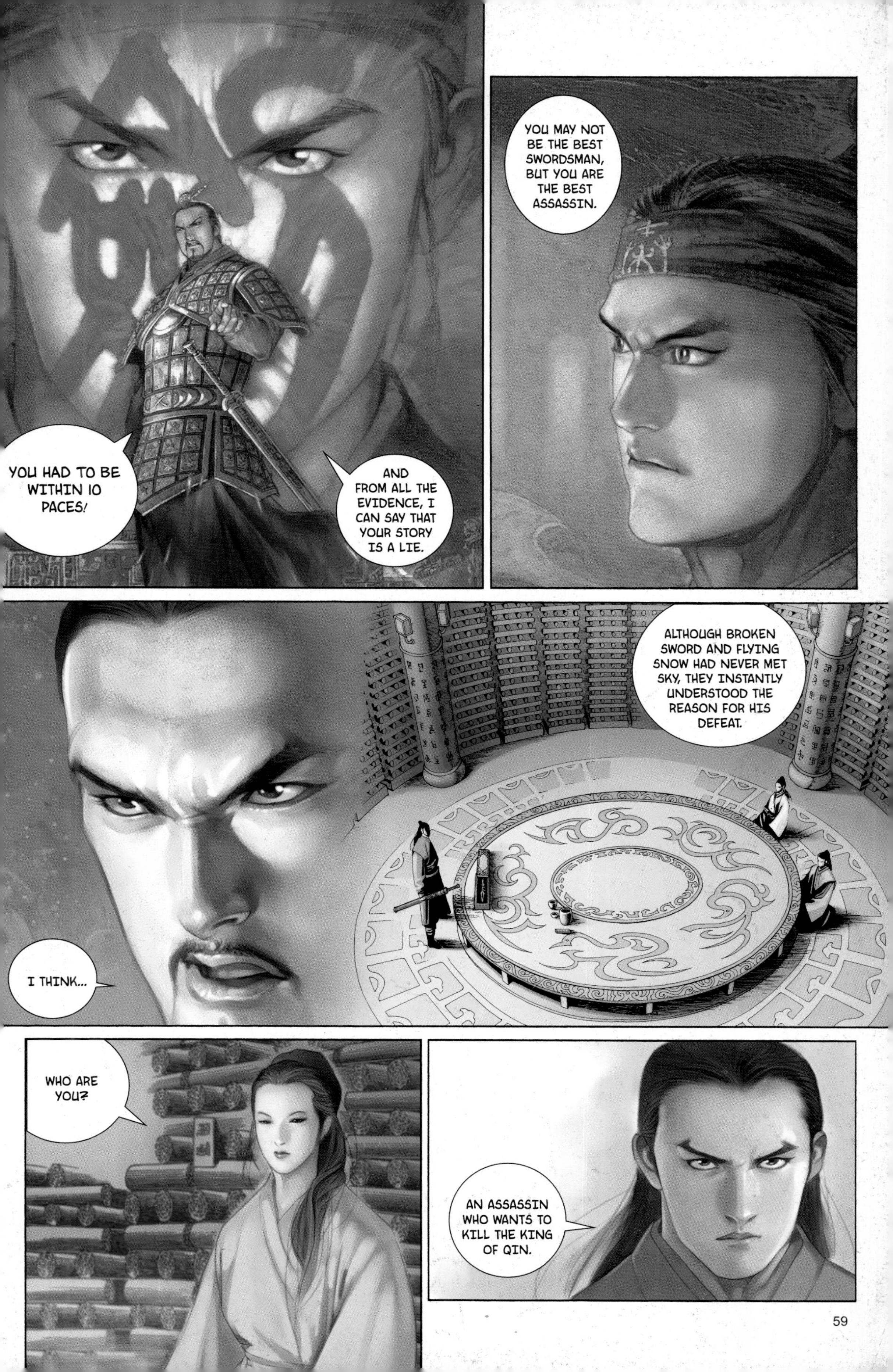
YOU HAD TO BE WITHIN 10 PACES!
AND FROM ALL THE EVIDENCE, I CAN SAY THAT YOUR STORY IS A LIE.
YOU MAY NOT BE THE BEST SWORDSMAN, BUT YOU ARE THE BEST ASSASSIN.
ALTHOUGH BROKEN SWORD AND FLYING SNOW HAD NEVER MET SKY, THEY INSTANTLY UNDERSTOOD THE REASON FOR HIS DEFEAT.
I THINK...
WHO ARE YOU?
AN ASSASSIN WHO WANTS TO KILL THE KING OF QIN.

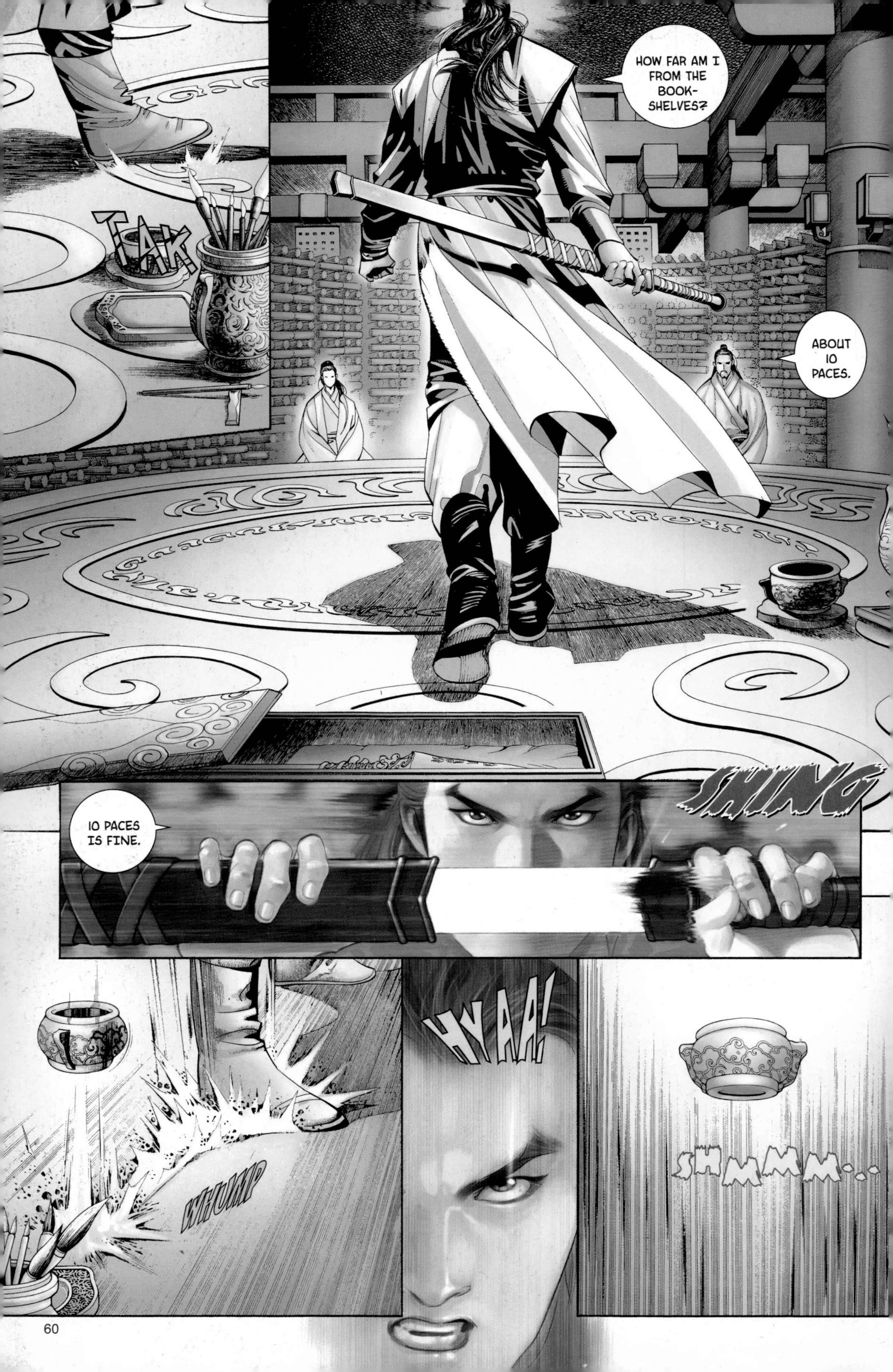
TAK
HOW FAR AM I FROM THE BOOK-SHELVES?
ABOUT 10 PACES.
SHING
10 PACES IS FINE.
WHUMP
HYAA!
SHMMM...

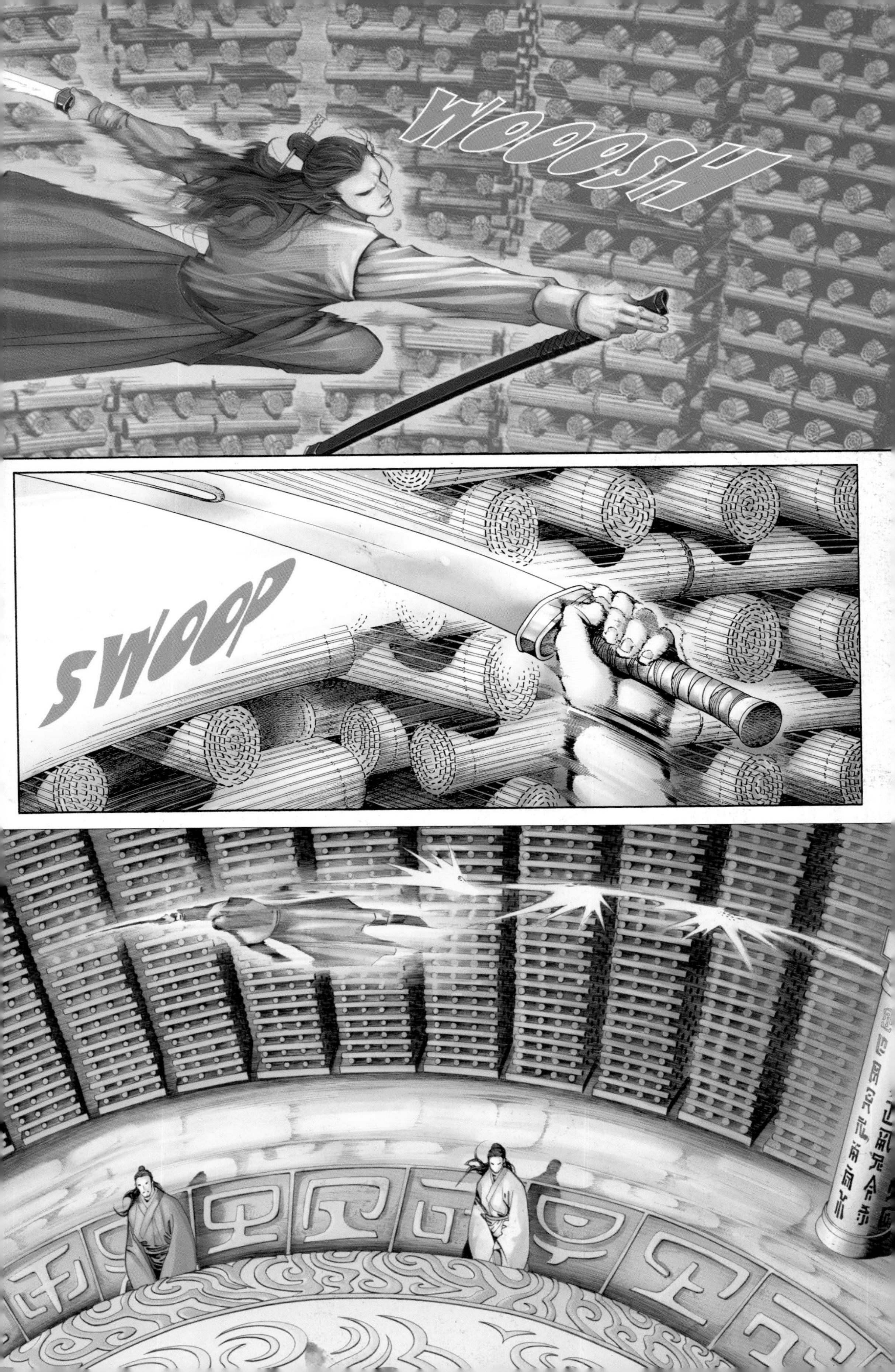
WOOOSH
SWOOP

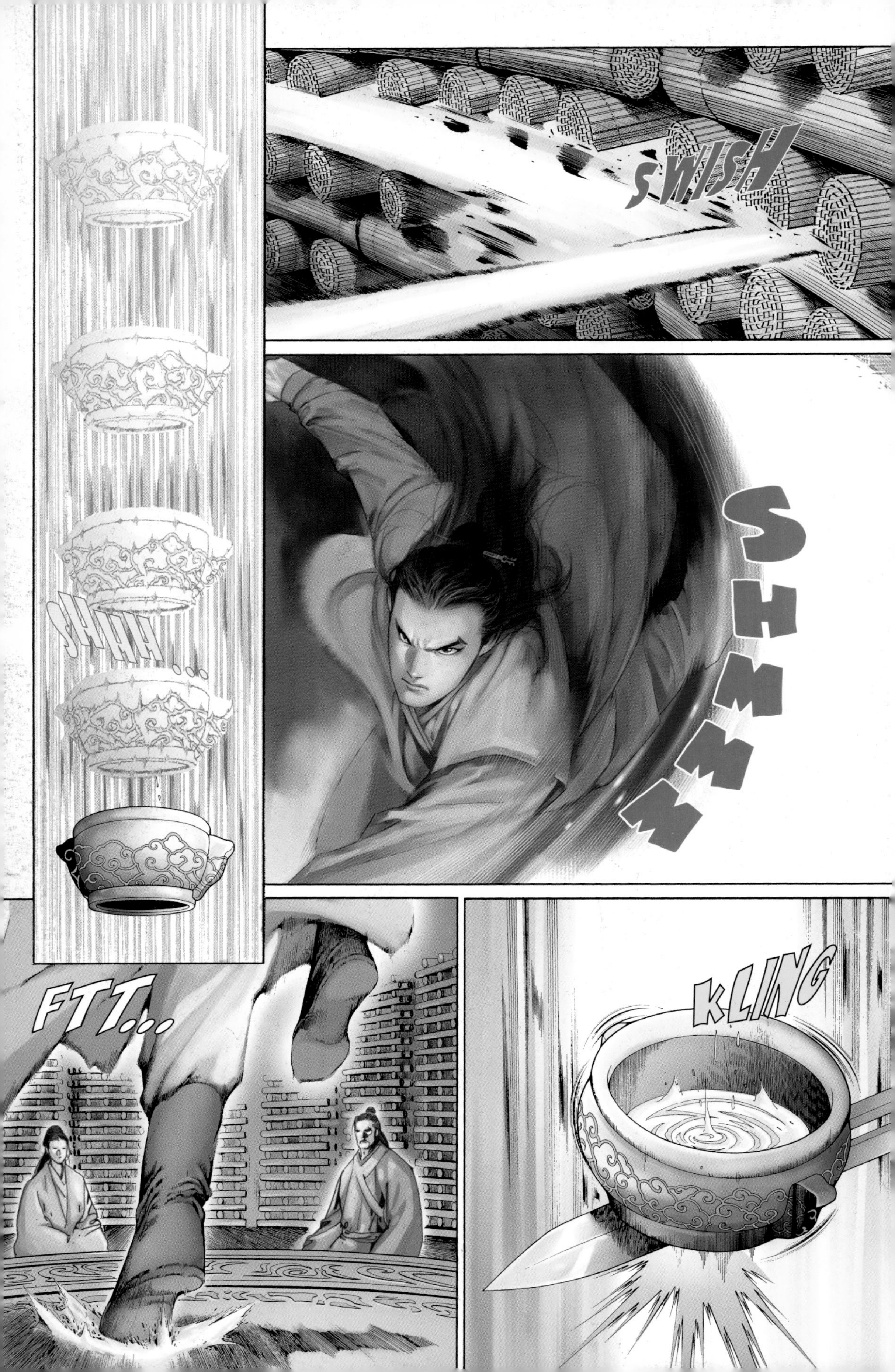
SWISH
SHHH...
SHMMMM
FTT...
KLING

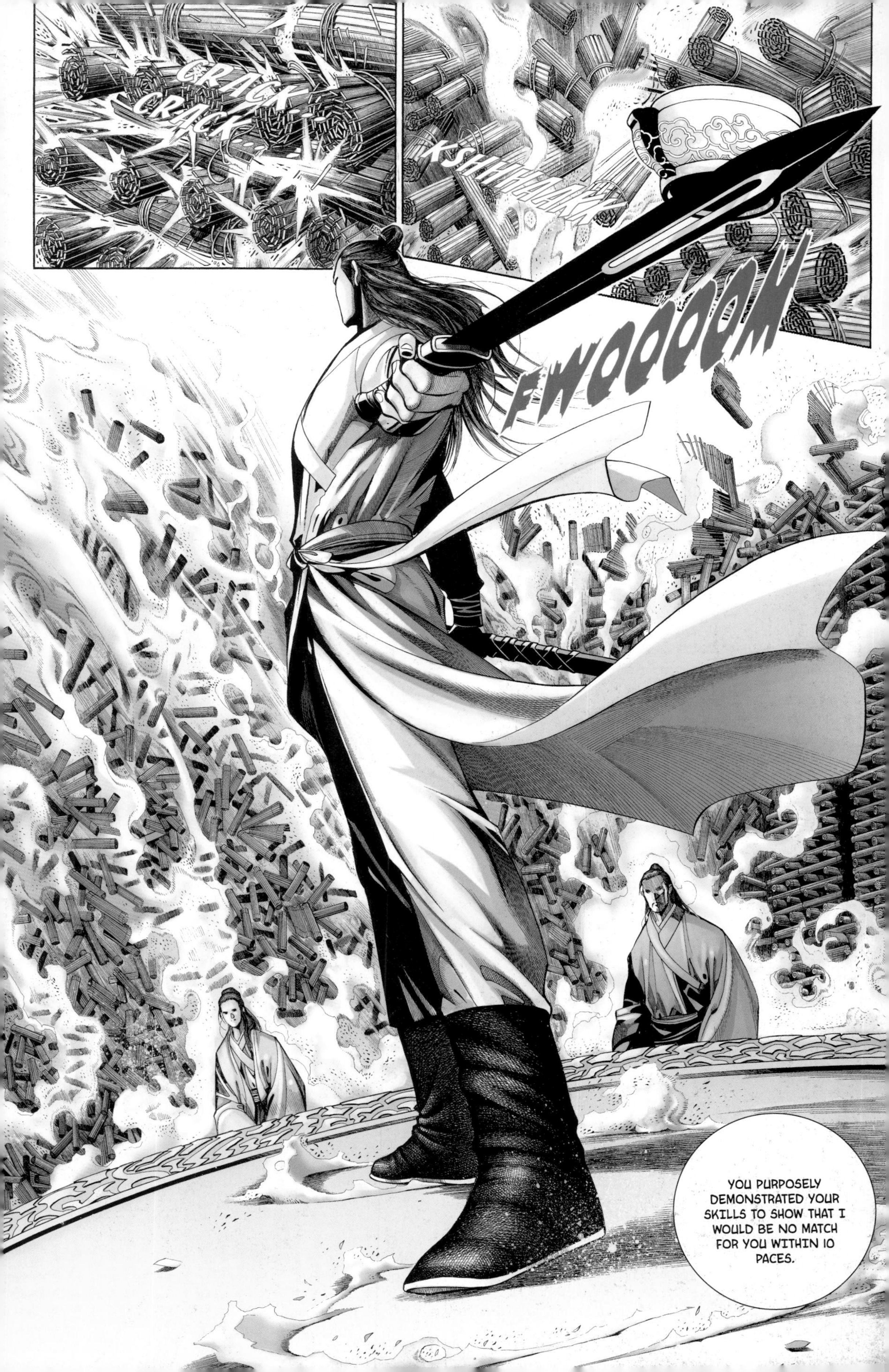
CRACK
CRACK
KSHHHAK
FWOOOOM
YOU PURPOSELY DEMONSTRATED YOUR SKILLS TO SHOW THAT I WOULD BE NO MATCH FOR YOU WITHIN 10 PACES.

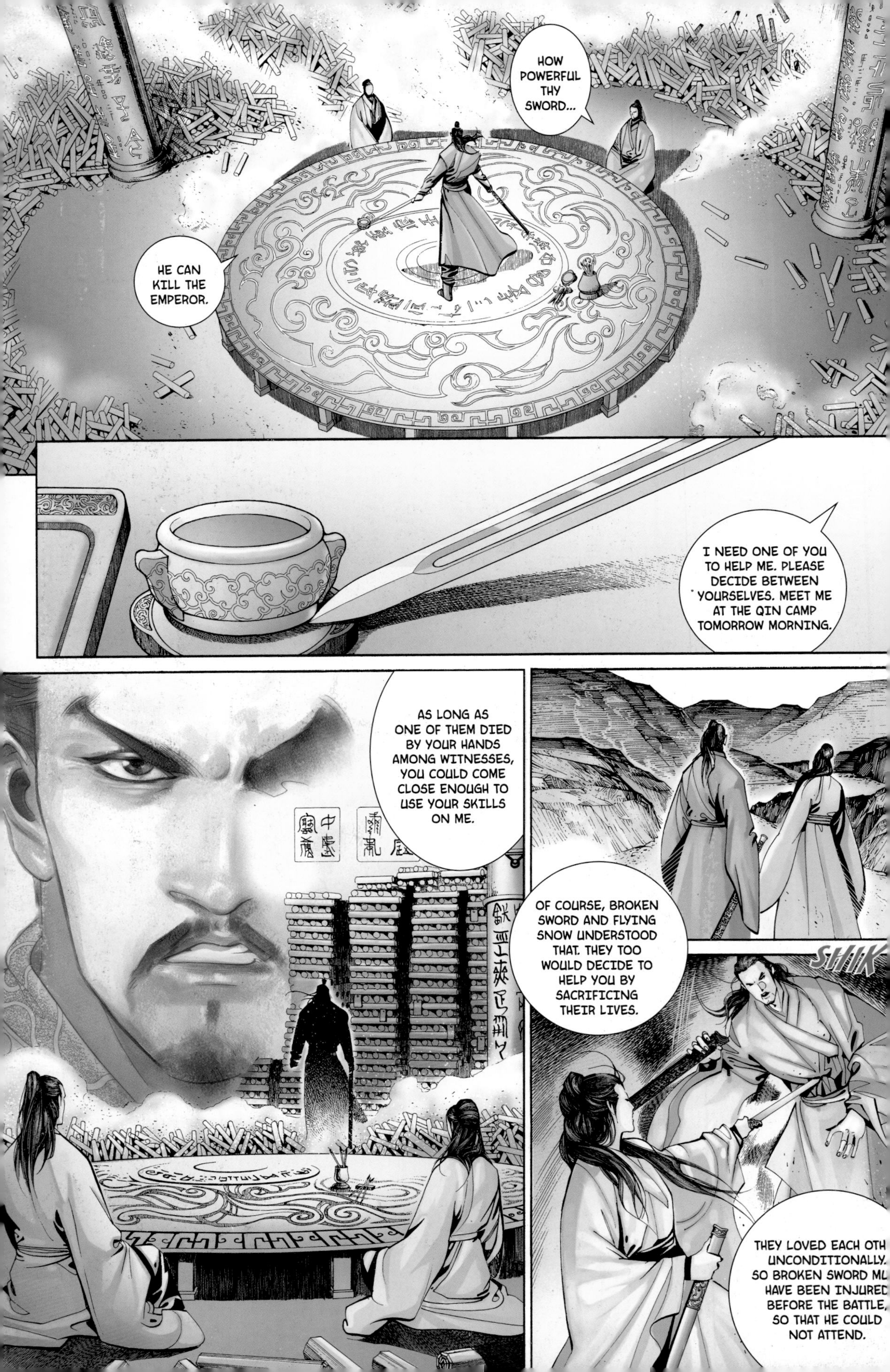
HOW POWERFUL THY SWORD...
HE CAN KILL THE EMPEROR.
I NEED ONE OF YOU TO HELP ME. PLEASE DECIDE BETWEEN YOURSELVES. MEET ME AT THE QIN CAMP TOMORROW MORNING.
AS LONG AS ONE OF THEM DIED BY YOUR HANDS AMONG WITNESSES, YOU COULD COME CLOSE ENOUGH TO USE YOUR SKILLS ON ME.
OF COURSE, BROKEN SWORD AND FLYING SNOW UNDERSTOOD THAT. THEY TOO WOULD DECIDE TO HELP YOU BY SACRIFICING THEIR LIVES.
SHIK
THEY LOVED EACH OTH
UNCONDITIONALLY.
SO BROKEN SWORD MU
HAVE BEEN INJURED
BEFORE THE BATTLE,
SO THAT HE COULD
NOT ATTEND.

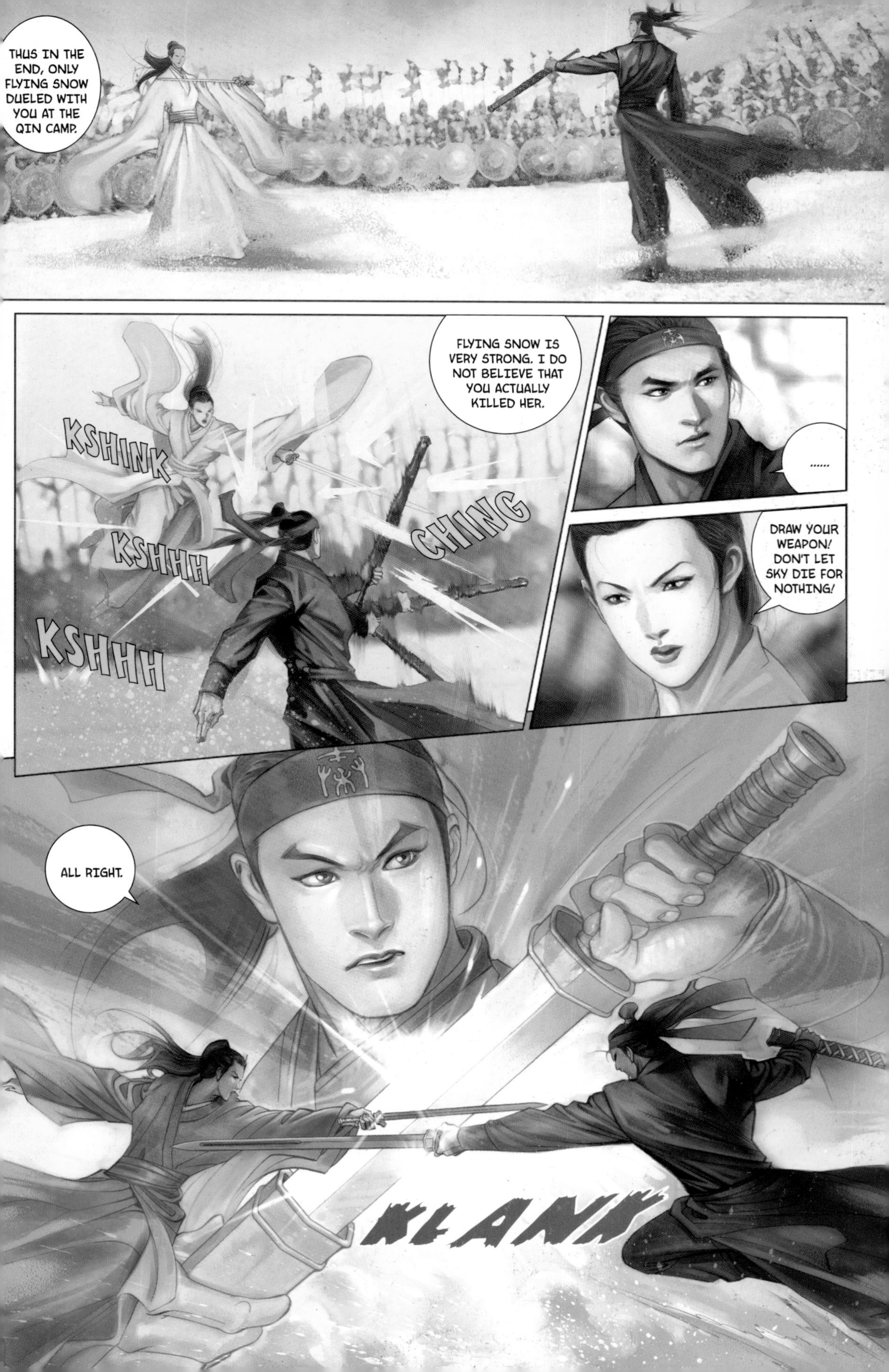
THUS IN THE END, ONLY FLYING SNOW DUELED WITH YOU AT THE QIN CAMP.
FLYING SNOW IS VERY STRONG. I DO NOT BELIEVE THAT YOU ACTUALLY KILLED HER.
KSHINK
KSHHH
KSHHH
CHING
......
DRAW YOUR WEAPON! DON'T LET SKY DIE FOR NOTHING!
ALL RIGHT.
KLANK

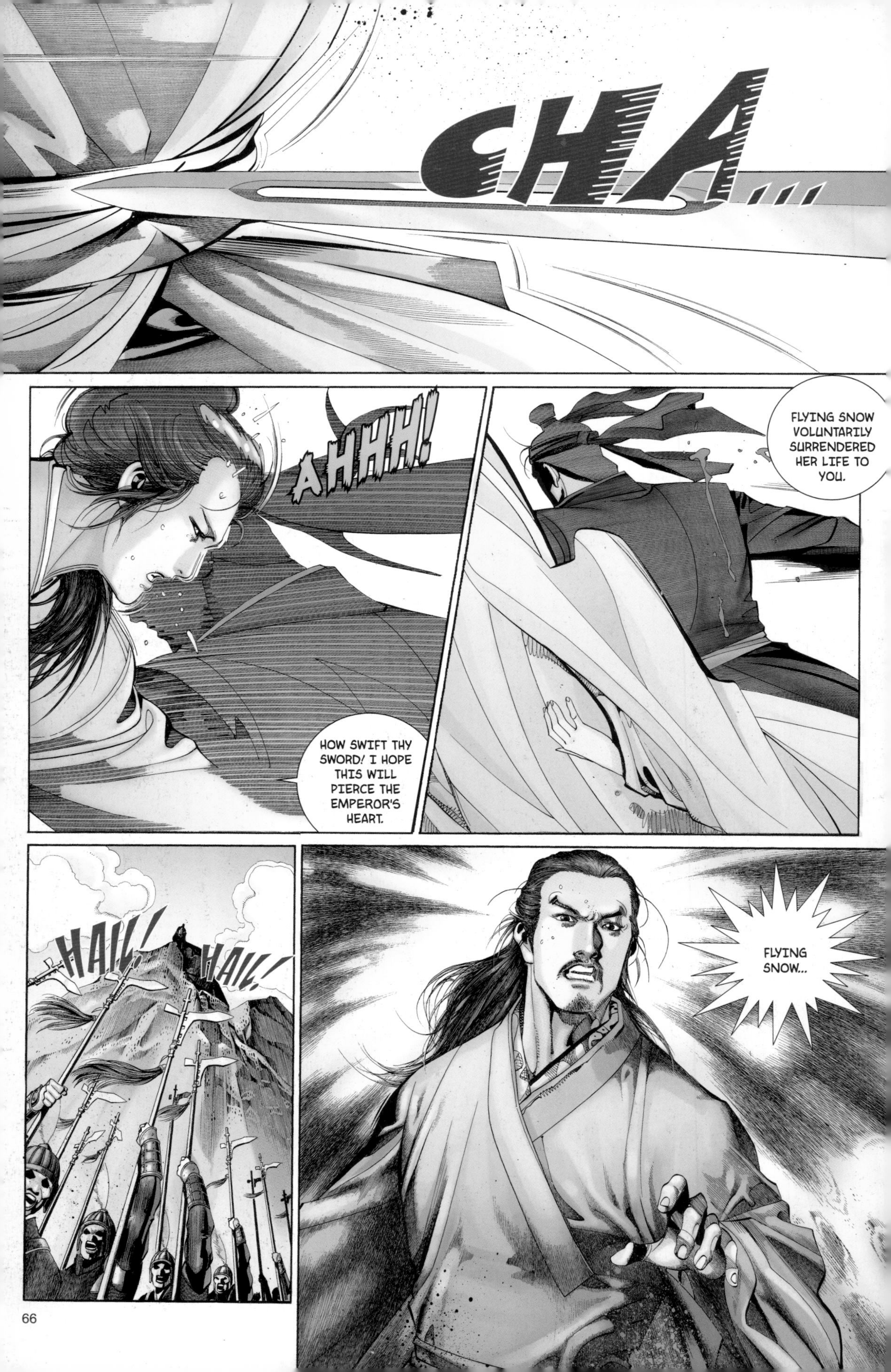
CHA...
AHHH!
HOW SWIFT THY SWORD! I HOPE THIS WILL PIERCE THE EMPEROR'S HEART.
FLYING SNOW VOLUNTARILY SURRENDERED HER LIFE TO YOU.
HAIL! HAIL!
FLYING SNOW...

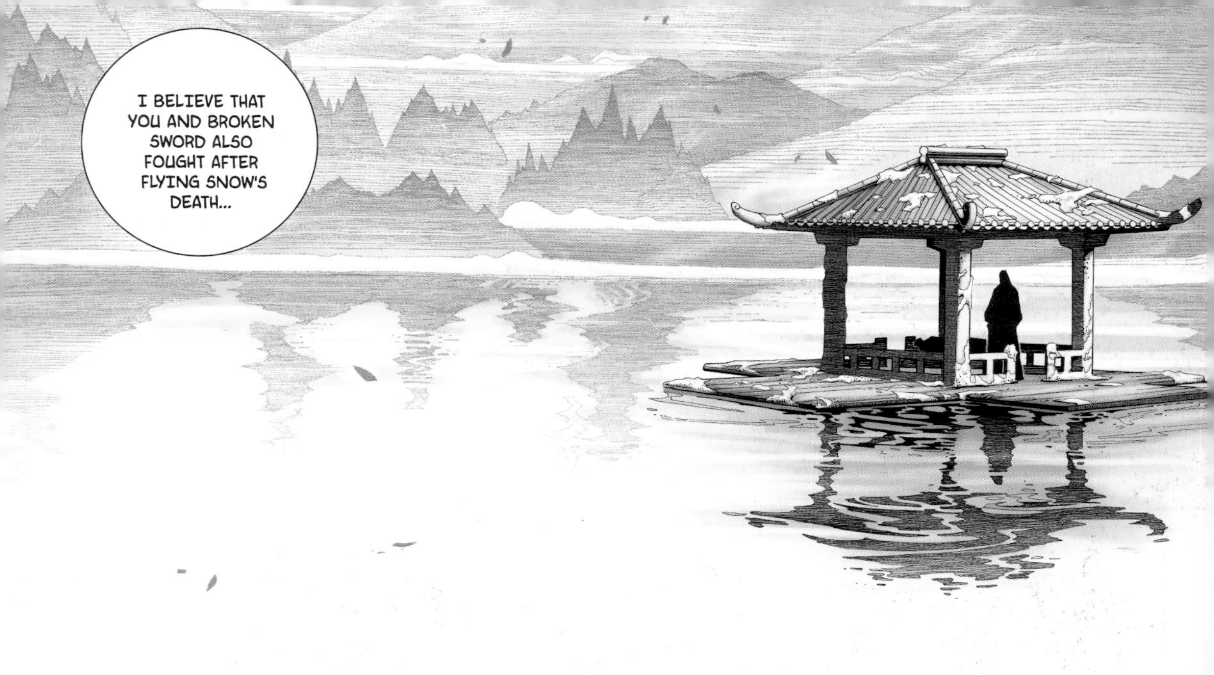
I BELIEVE THAT YOU AND BROKEN SWORD ALSO FOUGHT AFTER FLYING SNOW'S DEATH...

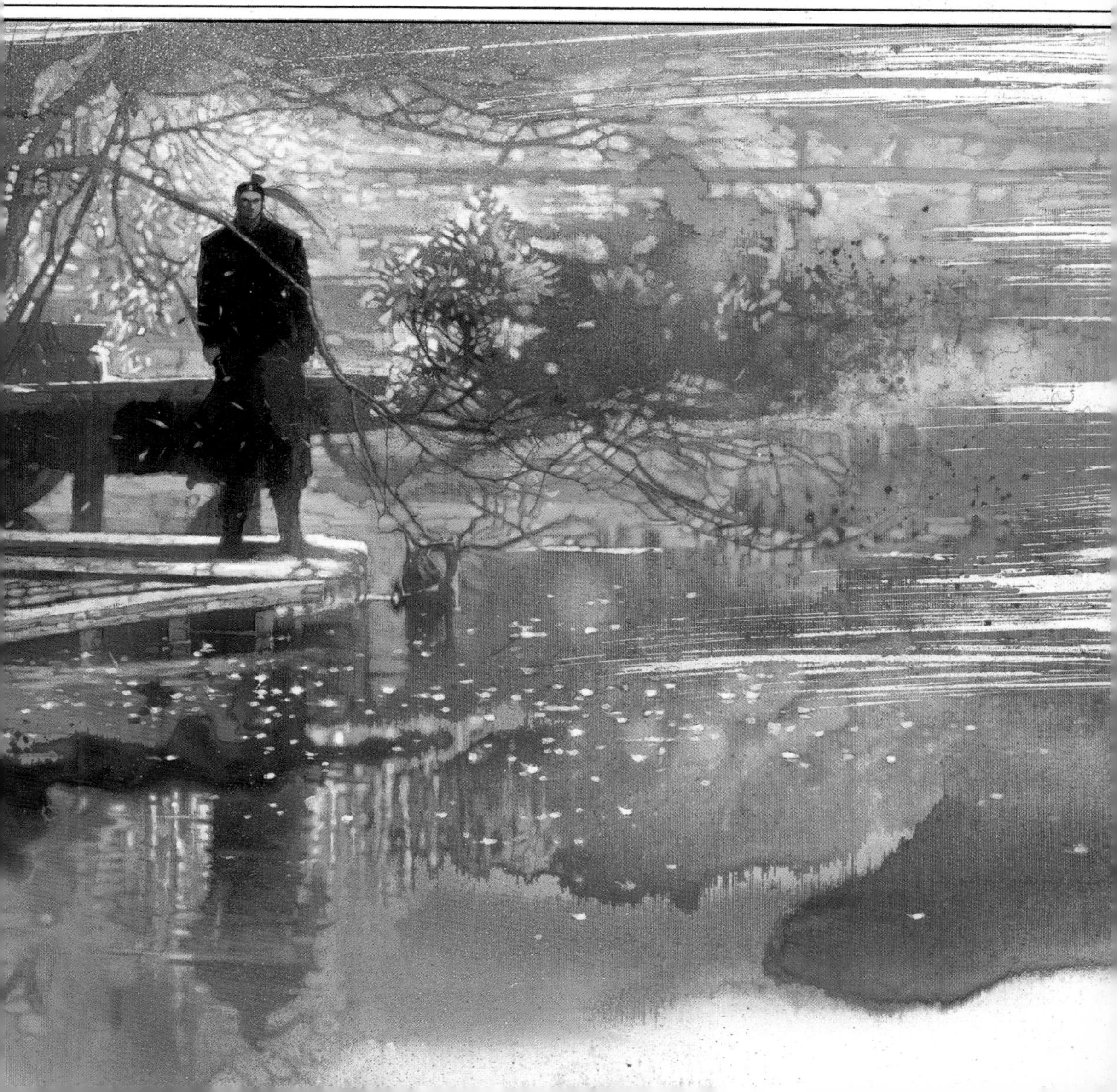

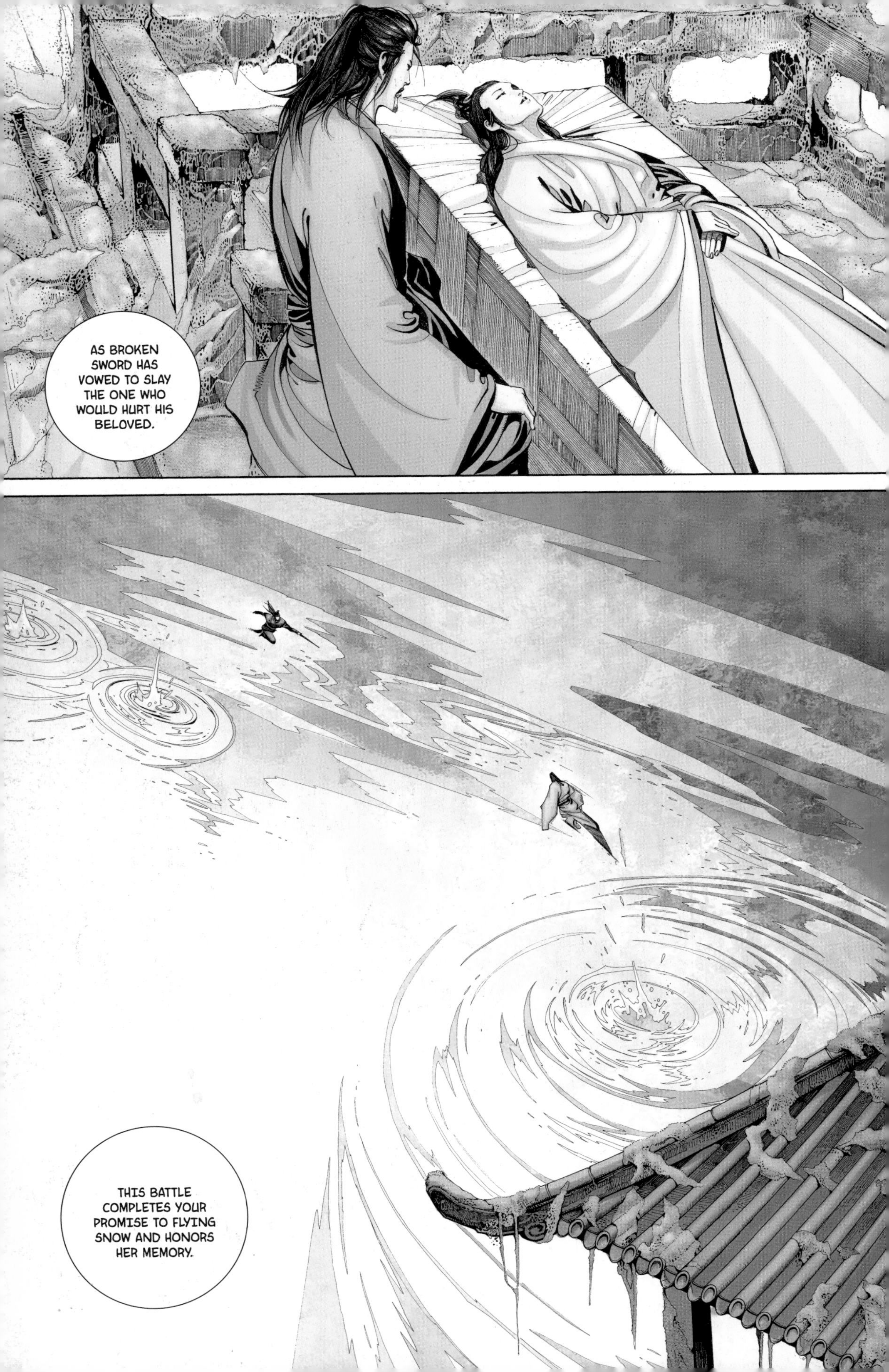
AS BROKEN SWORD HAS VOWED TO SLAY THE ONE WHO WOULD HURT HIS BELOVED.
THIS BATTLE COMPLETES YOUR PROMISE TO FLYING SNOW AND HONORS HER MEMORY.

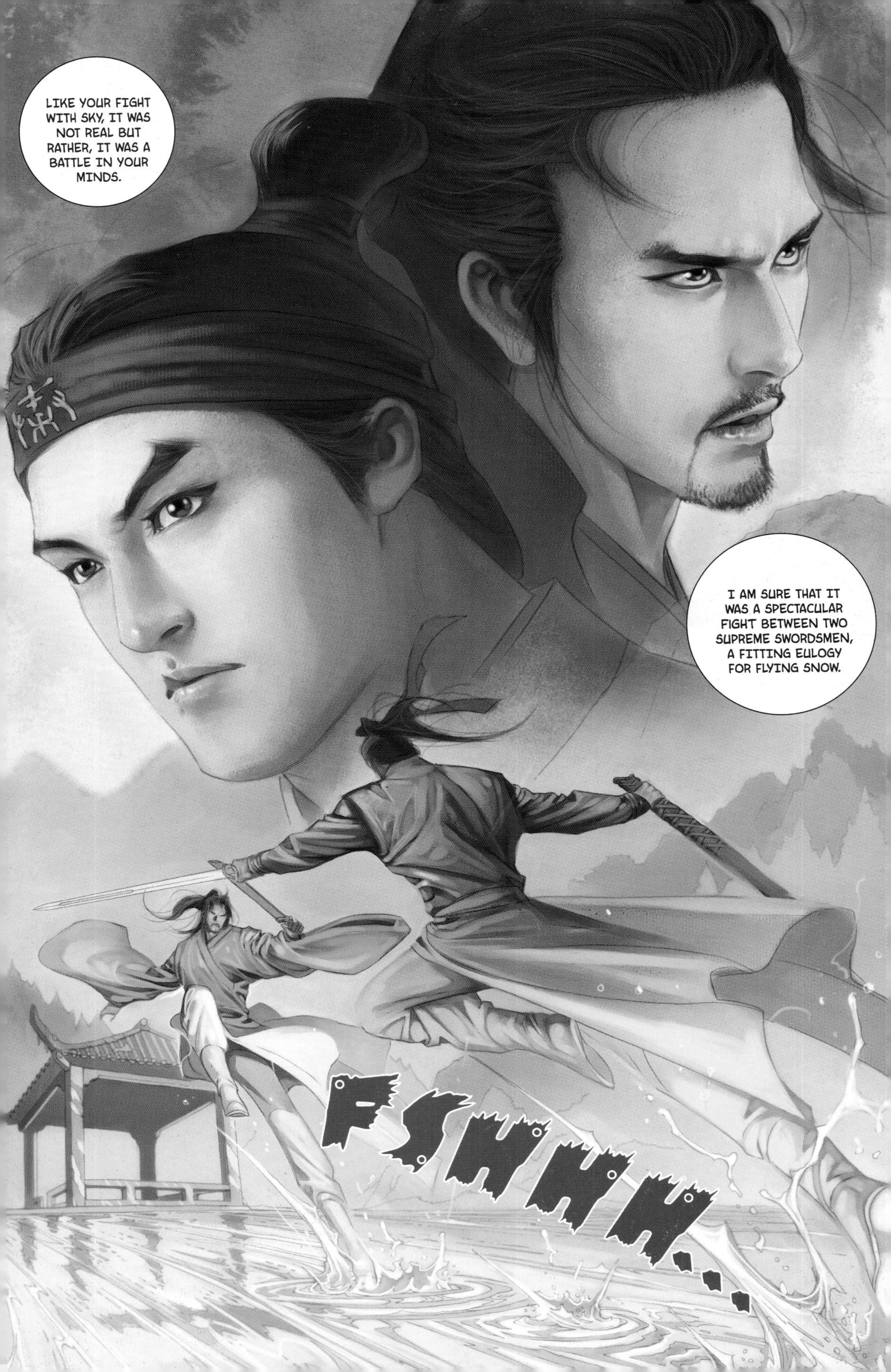
LIKE YOUR FIGHT WITH SKY, IT WAS NOT REAL BUT RATHER, IT WAS A BATTLE IN YOUR MINDS.
I AM SURE THAT IT WAS A SPECTACULAR FIGHT BETWEEN TWO SUPREME SWORDSMEN, A FITTING EULOGY FOR FLYING SNOW.
FSHHH...

HE AND SHE ARE BOUND IN LIFE AND DEATH. THEY WILL NEVER PART, NOR WILL THEIR SWORDS.

SHHHH...

BROKEN SWORD HAD INSTRUCTED MOON TO OFFER YOU HIS SWORD AFTER THE BATTLE -- TO FURTHER AID YOU ON YOUR MISSION.

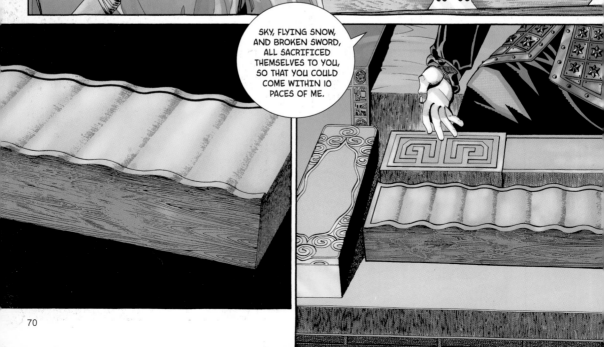

SKY, FLYING SNOW, AND BROKEN SWORD, ALL SACRIFICED THEMSELVES TO YOU, SO THAT YOU COULD COME WITHIN 10 PACES OF ME.

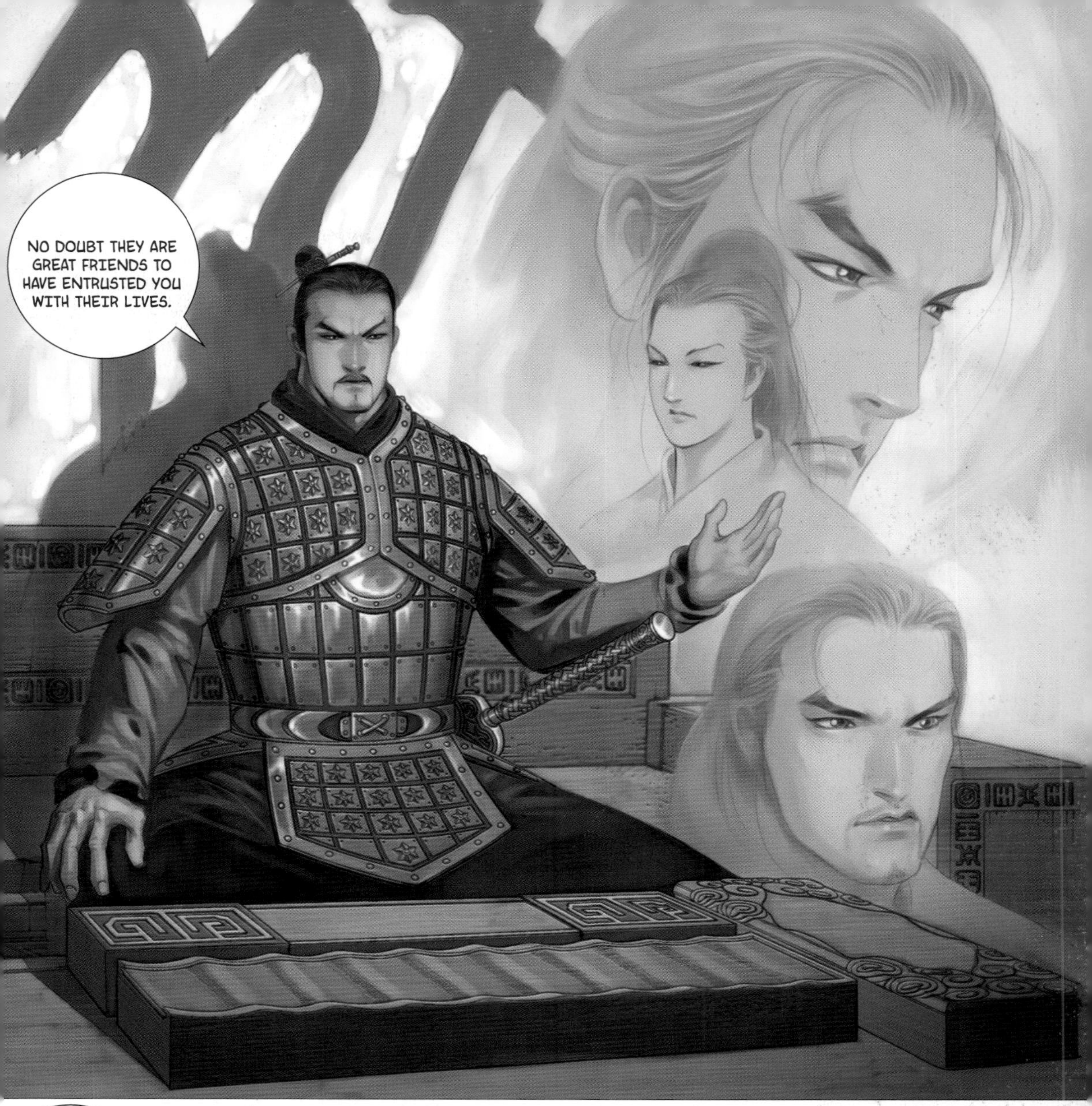
NO DOUBT THEY ARE GREAT FRIENDS TO HAVE ENTRUSTED YOU WITH THEIR LIVES.

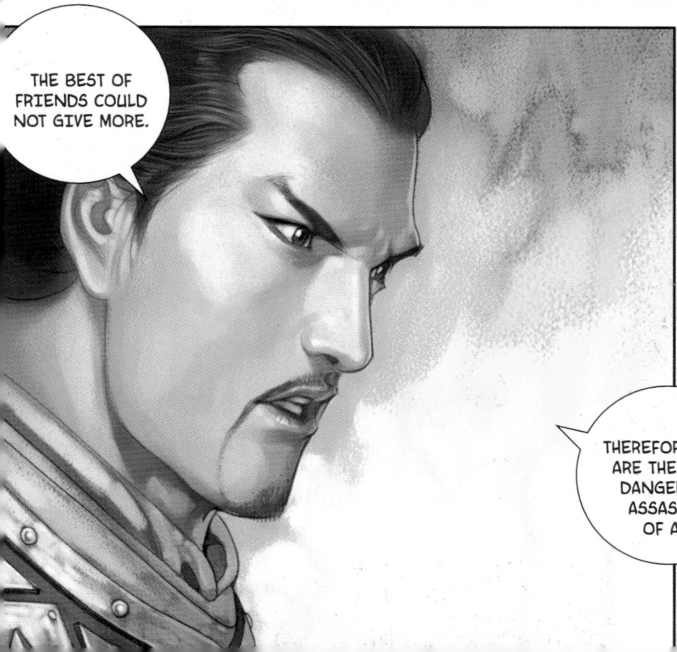
THE BEST OF FRIENDS COULD NOT GIVE MORE.

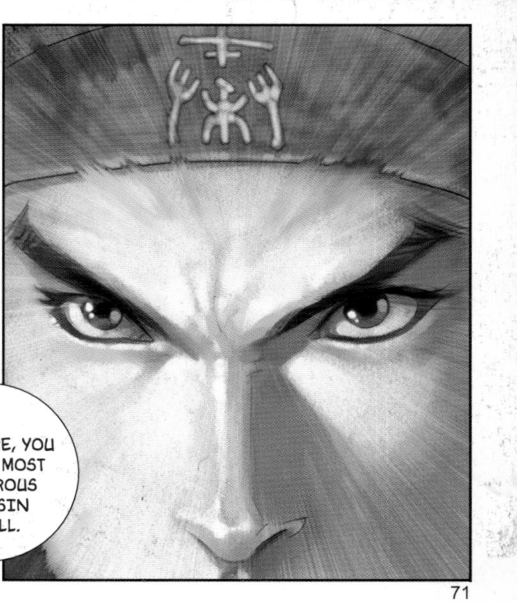
THEREFORE, YOU ARE THE MOST DANGEROUS ASSASSIN OF ALL.

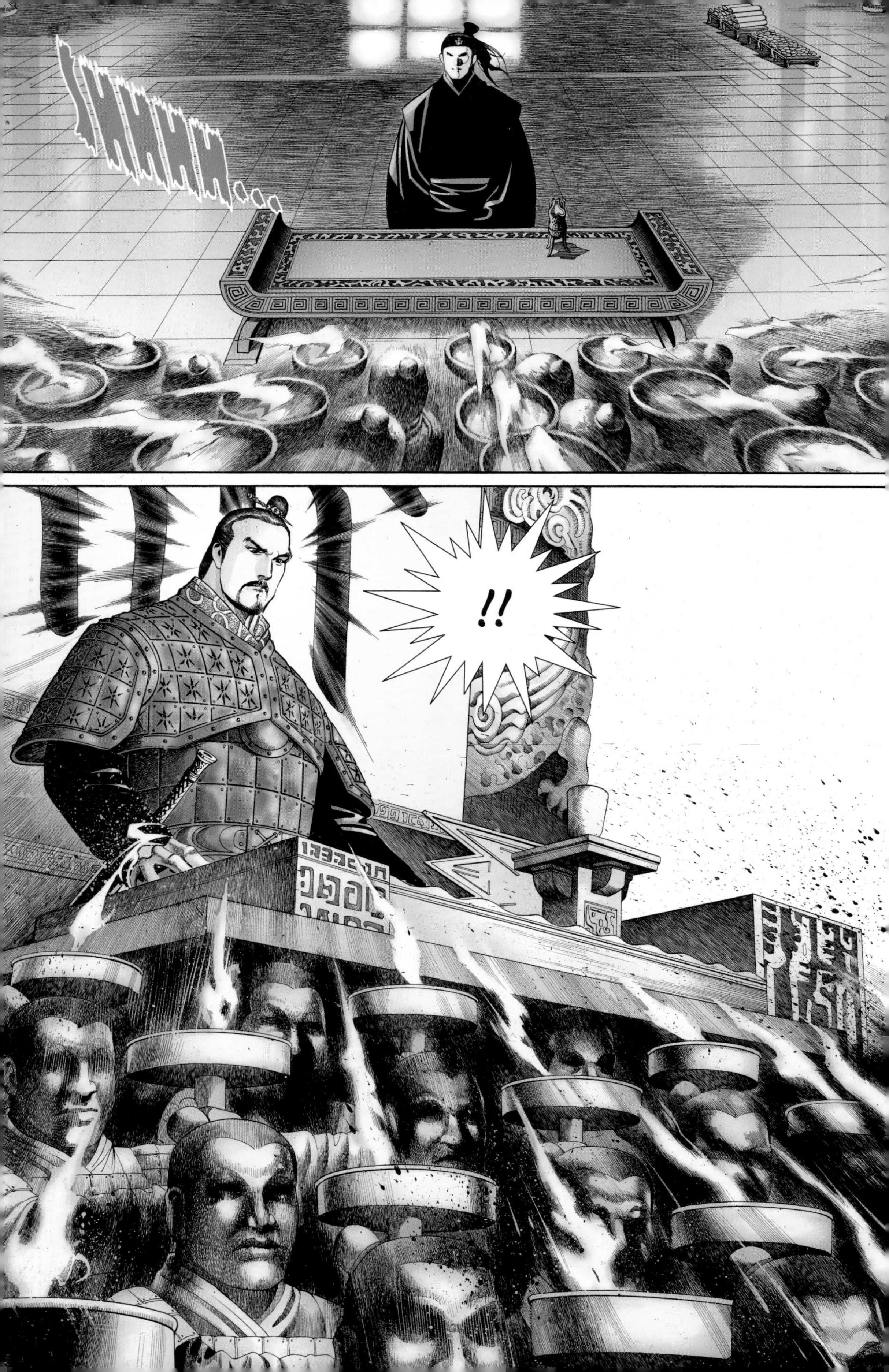
SHHHHH...
!!

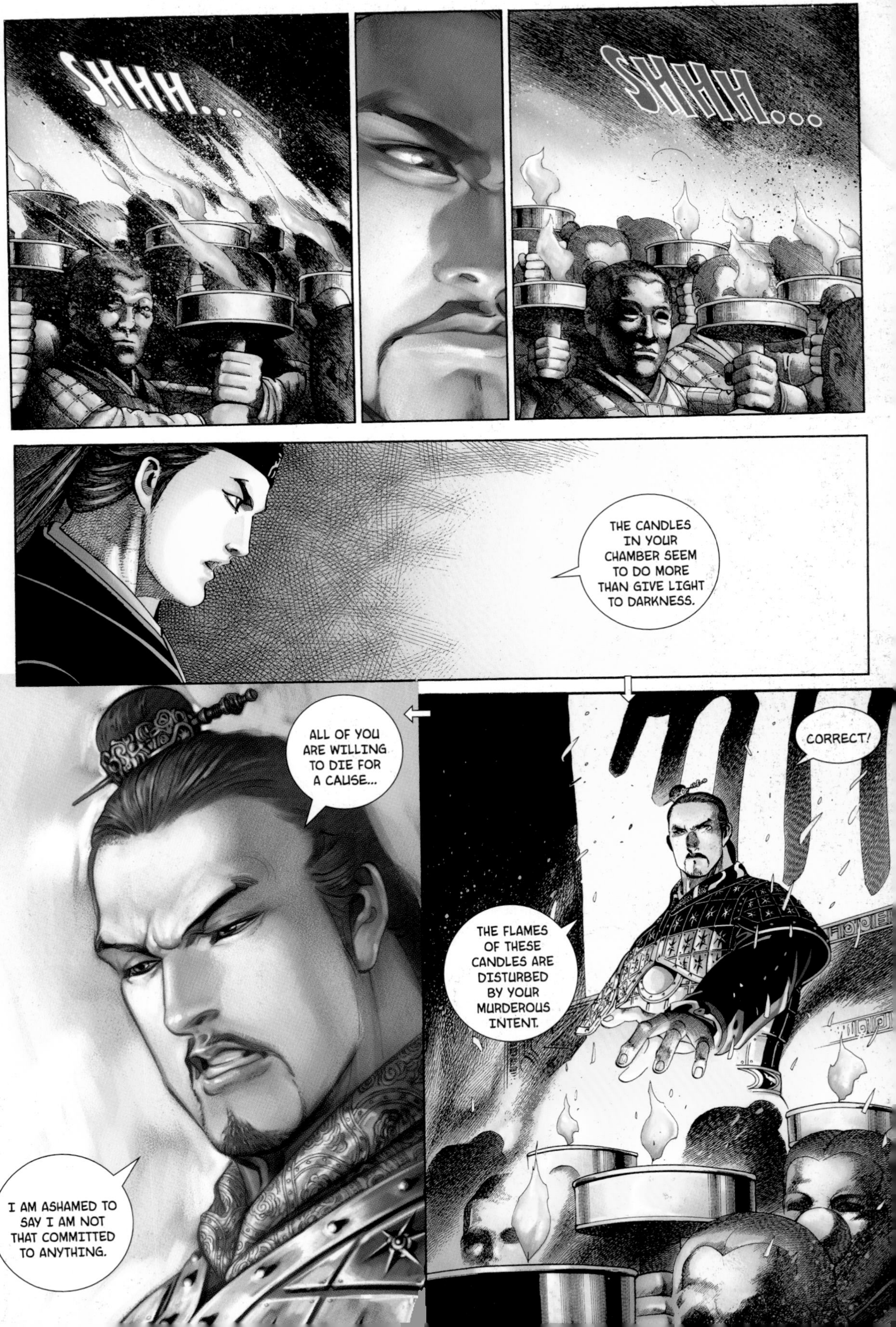
SHHH...
SHHH...
THE CANDLES IN YOUR CHAMBER SEEM TO DO MORE THAN GIVE LIGHT TO DARKNESS.
ALL OF YOU ARE WILLING TO DIE FOR A CAUSE...
I AM ASHAMED TO SAY I AM NOT THAT COMMITTED TO ANYTHING.
CORRECT!
THE FLAMES OF THESE CANDLES ARE DISTURBED BY YOUR MURDEROUS INTENT.

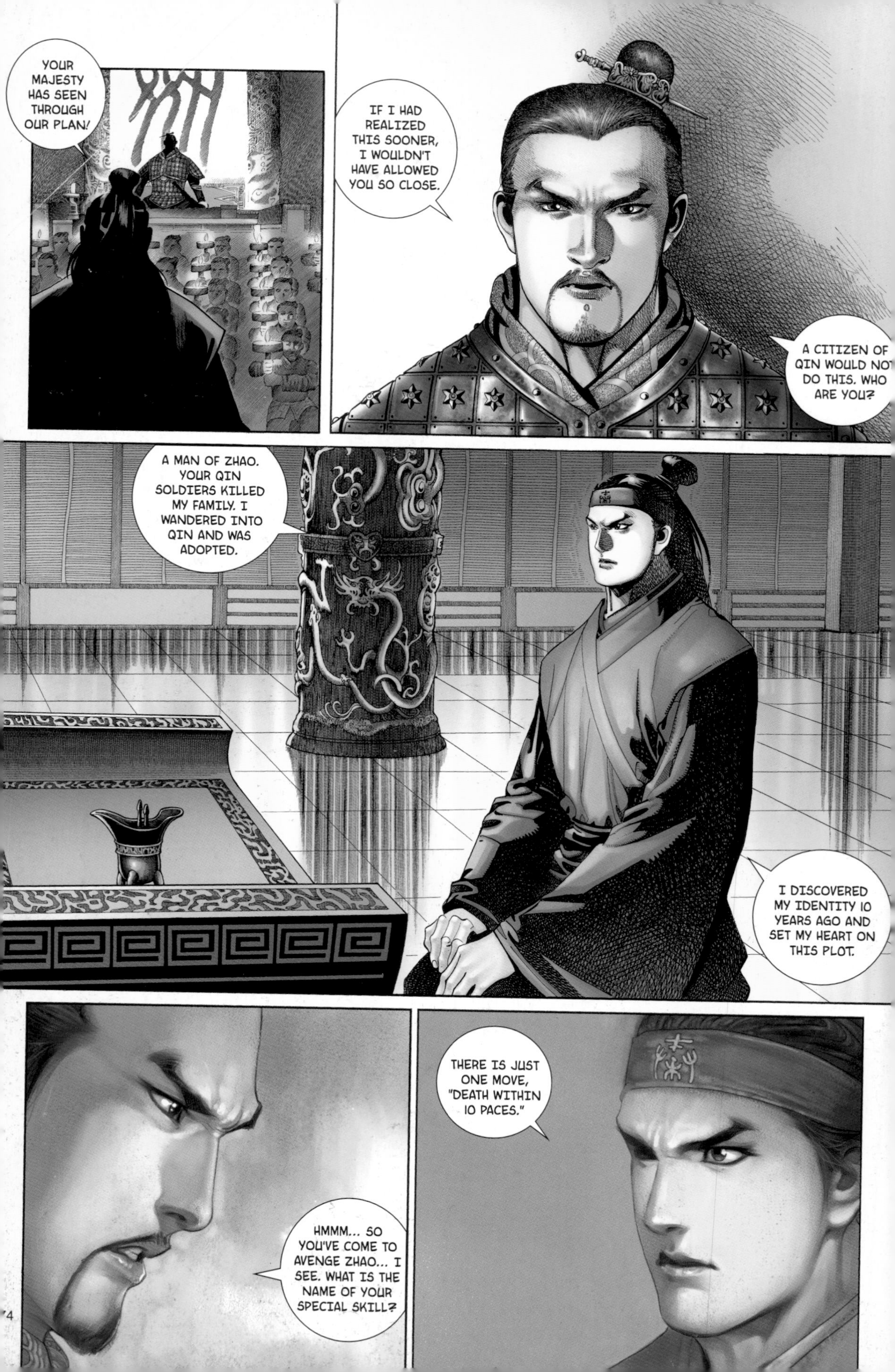
YOUR MAJESTY HAS SEEN THROUGH OUR PLAN!
IF I HAD REALIZED THIS SOONER, I WOULDN'T HAVE ALLOWED YOU SO CLOSE.
A CITIZEN OF QIN WOULD NOT DO THIS. WHO ARE YOU?
A MAN OF ZHAO. YOUR QIN SOLDIERS KILLED MY FAMILY. I WANDERED INTO QIN AND WAS ADOPTED.
I DISCOVERED MY IDENTITY 10 YEARS AGO AND SET MY HEART ON THIS PLOT.
HMMM... SO YOU'VE COME TO AVENGE ZHAO... I SEE. WHAT IS THE NAME OF YOUR SPECIAL SKILL?
THERE IS JUST ONE MOVE, "DEATH WITHIN 10 PACES."

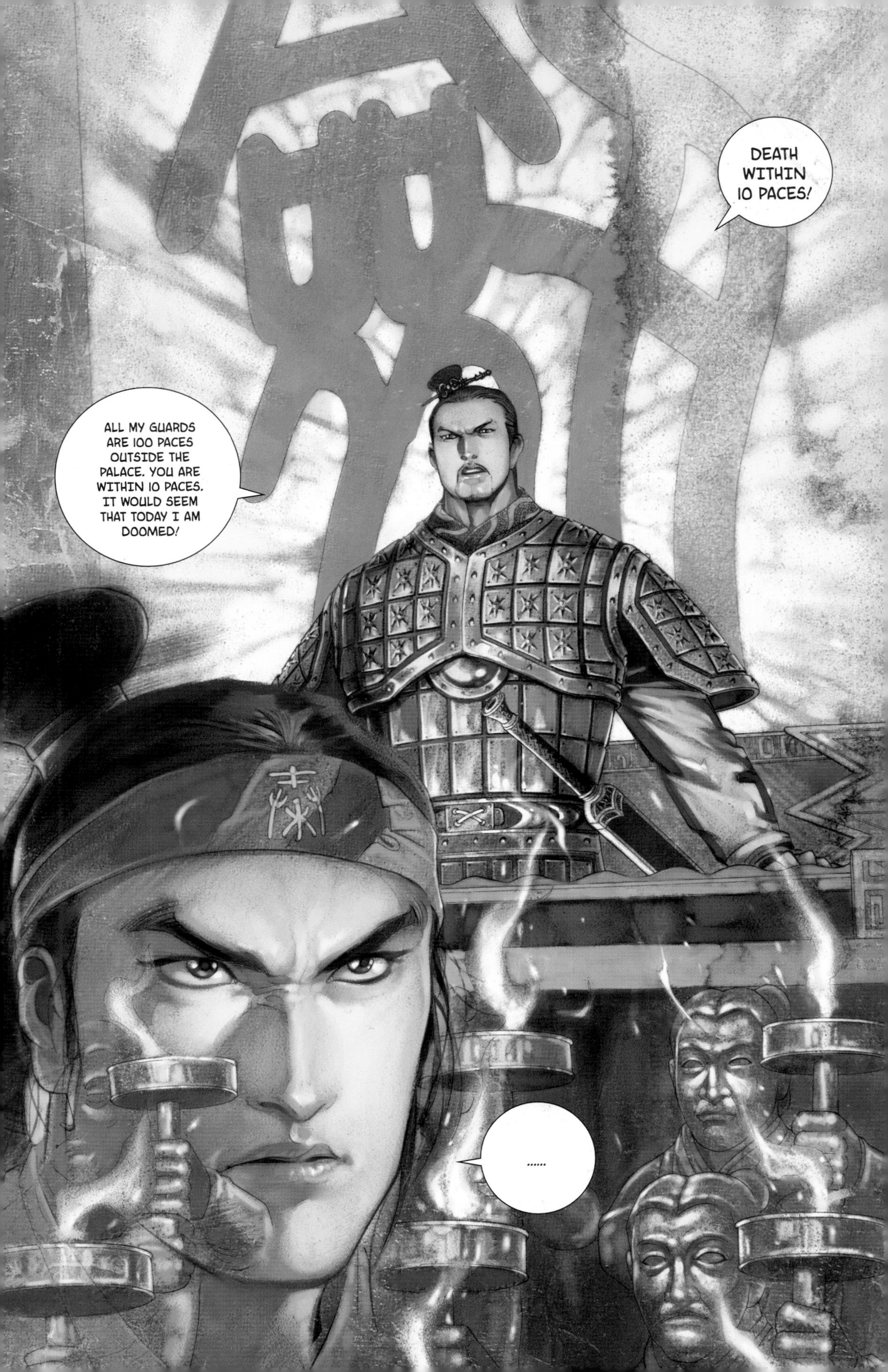
DEATH WITHIN 10 PACES!
ALL MY GUARDS ARE 100 PACES OUTSIDE THE PALACE. YOU ARE WITHIN 10 PACES. IT WOULD SEEM THAT TODAY I AM DOOMED!
......

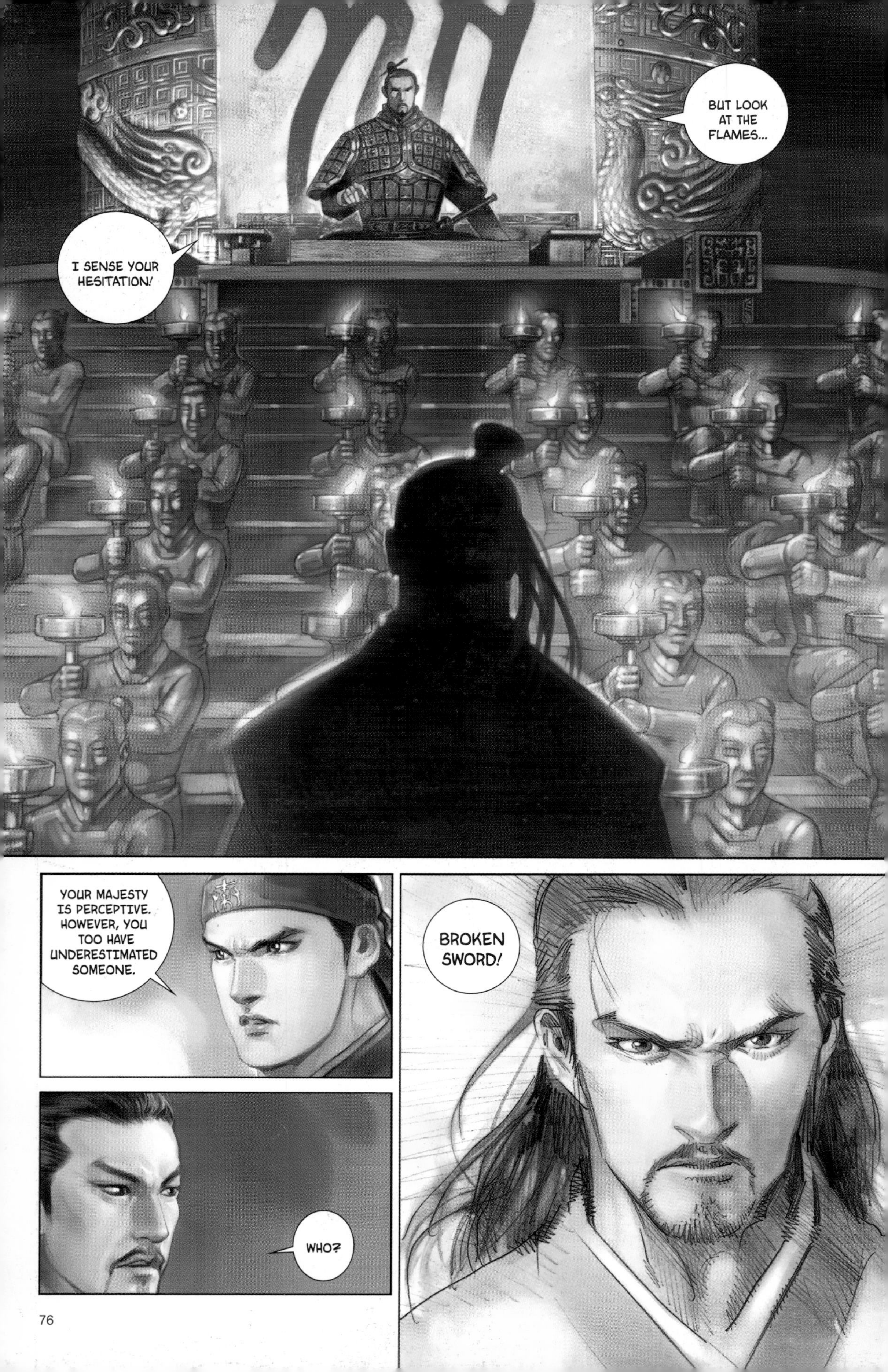
BUT LOOK AT THE FLAMES...
I SENSE YOUR HESITATION!
YOUR MAJESTY IS PERCEPTIVE. HOWEVER, YOU TOO HAVE UNDERESTIMATED SOMEONE.
WHO?
BROKEN SWORD!

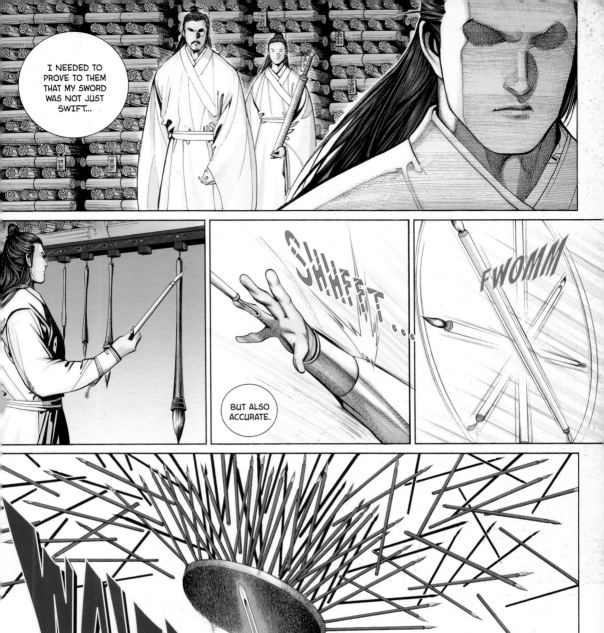

I NEEDED TO PROVE TO THEM THAT MY SWORD WAS NOT JUST SWIFT...

SHHFFT...

BUT ALSO ACCURATE.

FWOMM

WAHH!

BEING SWIFT IS NOT ENOUGH TO KILL THE EMPEROR.

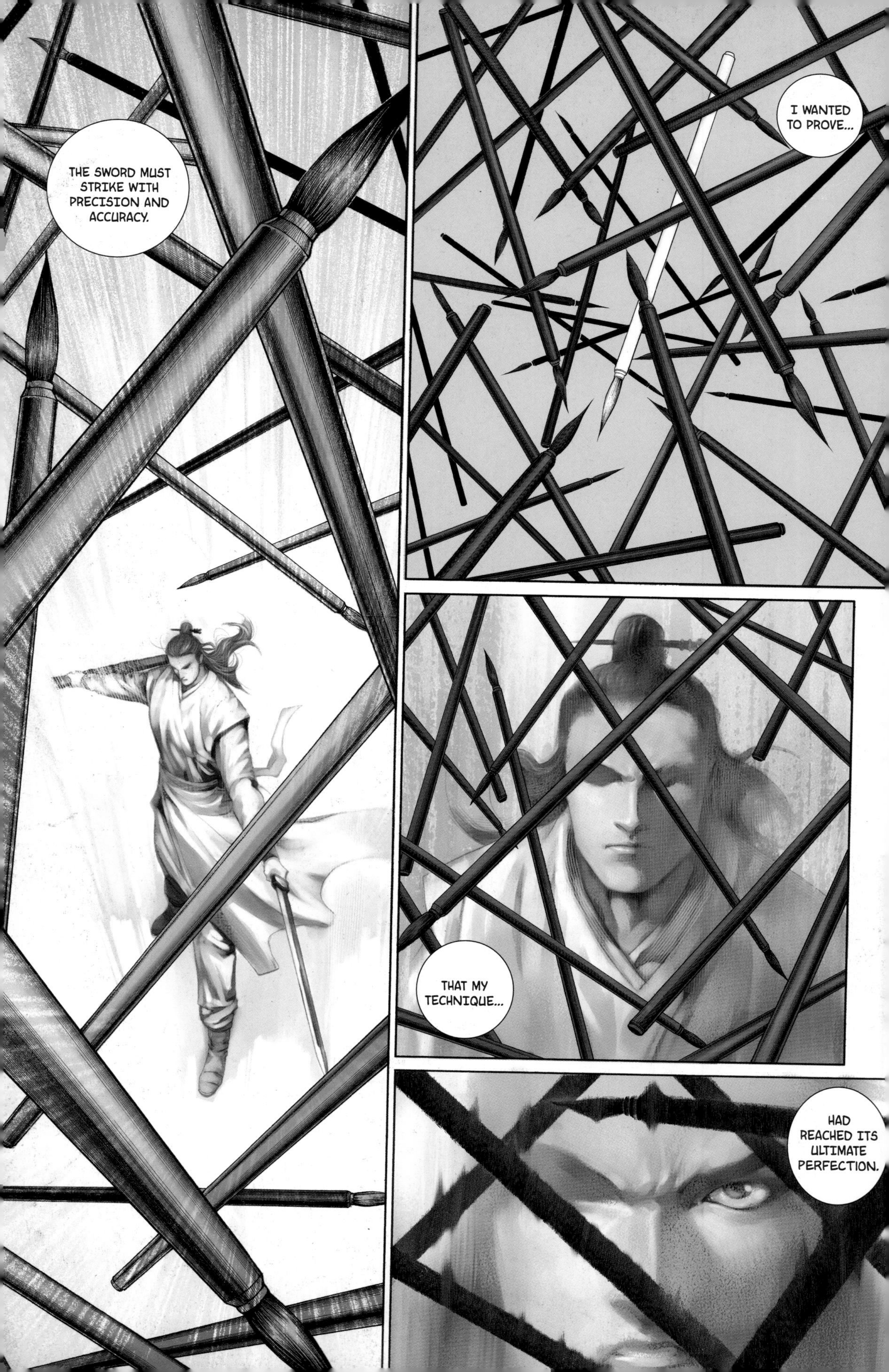
THE SWORD MUST STRIKE WITH PRECISION AND ACCURACY.
I WANTED TO PROVE...
THAT MY TECHNIQUE...
HAD REACHED ITS ULTIMATE PERFECTION.

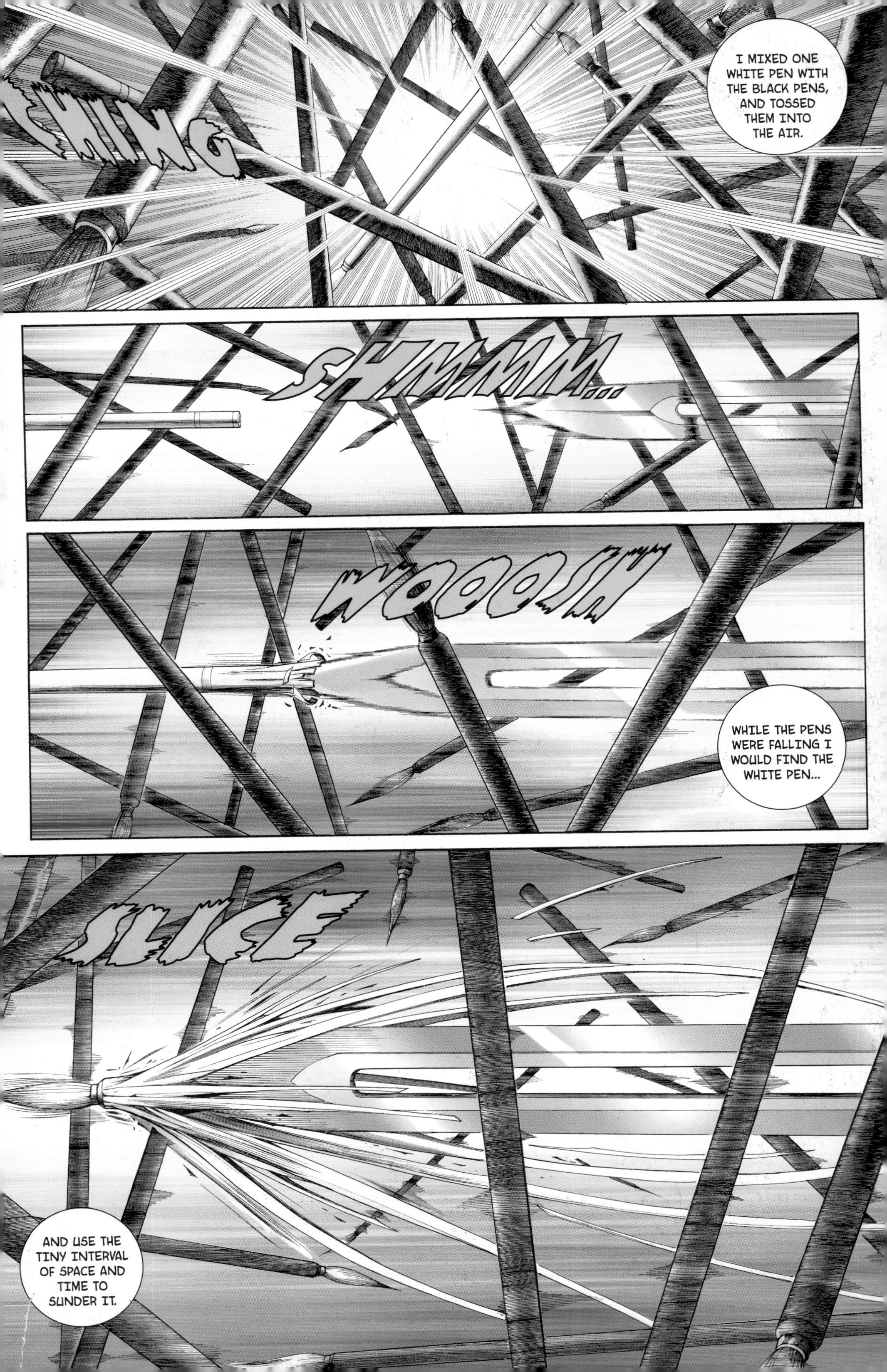
SHING
I MIXED ONE WHITE PEN WITH THE BLACK PENS, AND TOSSED THEM INTO THE AIR.
SHMMM...
WOOOSH
WHILE THE PENS WERE FALLING I WOULD FIND THE WHITE PEN...
SLICE
AND USE THE TINY INTERVAL OF SPACE AND TIME TO SUNDER IT.

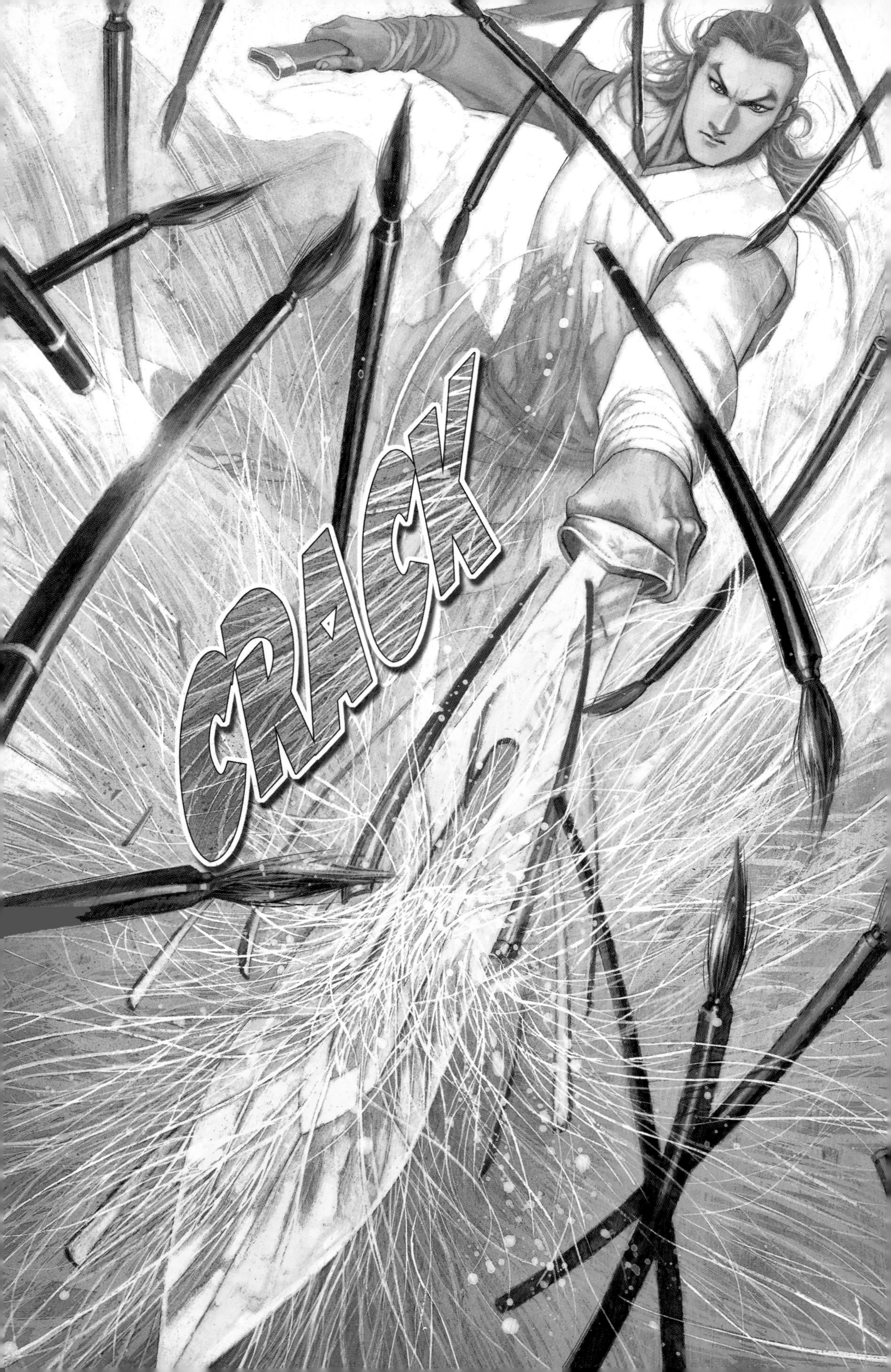
CRACK

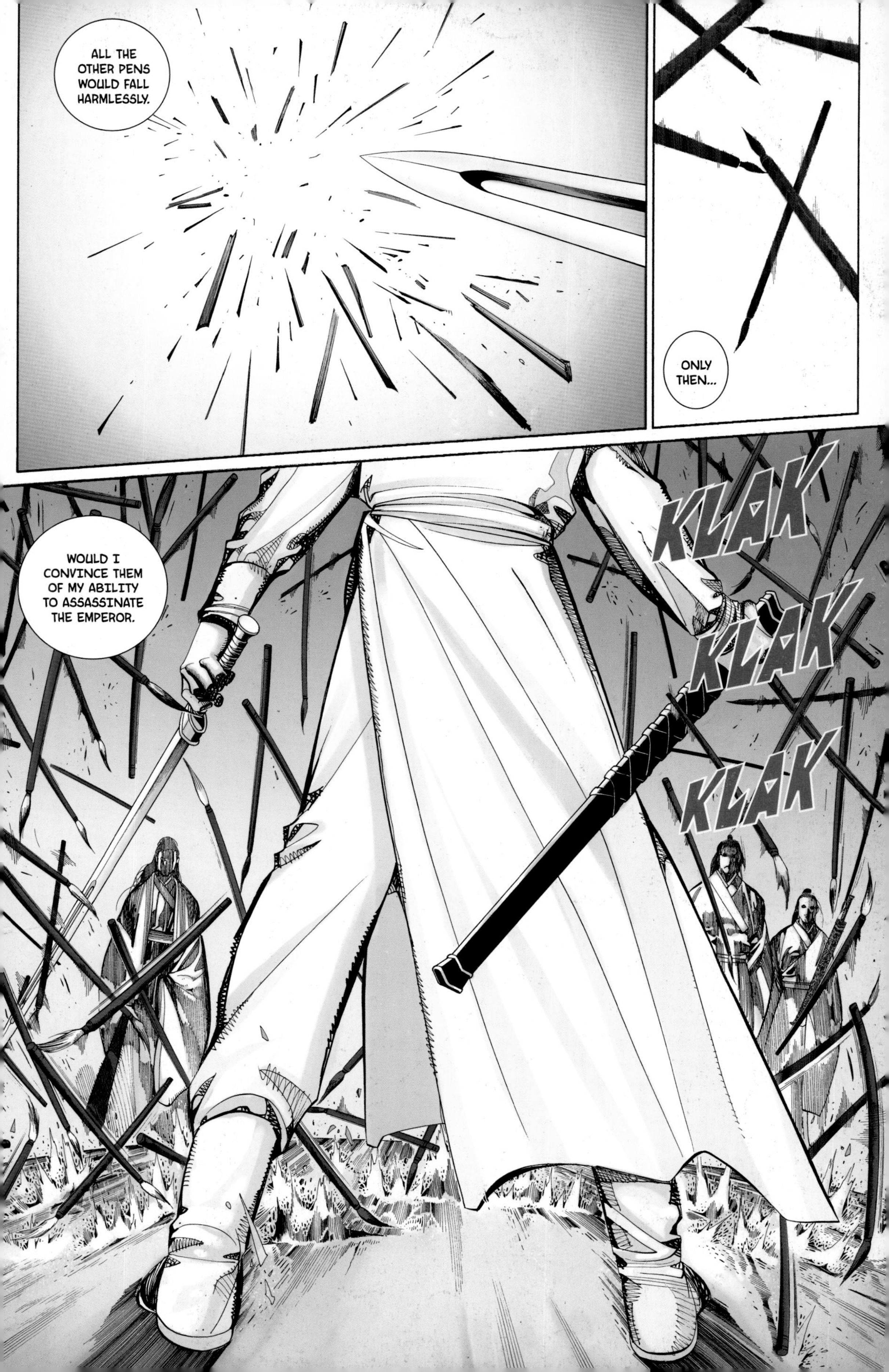
ALL THE OTHER PENS WOULD FALL HARMLESSLY.
ONLY THEN...
WOULD I CONVINCE THEM OF MY ABILITY TO ASSASSINATE THE EMPEROR.
KLAK
KLAK
KLAK

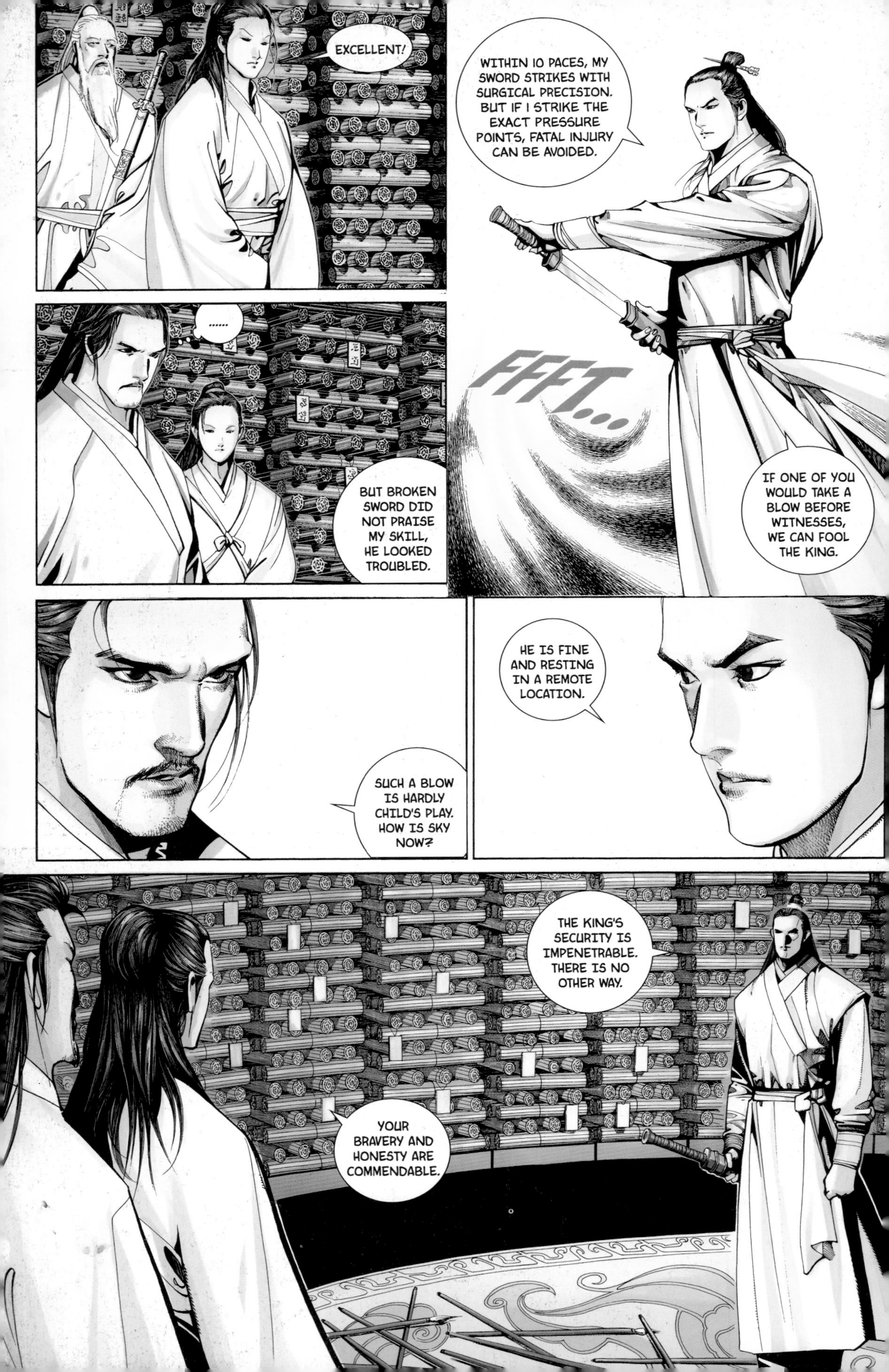
EXCELLENT!
WITHIN 10 PACES, MY SWORD STRIKES WITH SURGICAL PRECISION. BUT IF I STRIKE THE EXACT PRESSURE POINTS, FATAL INJURY CAN BE AVOIDED.
......
BUT BROKEN SWORD DID NOT PRAISE MY SKILL, HE LOOKED TROUBLED.
FFFT...
IF ONE OF YOU WOULD TAKE A BLOW BEFORE WITNESSES, WE CAN FOOL THE KING.
SUCH A BLOW IS HARDLY CHILD'S PLAY. HOW IS SKY NOW?
HE IS FINE AND RESTING IN A REMOTE LOCATION.
THE KING'S SECURITY IS IMPENETRABLE. THERE IS NO OTHER WAY.
YOUR BRAVERY AND HONESTY ARE COMMENDABLE.

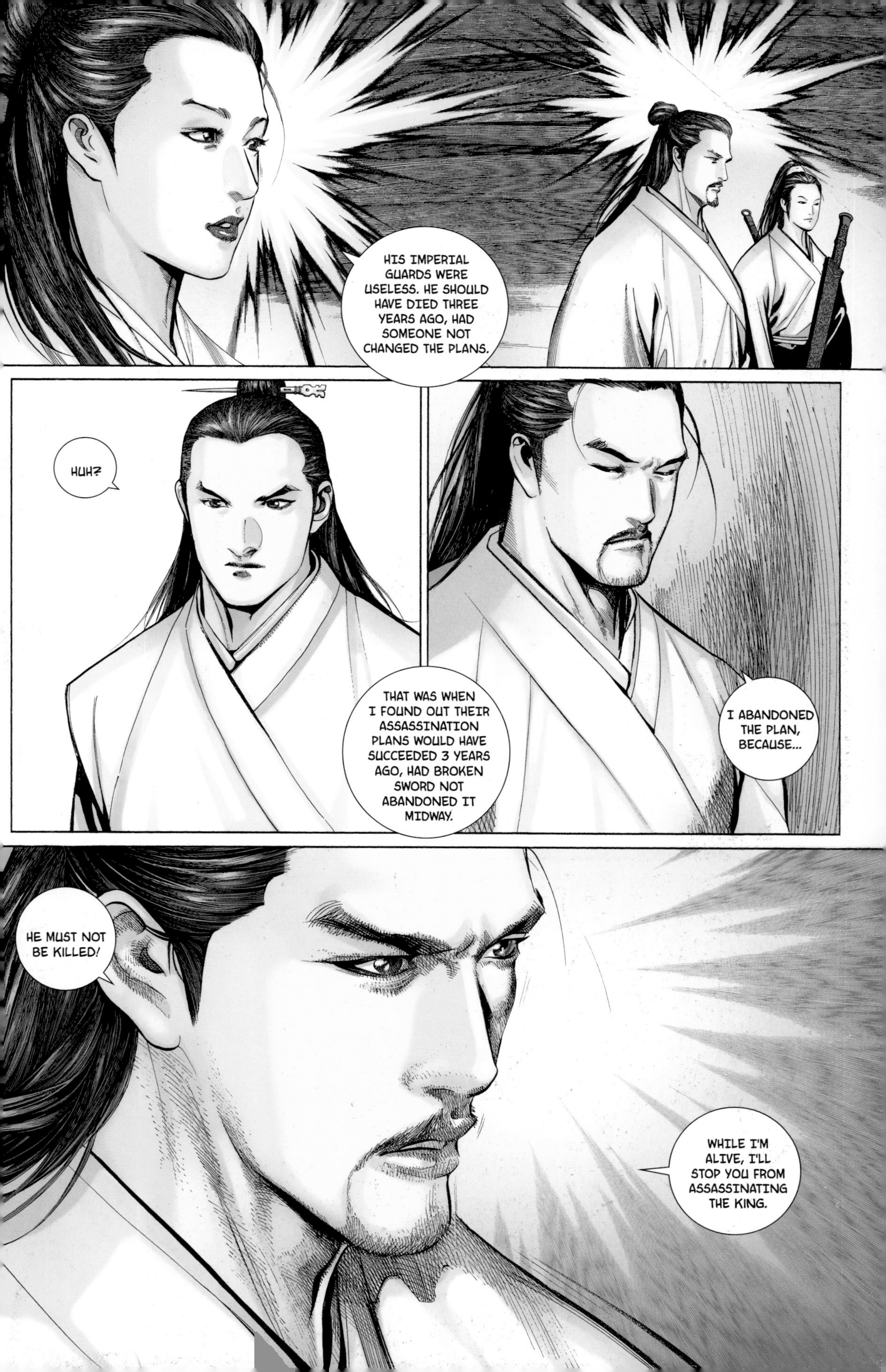
HIS IMPERIAL GUARDS WERE USELESS. HE SHOULD HAVE DIED THREE YEARS AGO, HAD SOMEONE NOT CHANGED THE PLANS.
HUH?
I ABANDONED THE PLAN, BECAUSE...
THAT WAS WHEN I FOUND OUT THEIR ASSASSINATION PLANS WOULD HAVE SUCCEEDED 3 YEARS AGO, HAD BROKEN SWORD NOT ABANDONED IT MIDWAY.
HE MUST NOT BE KILLED!
WHILE I'M ALIVE, I'LL STOP YOU FROM ASSASSINATING THE KING.

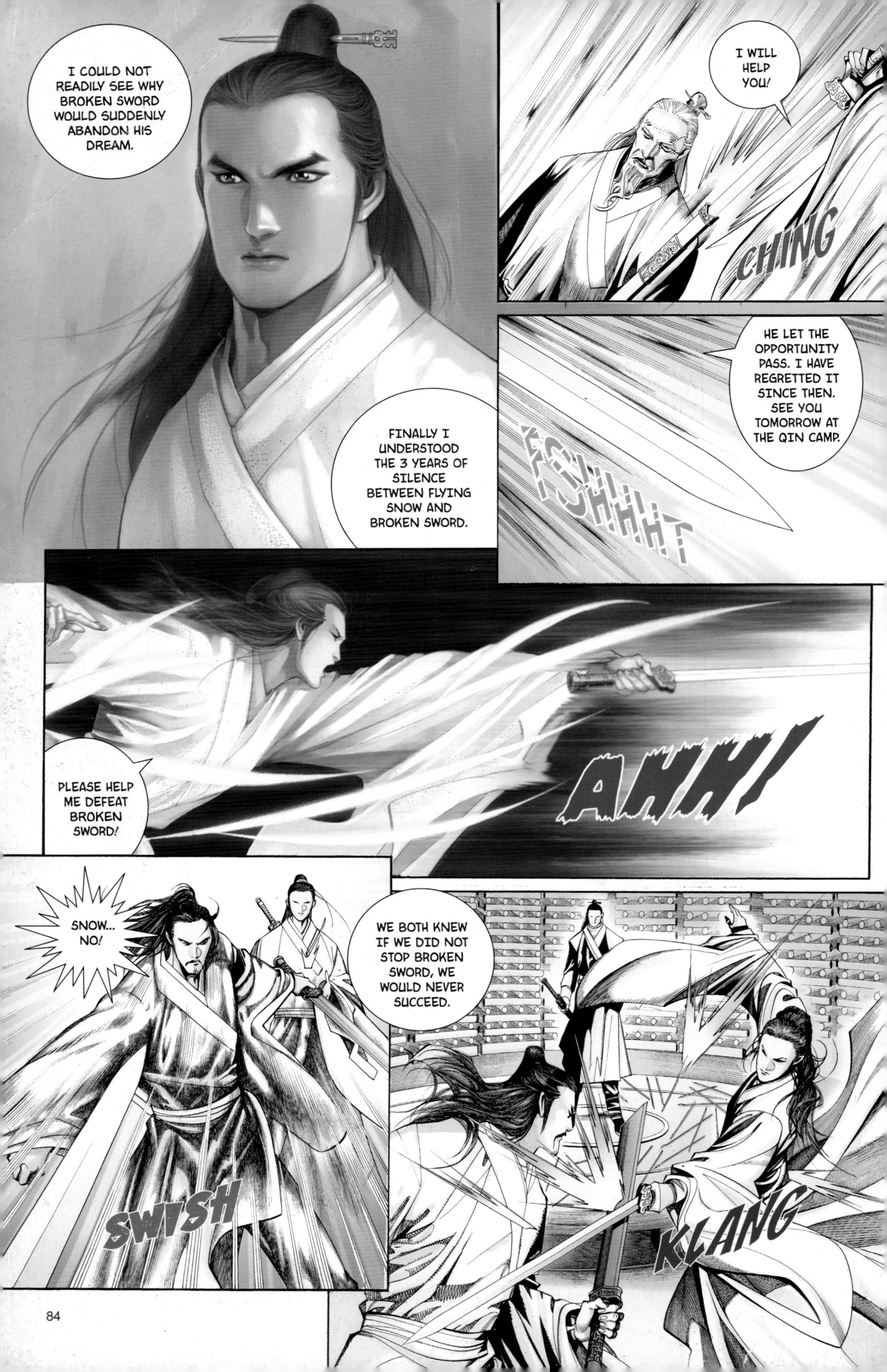
I COULD NOT READILY SEE WHY BROKEN SWORD WOULD SUDDENLY ABANDON HIS DREAM.
FINALLY I UNDERSTOOD THE 3 YEARS OF SILENCE BETWEEN FLYING SNOW AND BROKEN SWORD.
I WILL HELP YOU!
CHING
HE LET THE OPPORTUNITY PASS. I HAVE REGRETTED IT SINCE THEN. SEE YOU TOMORROW AT THE QIN CAMP.
SHHHHT
PLEASE HELP ME DEFEAT BROKEN SWORD!
AHH!
SNOW... NO!
SWISH
WE BOTH KNEW IF WE DID NOT STOP BROKEN SWORD, WE WOULD NEVER SUCCEED.
KLANG

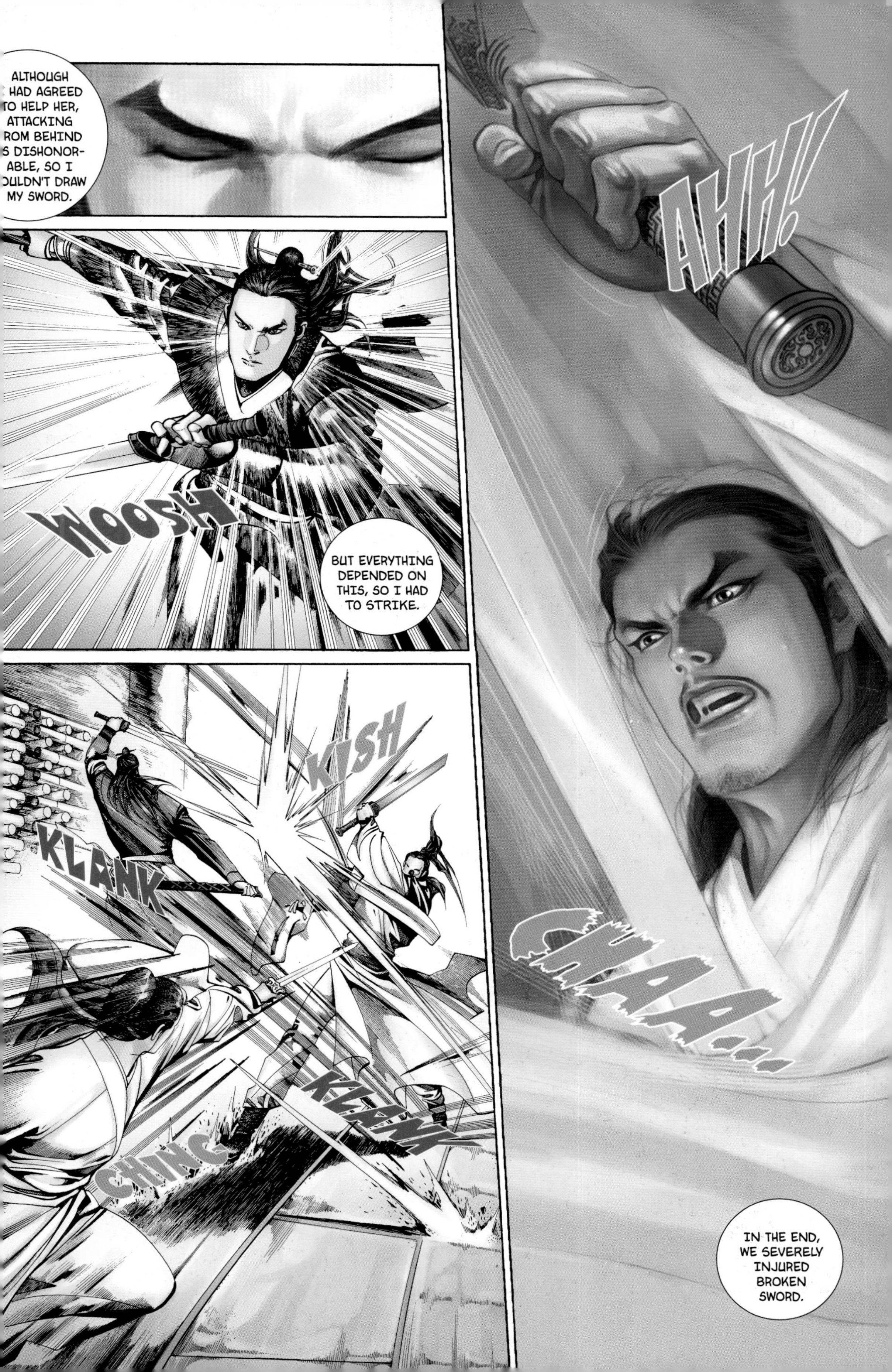

ALTHOUGH HAD AGREED TO HELP HER, ATTACKING ROM BEHIND S DISHONOR-ABLE, SO I OULDN'T DRAW MY SWORD.
WOOSH
BUT EVERYTHING DEPENDED ON THIS, SO I HAD TO STRIKE.
KISH
KLANK
KLANK
CHING
AHH!!
CHAA...
IN THE END, WE SEVERELY INJURED BROKEN SWORD.

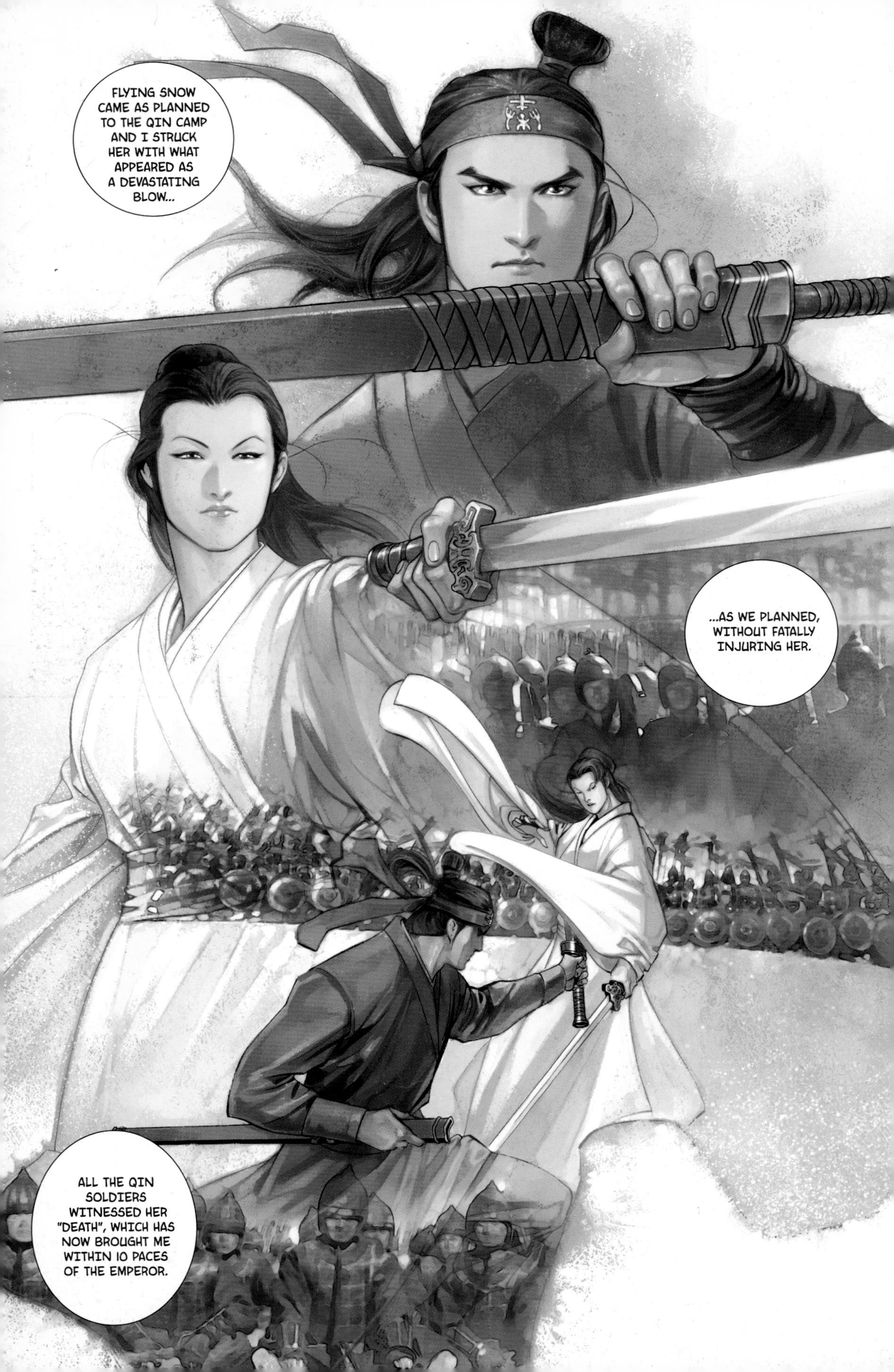
FLYING SNOW CAME AS PLANNED TO THE QIN CAMP AND I STRUCK HER WITH WHAT APPEARED AS A DEVASTATING BLOW...
...AS WE PLANNED, WITHOUT FATALLY INJURING HER.
ALL THE QIN SOLDIERS WITNESSED HER "DEATH", WHICH HAS NOW BROUGHT ME WITHIN 10 PACES OF THE EMPEROR.

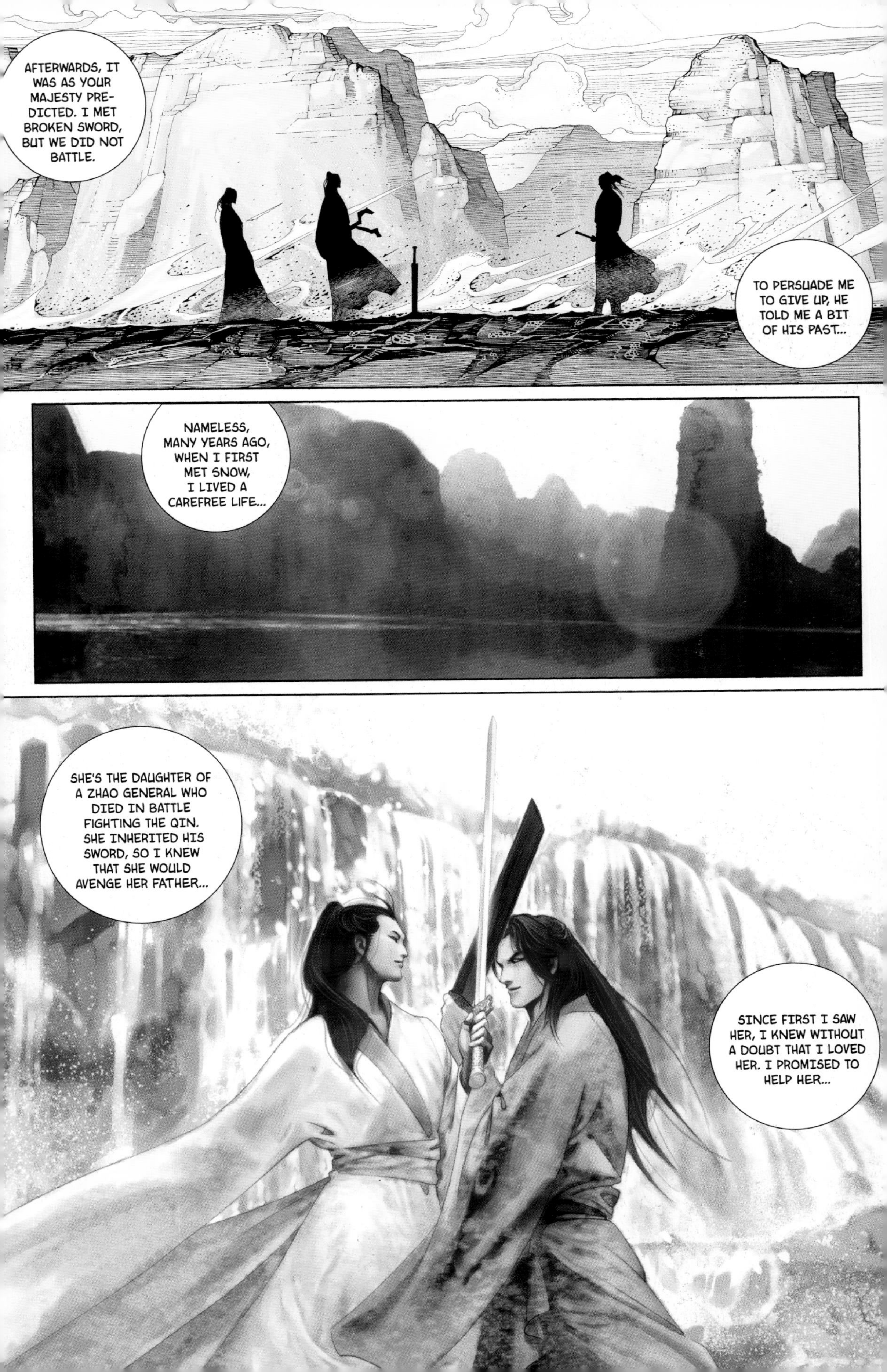
AFTERWARDS, IT WAS AS YOUR MAJESTY PRE-DICTED. I MET BROKEN SWORD, BUT WE DID NOT BATTLE.
TO PERSUADE ME TO GIVE UP, HE TOLD ME A BIT OF HIS PAST...
NAMELESS, MANY YEARS AGO, WHEN I FIRST MET SNOW, I LIVED A CAREFREE LIFE...
SHE'S THE DAUGHTER OF A ZHAO GENERAL WHO DIED IN BATTLE FIGHTING THE QIN. SHE INHERITED HIS SWORD, SO I KNEW THAT SHE WOULD AVENGE HER FATHER...
SINCE FIRST I SAW HER, I KNEW WITHOUT A DOUBT THAT I LOVED HER. I PROMISED TO HELP HER...

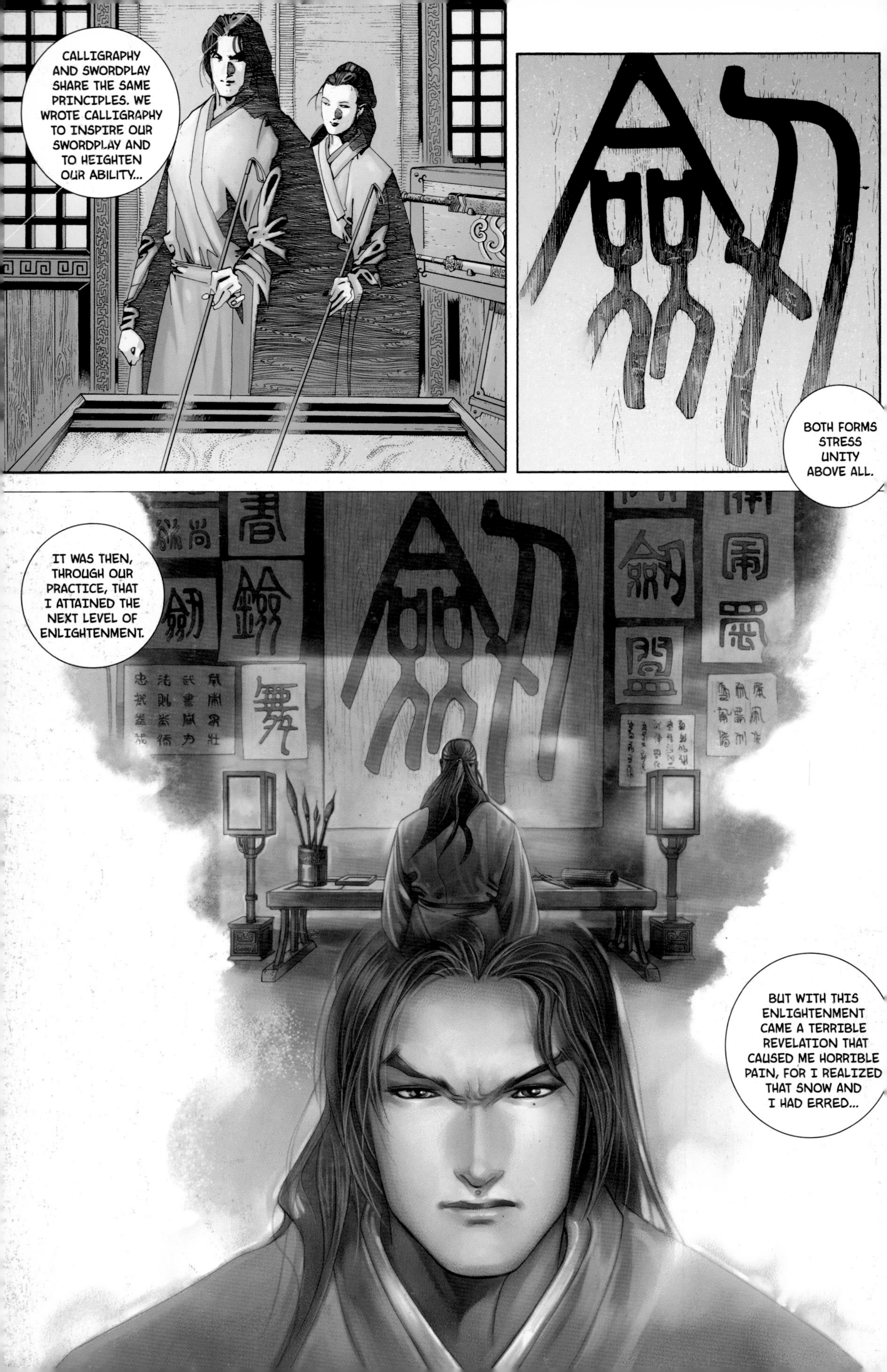
CALLIGRAPHY AND SWORDPLAY SHARE THE SAME PRINCIPLES. WE WROTE CALLIGRAPHY TO INSPIRE OUR SWORDPLAY AND TO HEIGHTEN OUR ABILITY...
BOTH FORMS STRESS UNITY ABOVE ALL.
IT WAS THEN, THROUGH OUR PRACTICE, THAT I ATTAINED THE NEXT LEVEL OF ENLIGHTENMENT.
BUT WITH THIS ENLIGHTENMENT CAME A TERRIBLE REVELATION THAT CAUSED ME HORRIBLE PAIN, FOR I REALIZED THAT SNOW AND I HAD ERRED...

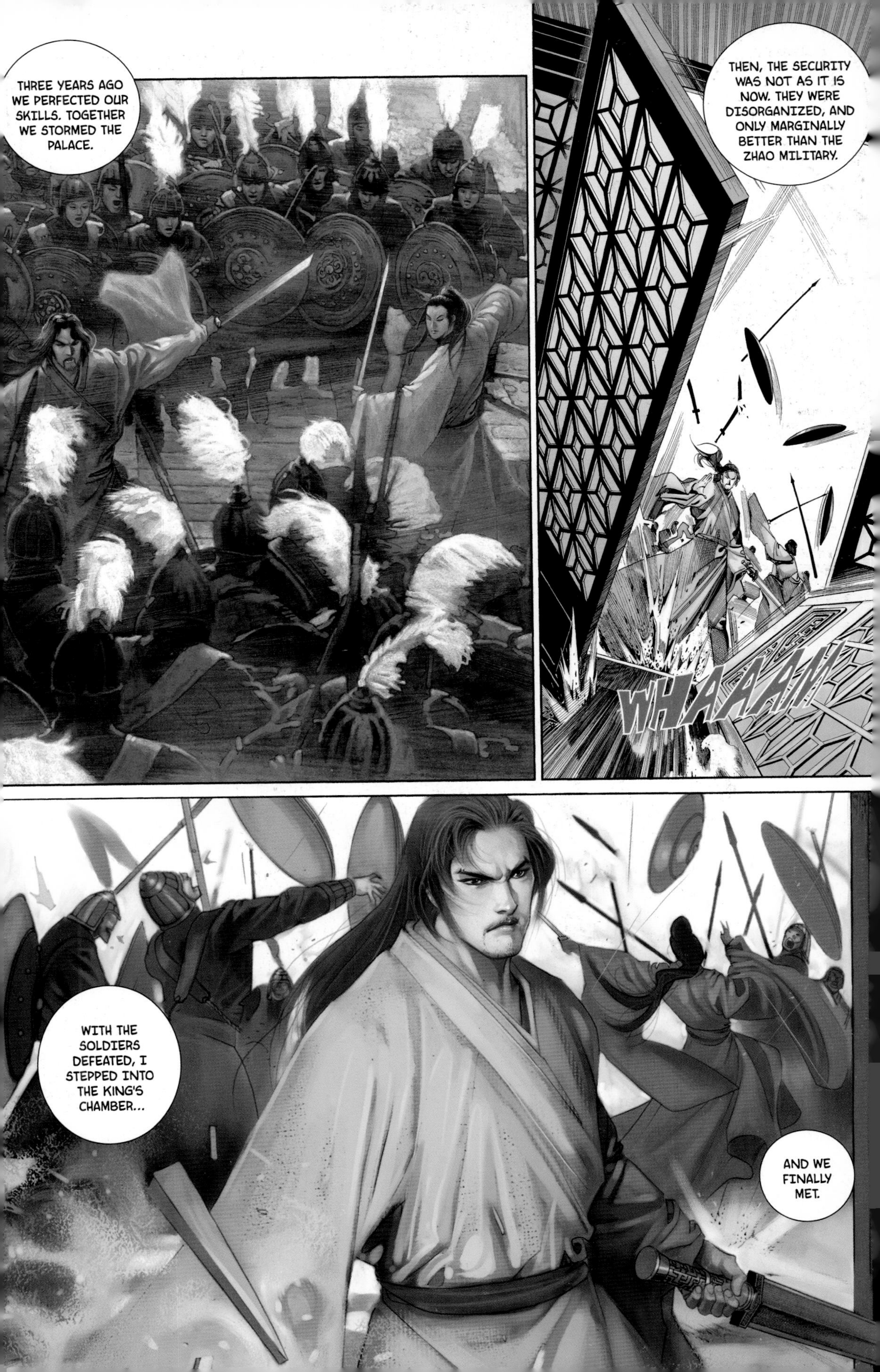
THREE YEARS AGO WE PERFECTED OUR SKILLS. TOGETHER WE STORMED THE PALACE.
THEN, THE SECURITY WAS NOT AS IT IS NOW. THEY WERE DISORGANIZED, AND ONLY MARGINALLY BETTER THAN THE ZHAO MILITARY.
WHAAAAM
WITH THE SOLDIERS DEFEATED, I STEPPED INTO THE KING'S CHAMBER...
AND WE FINALLY MET.

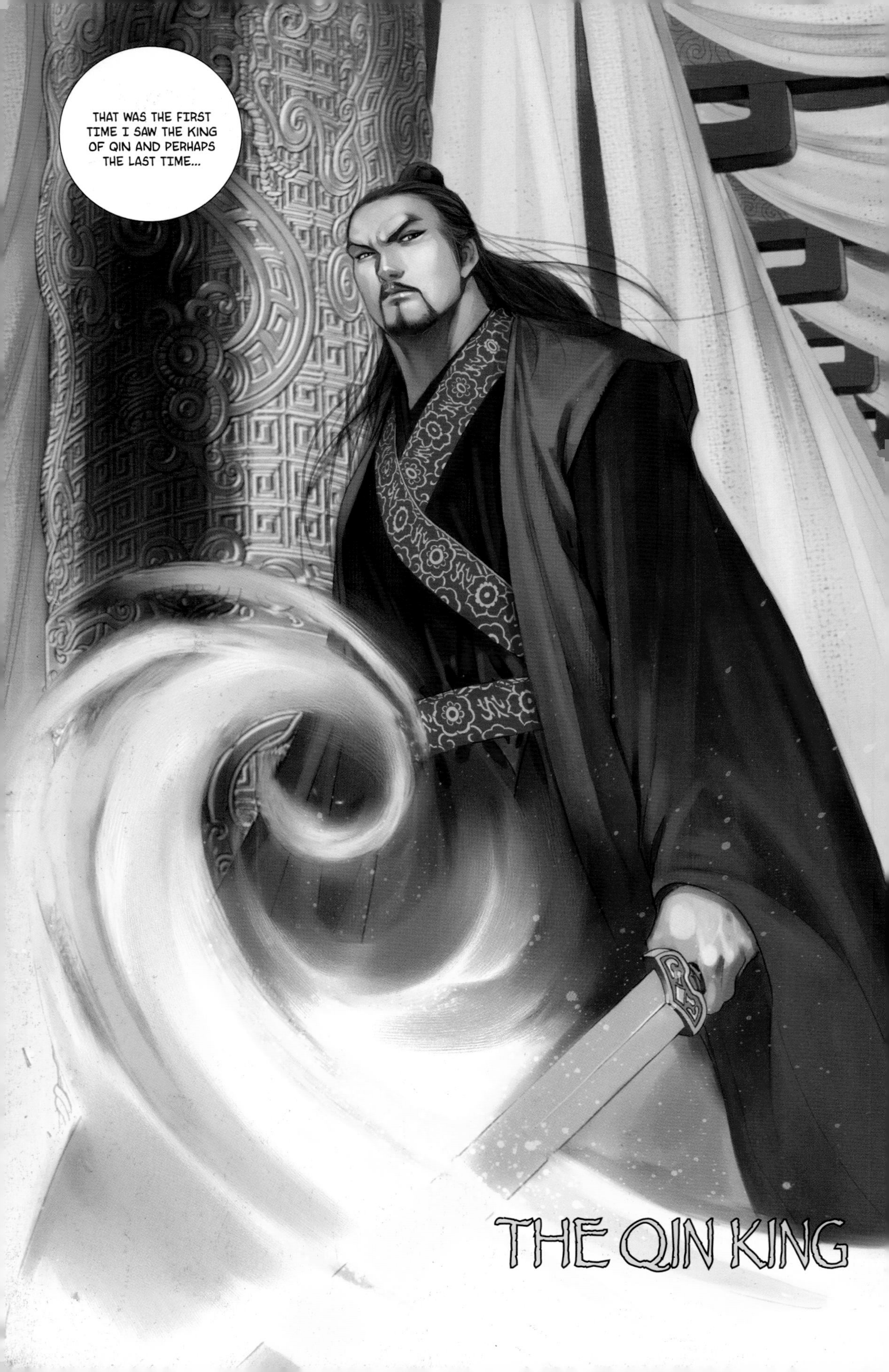
THAT WAS THE FIRST TIME I SAW THE KING OF QIN AND PERHAPS THE LAST TIME...
THE QIN KING

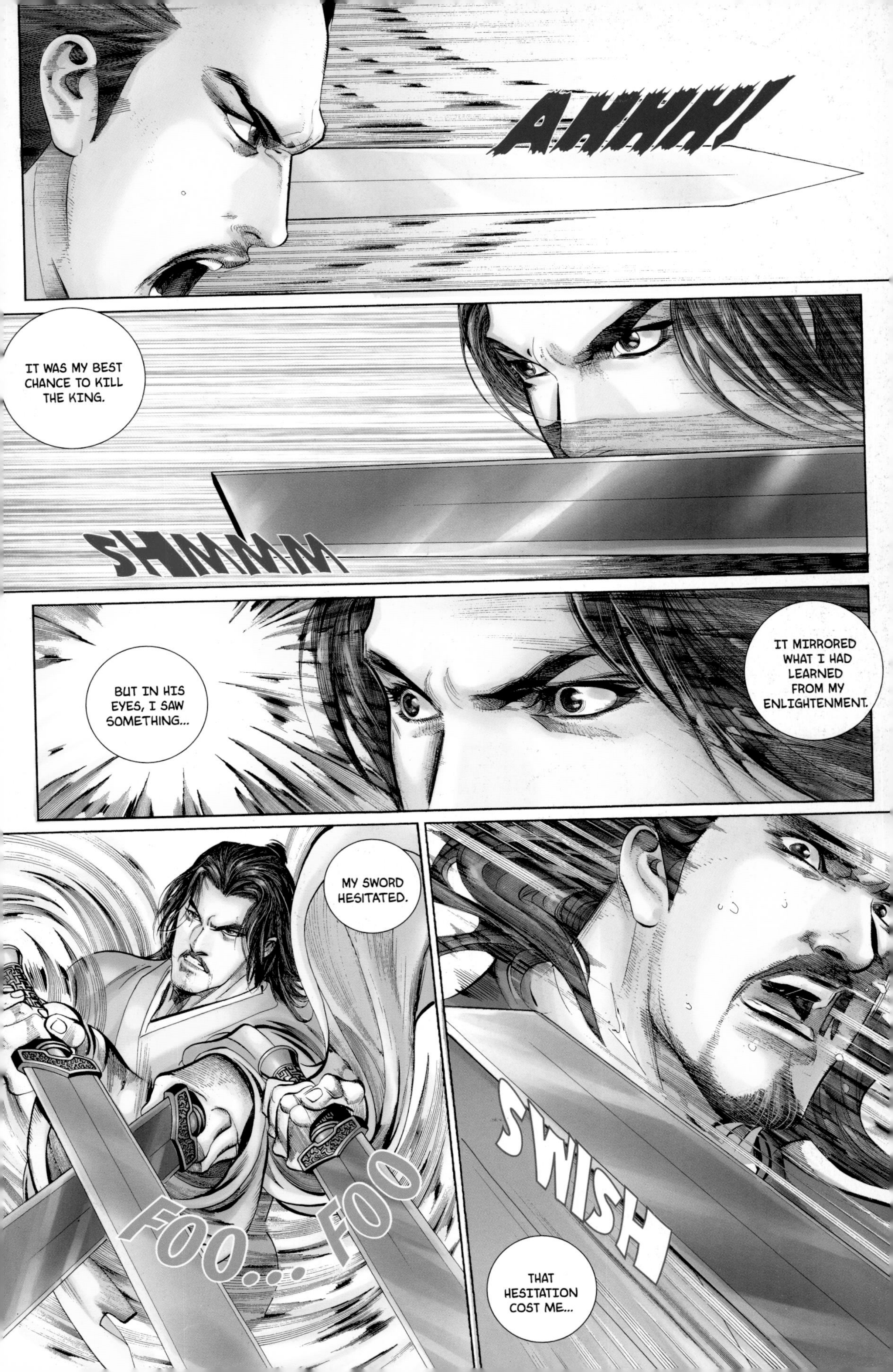
AHHH!
IT WAS MY BEST CHANCE TO KILL THE KING.
SHMMM
BUT IN HIS EYES, I SAW SOMETHING...
IT MIRRORED WHAT I HAD LEARNED FROM MY ENLIGHTENMENT.
MY SWORD HESITATED.
FOO... FOO
SWISH
THAT HESITATION COST ME...

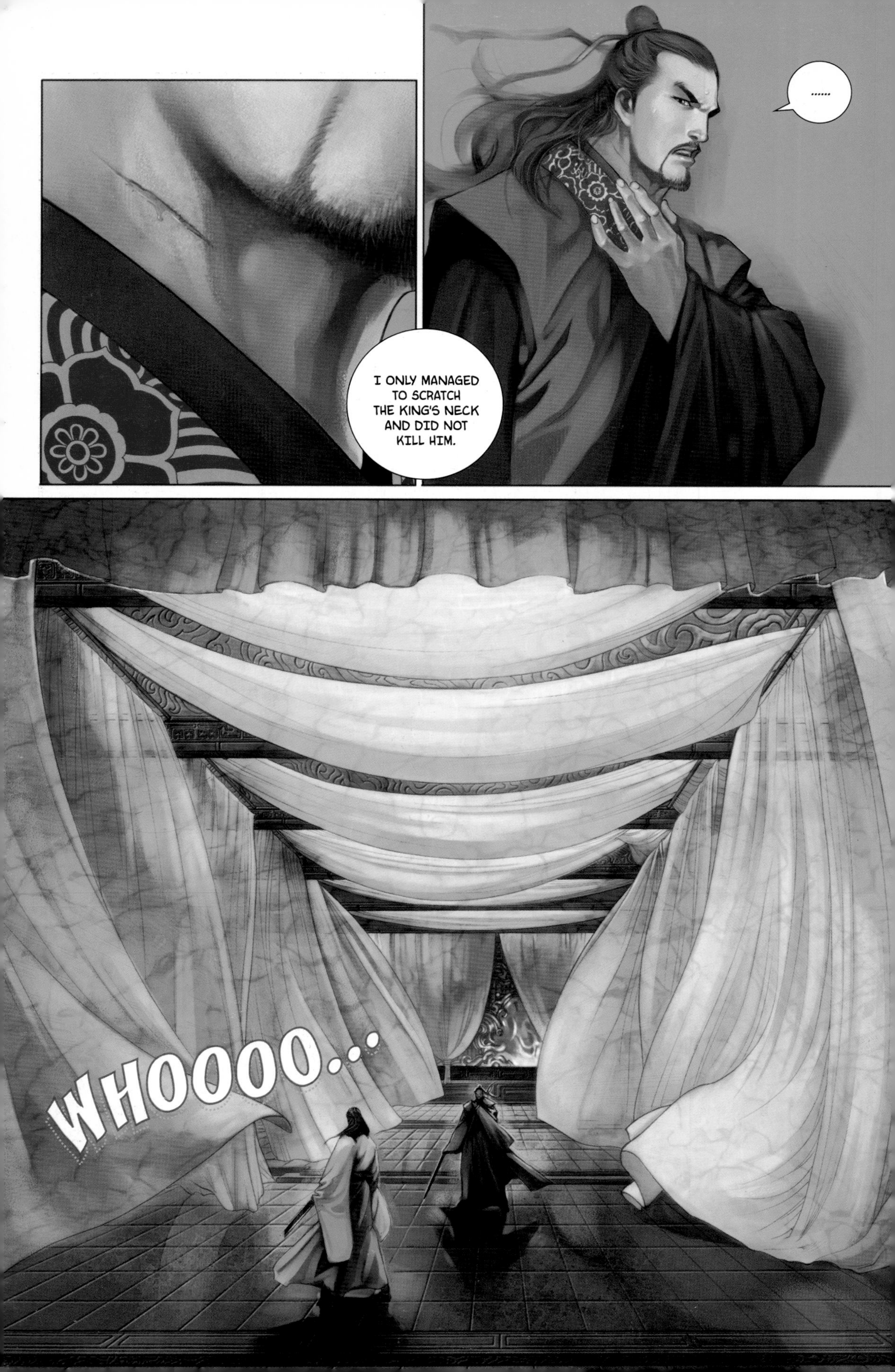
......
I ONLY MANAGED TO SCRATCH THE KING'S NECK AND DID NOT KILL HIM.
WHOOOO...

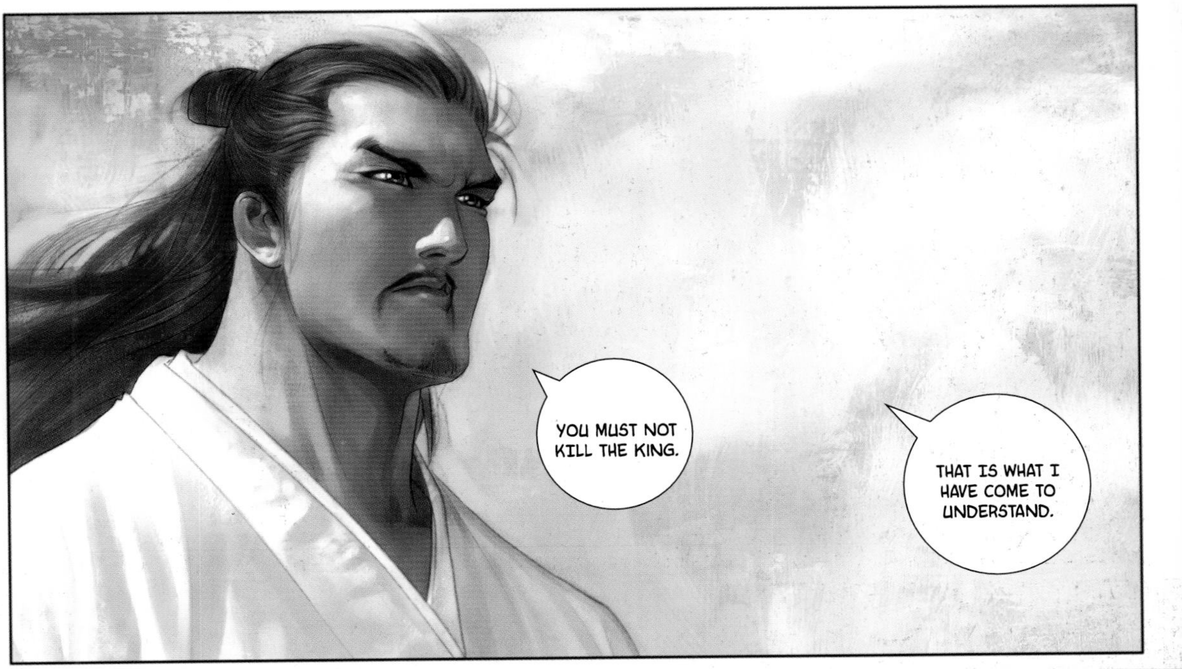
YOU MUST NOT KILL THE KING.
THAT IS WHAT I HAVE COME TO UNDERSTAND.

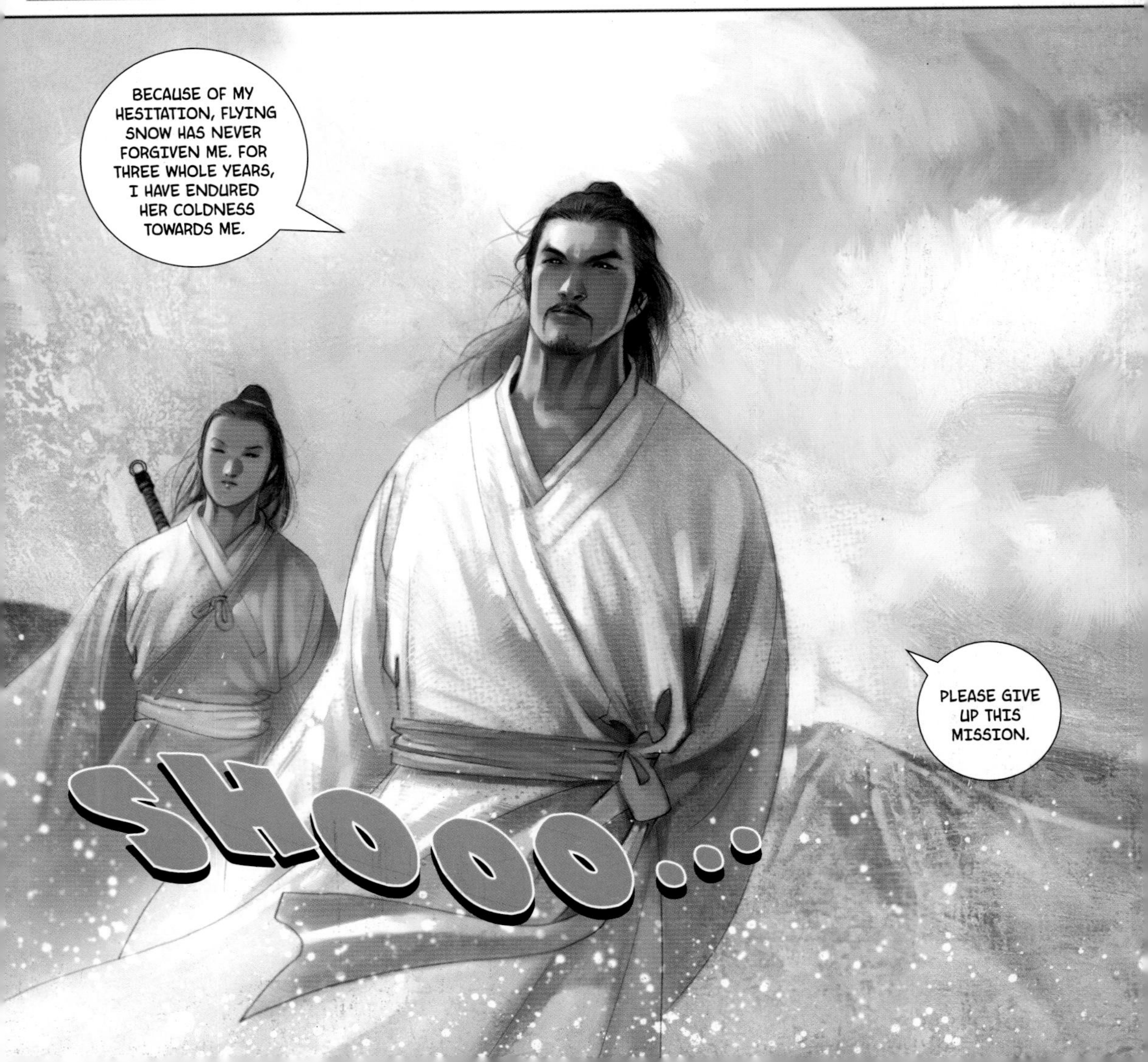
BECAUSE OF MY HESITATION, FLYING SNOW HAS NEVER FORGIVEN ME. FOR THREE WHOLE YEARS, I HAVE ENDURED HER COLDNESS TOWARDS ME.
PLEASE GIVE UP THIS MISSION.
SHOOO...

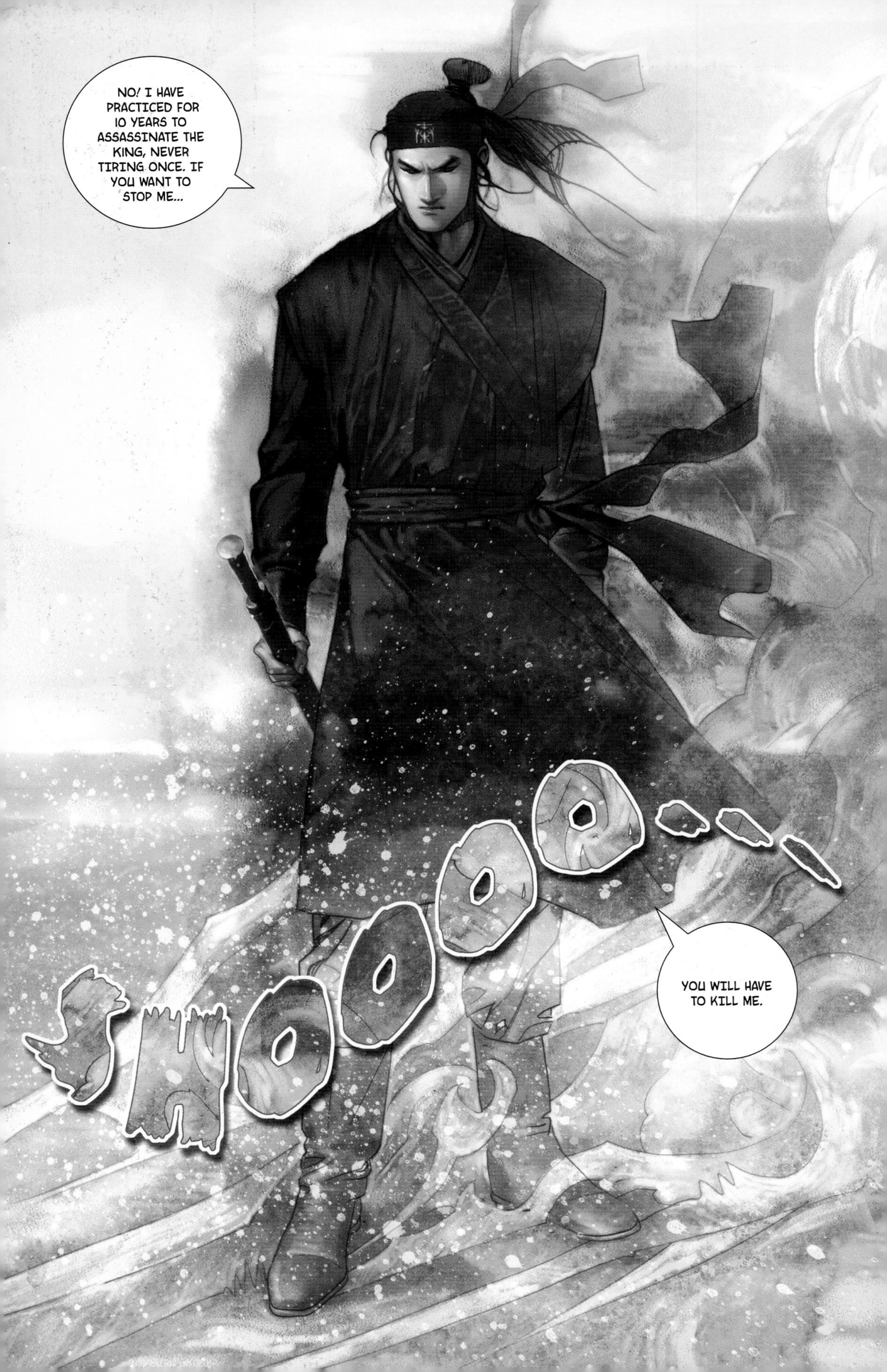
NO! I HAVE PRACTICED FOR 10 YEARS TO ASSASSINATE THE KING, NEVER TIRING ONCE. IF YOU WANT TO STOP ME...
SHOOOOO...
YOU WILL HAVE TO KILL ME.

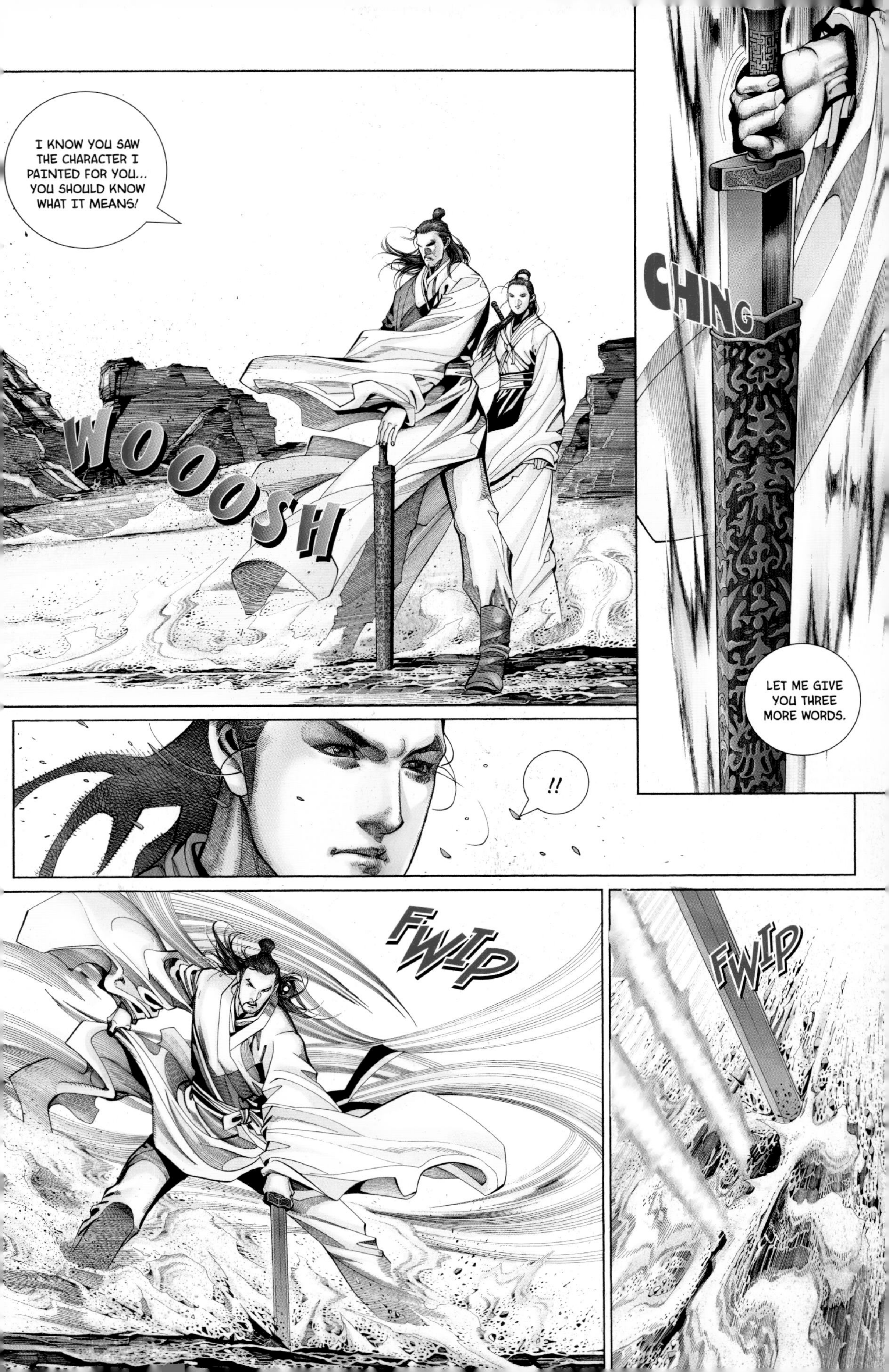
I KNOW YOU SAW THE CHARACTER I PAINTED FOR YOU... YOU SHOULD KNOW WHAT IT MEANS!
WOOOOSH
CHING
LET ME GIVE YOU THREE MORE WORDS.
!!
FWIP
FWIP

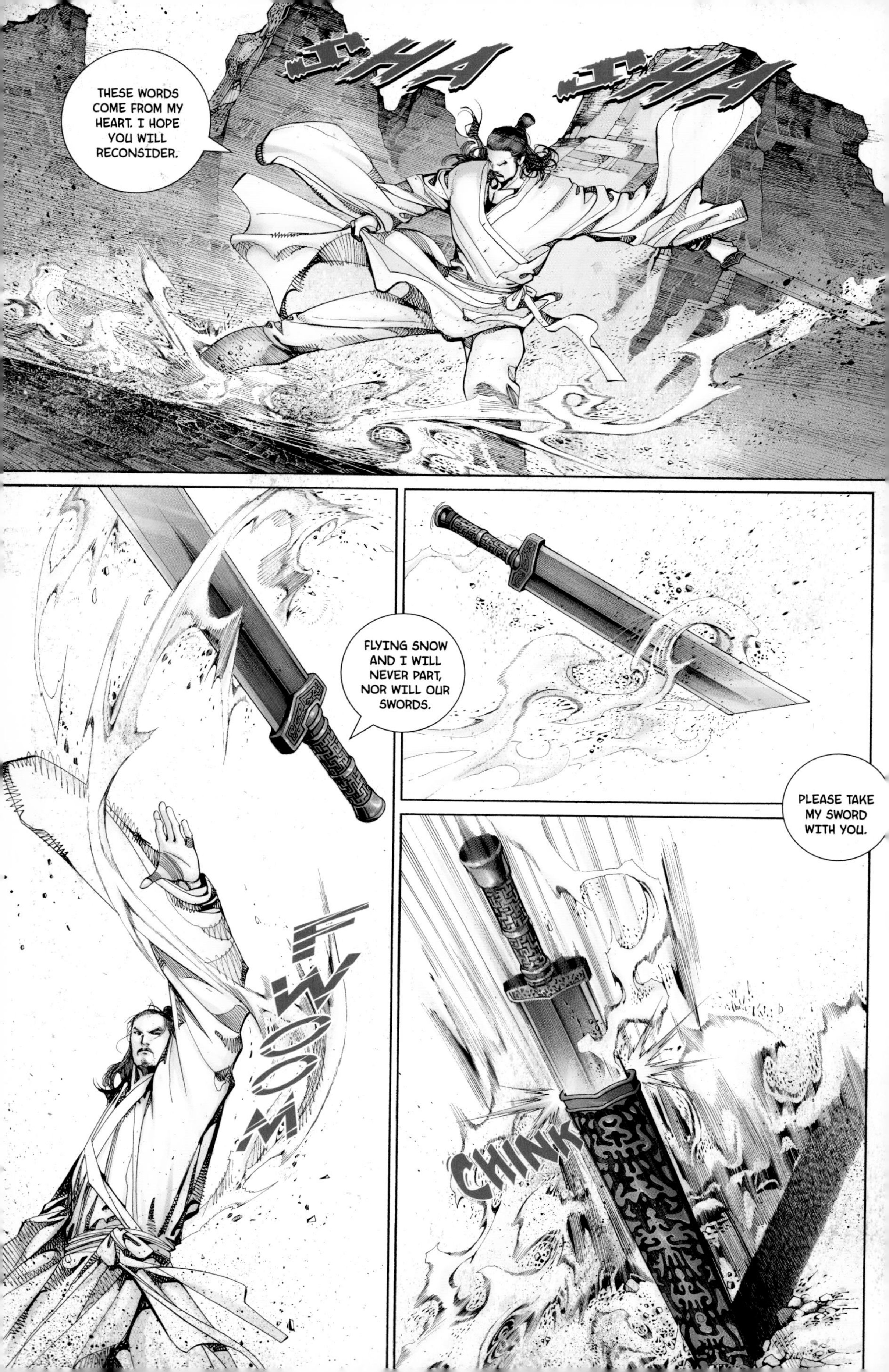
THESE WORDS COME FROM MY HEART. I HOPE YOU WILL RECONSIDER.
HA HA
FLYING SNOW AND I WILL NEVER PART, NOR WILL OUR SWORDS.
FWOOM
PLEASE TAKE MY SWORD WITH YOU.
CHINK

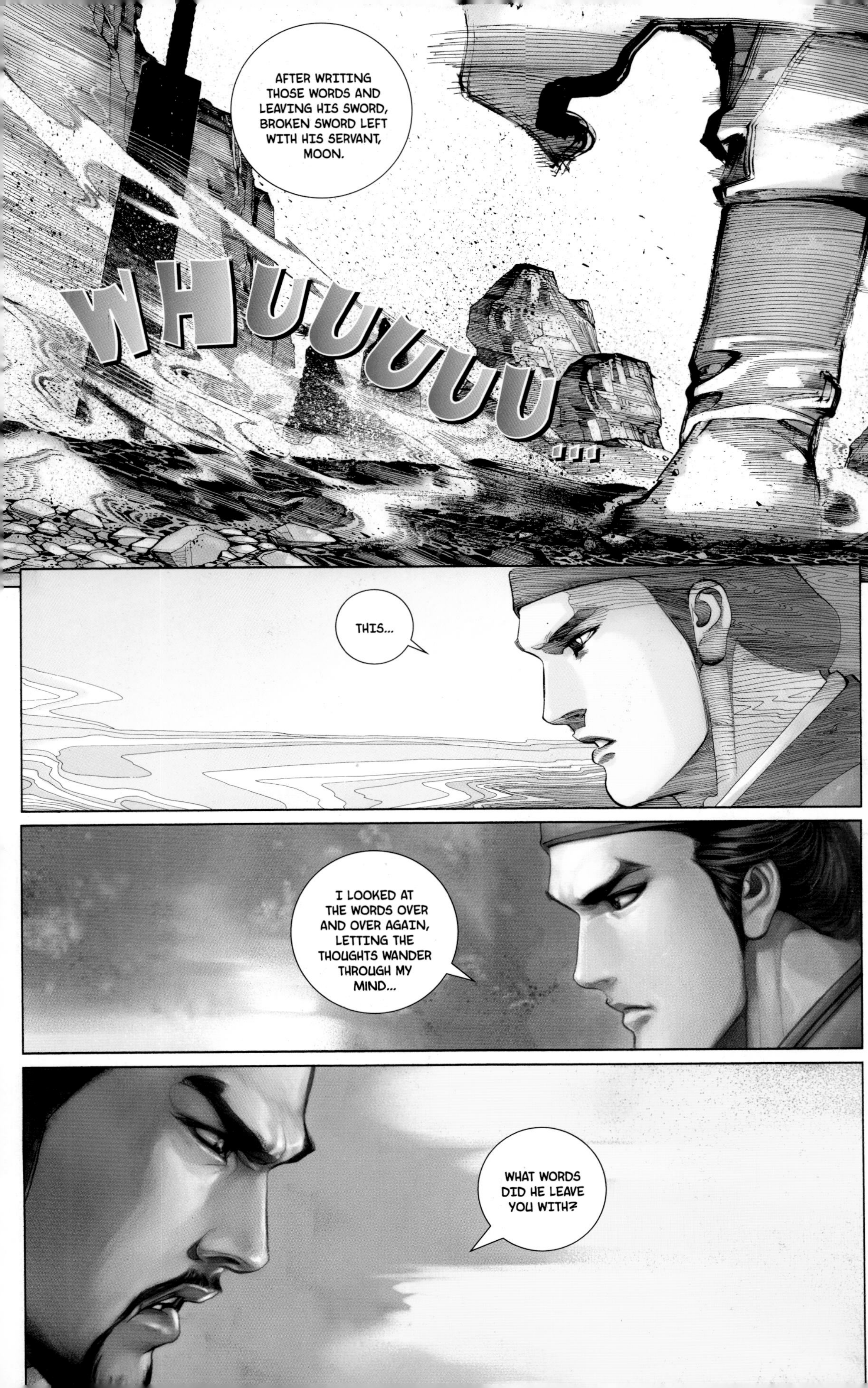
AFTER WRITING THOSE WORDS AND LEAVING HIS SWORD, BROKEN SWORD LEFT WITH HIS SERVANT, MOON.
WHUUUUUU...
THIS...
I LOOKED AT THE WORDS OVER AND OVER AGAIN, LETTING THE THOUGHTS WANDER THROUGH MY MIND...
WHAT WORDS DID HE LEAVE YOU WITH?

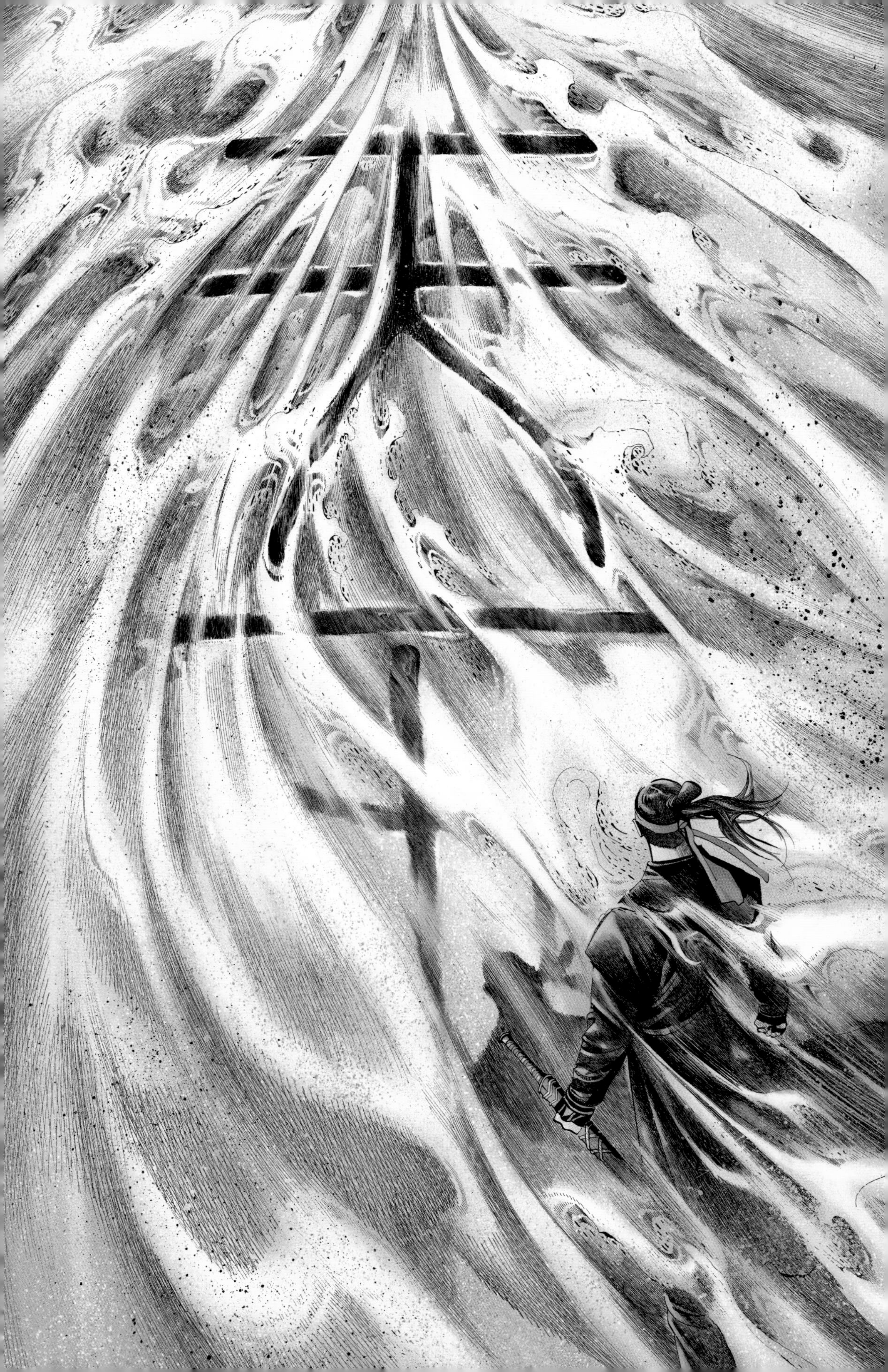

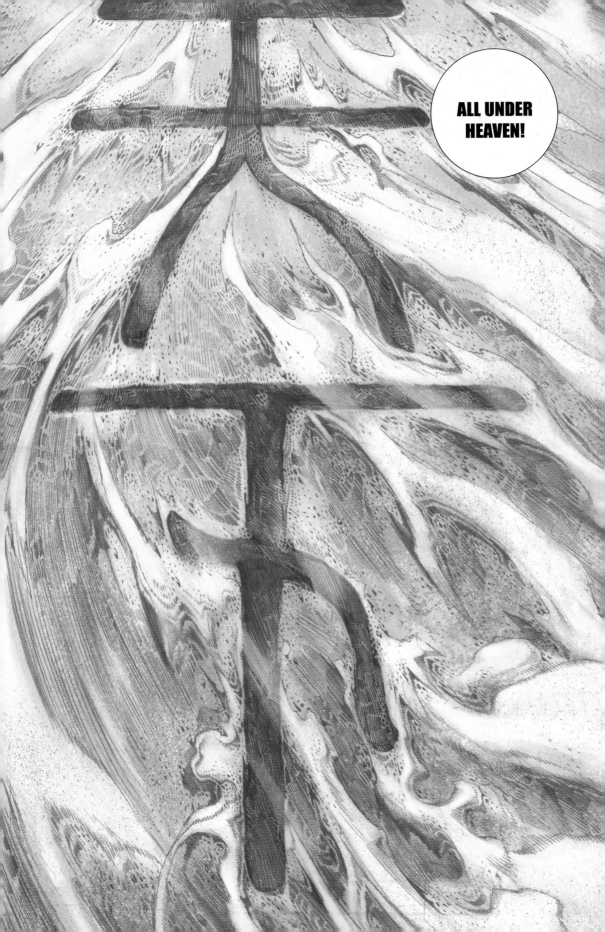

ALL UNDER HEAVEN!

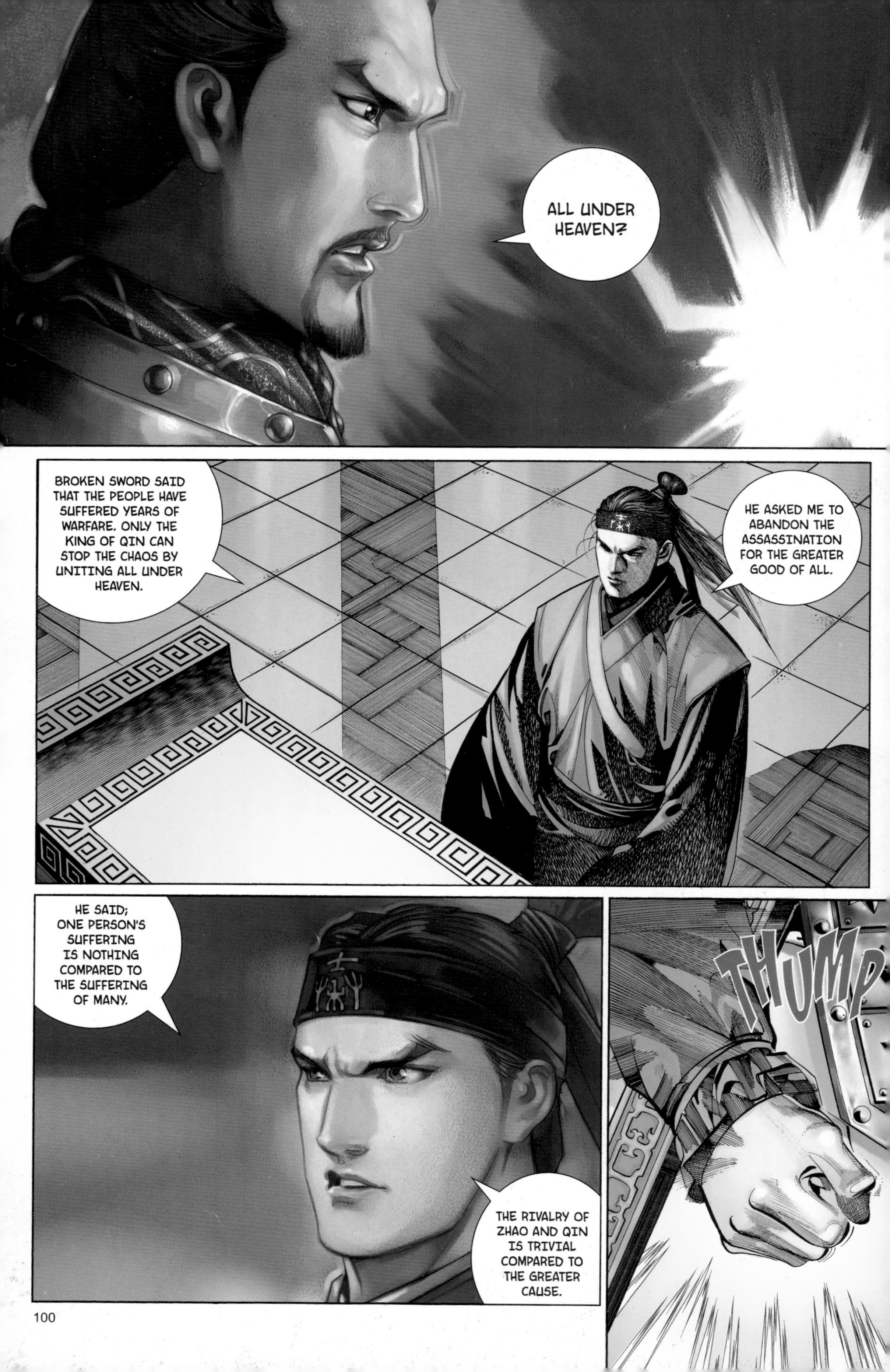
ALL UNDER HEAVEN?
BROKEN SWORD SAID THAT THE PEOPLE HAVE SUFFERED YEARS OF WARFARE. ONLY THE KING OF QIN CAN STOP THE CHAOS BY UNITING ALL UNDER HEAVEN.
HE ASKED ME TO ABANDON THE ASSASSINATION FOR THE GREATER GOOD OF ALL.
HE SAID; ONE PERSON'S SUFFERING IS NOTHING COMPARED TO THE SUFFERING OF MANY.
THE RIVALRY OF ZHAO AND QIN IS TRIVIAL COMPARED TO THE GREATER CAUSE.
THUMP

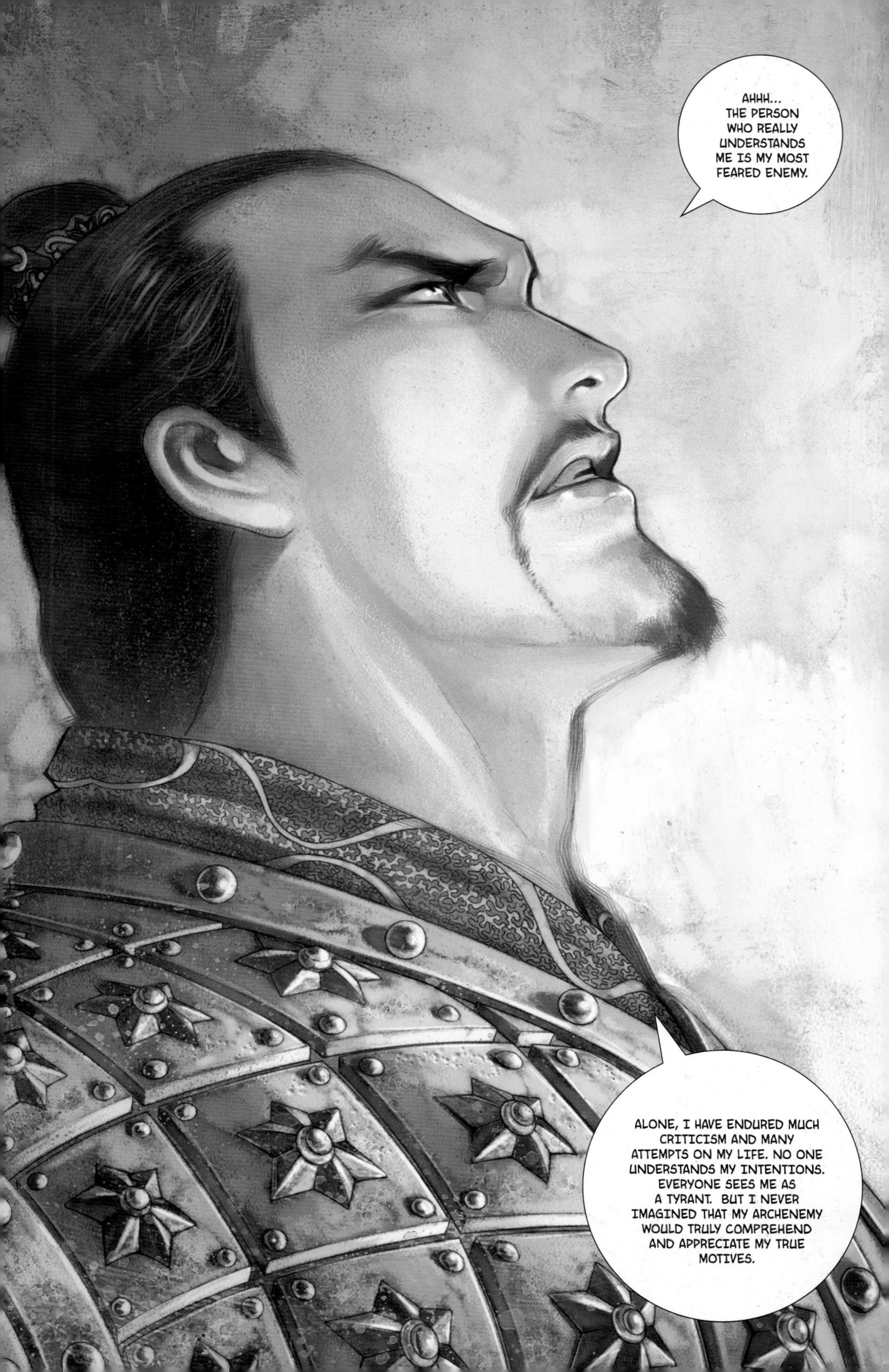
AHHH... THE PERSON WHO REALLY UNDERSTANDS ME IS MY MOST FEARED ENEMY.
ALONE, I HAVE ENDURED MUCH CRITICISM AND MANY ATTEMPTS ON MY LIFE. NO ONE UNDERSTANDS MY INTENTIONS. EVERYONE SEES ME AS A TYRANT. BUT I NEVER IMAGINED THAT MY ARCHENEMY WOULD TRULY COMPREHEND AND APPRECIATE MY TRUE MOTIVES.

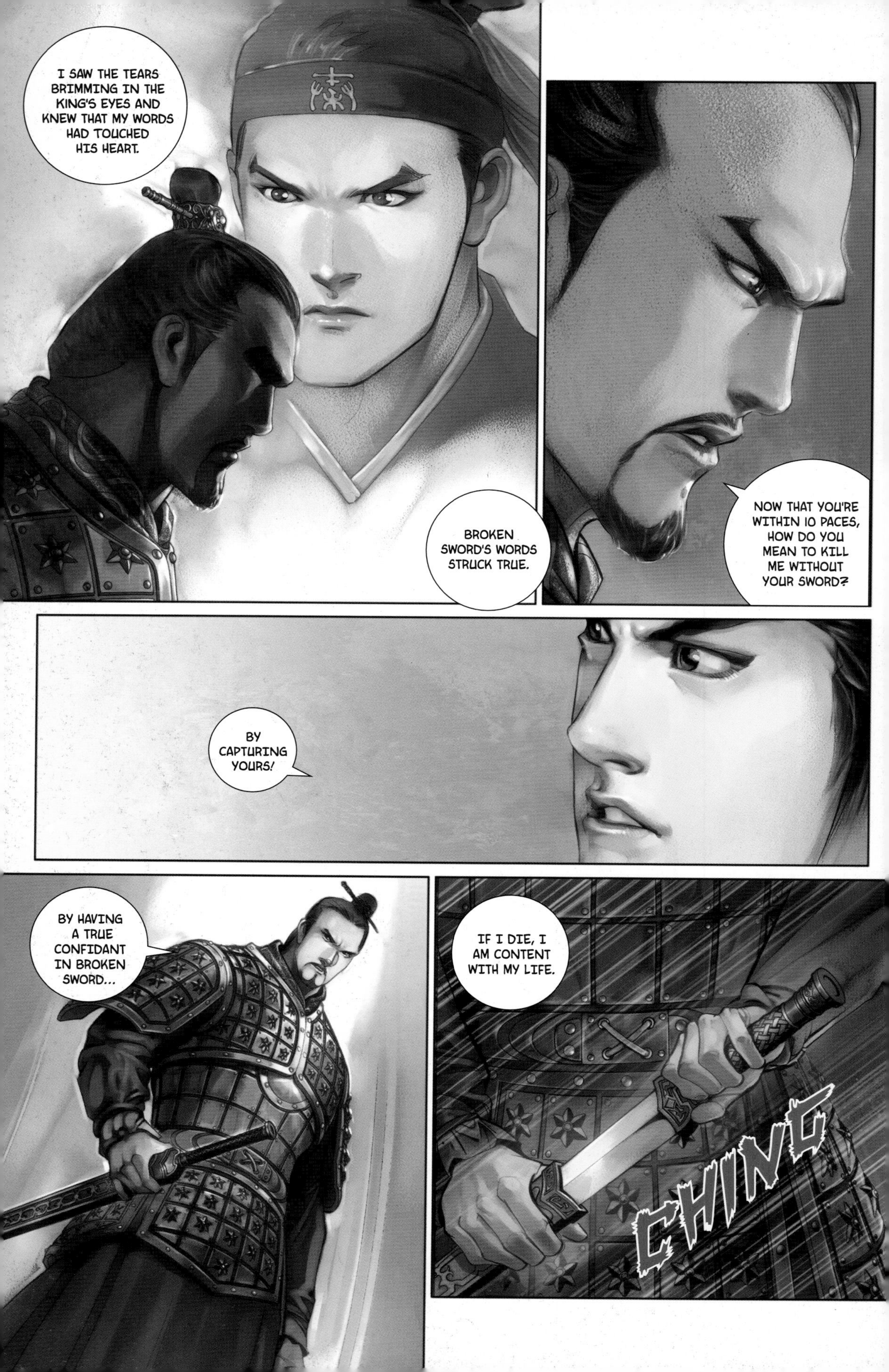
I SAW THE TEARS BRIMMING IN THE KING'S EYES AND KNEW THAT MY WORDS HAD TOUCHED HIS HEART.
BROKEN SWORD'S WORDS STRUCK TRUE.
NOW THAT YOU'RE WITHIN 10 PACES, HOW DO YOU MEAN TO KILL ME WITHOUT YOUR SWORD?
BY CAPTURING YOURS!
BY HAVING A TRUE CONFIDANT IN BROKEN SWORD...
IF I DIE, I AM CONTENT WITH MY LIFE.
CHING

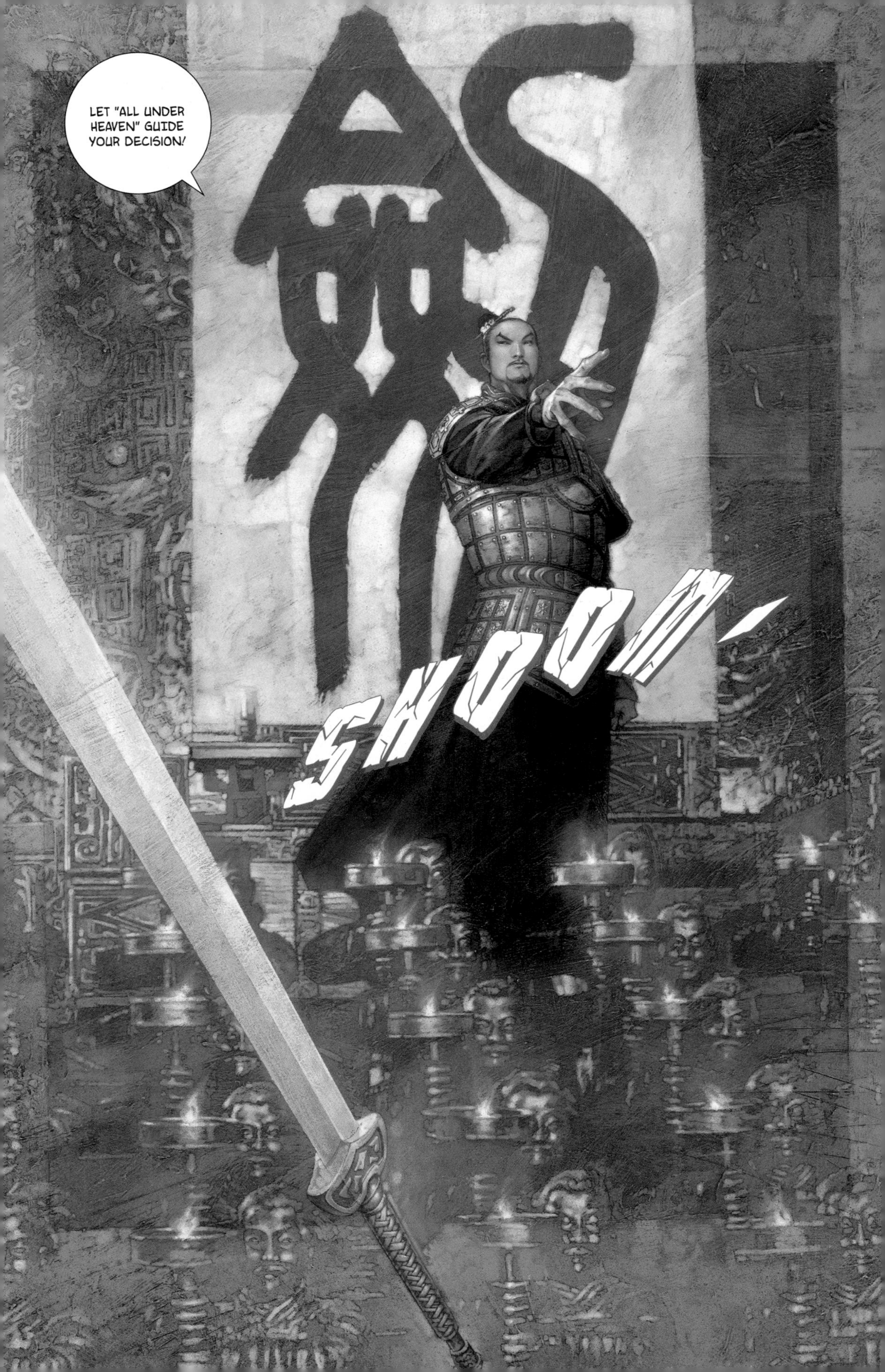
LET "ALL UNDER HEAVEN" GUIDE YOUR DECISION!
SHOOM

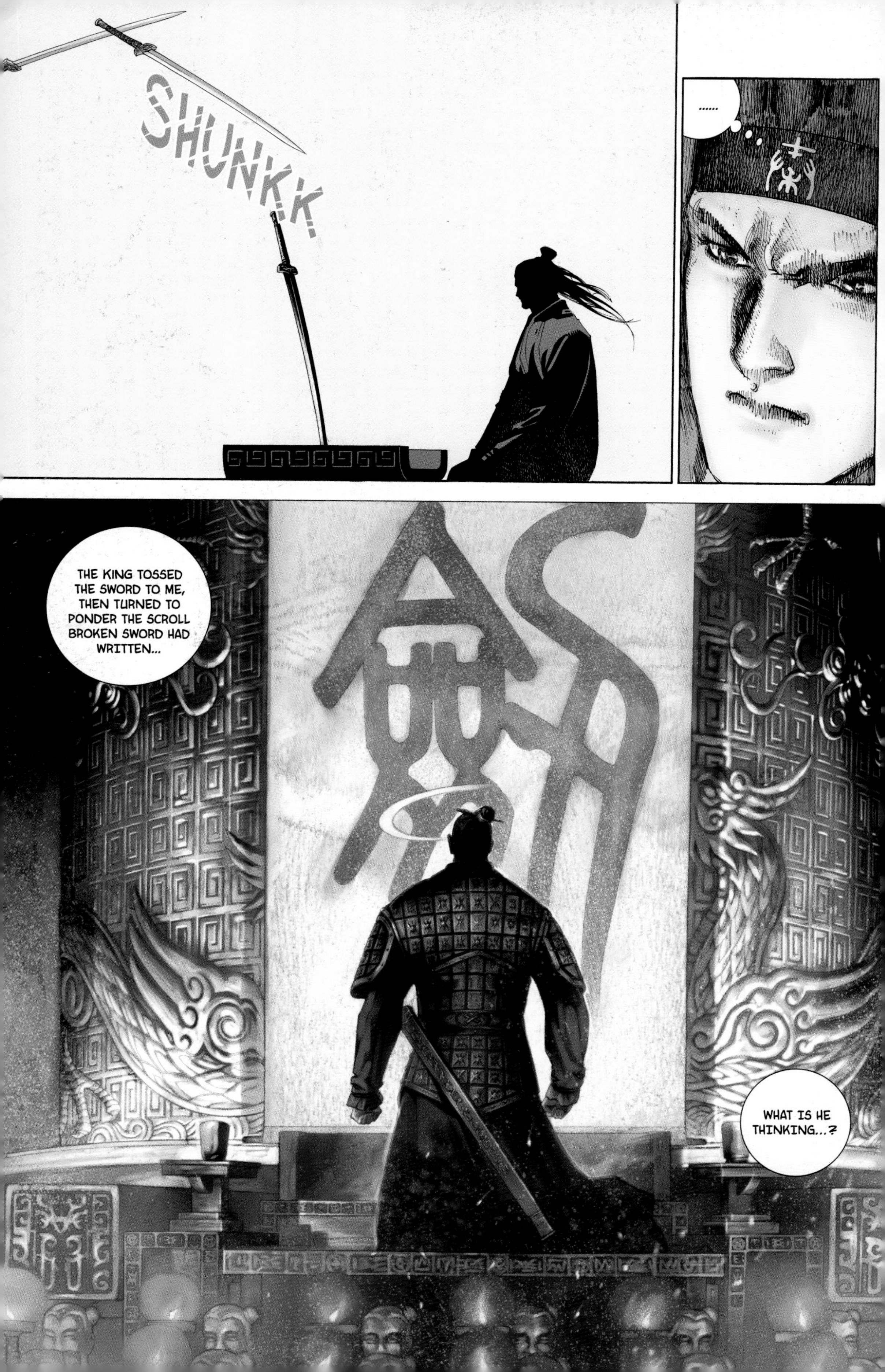
SHUNKK
......
THE KING TOSSED THE SWORD TO ME, THEN TURNED TO PONDER THE SCROLL BROKEN SWORD HAD WRITTEN...
WHAT IS HE THINKING...?

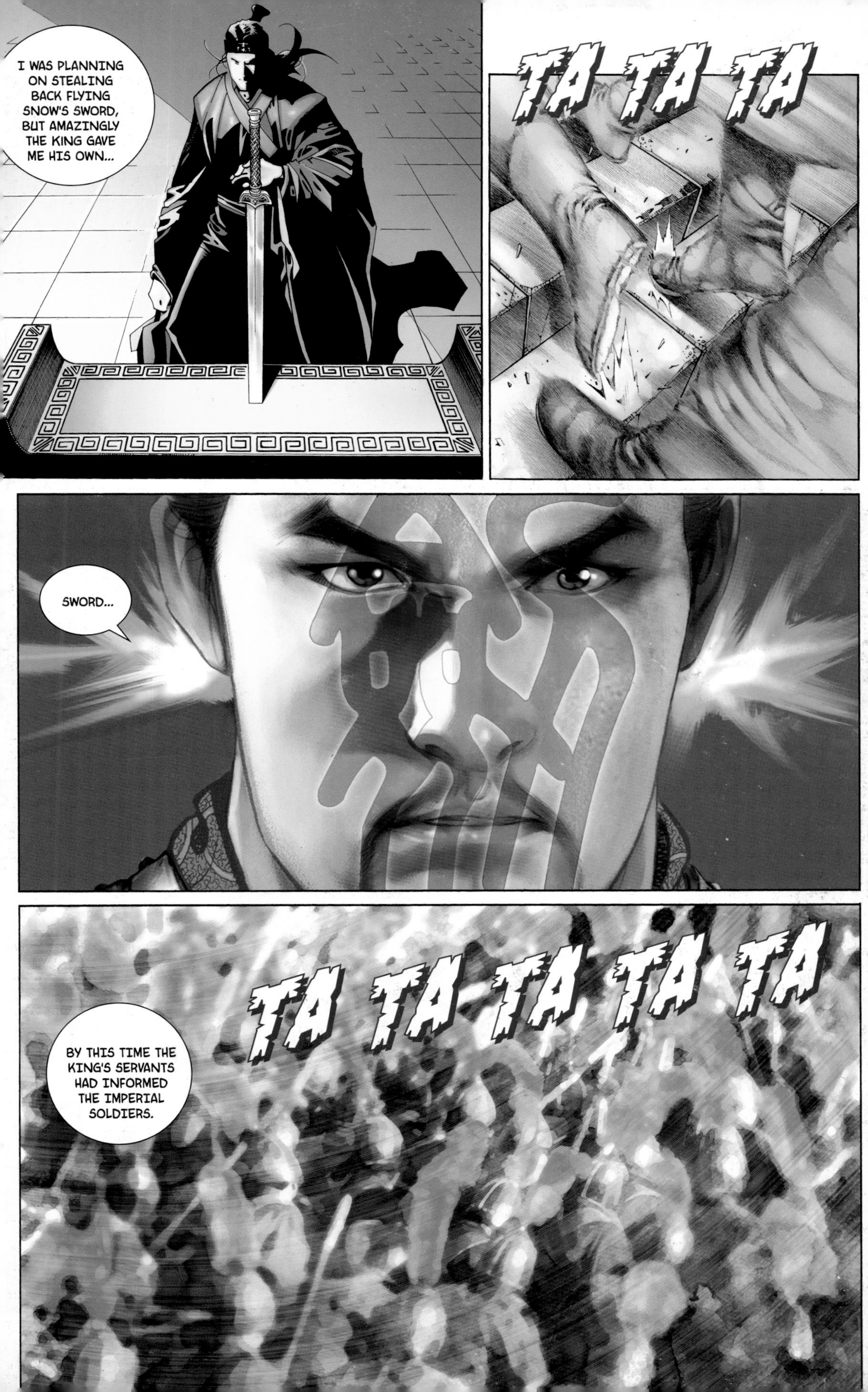
I WAS PLANNING ON STEALING BACK FLYING SNOW'S SWORD, BUT AMAZINGLY THE KING GAVE ME HIS OWN...
TA TA TA
SWORD...
TA TA TA TA TA
BY THIS TIME THE KING'S SERVANTS HAD INFORMED THE IMPERIAL SOLDIERS.

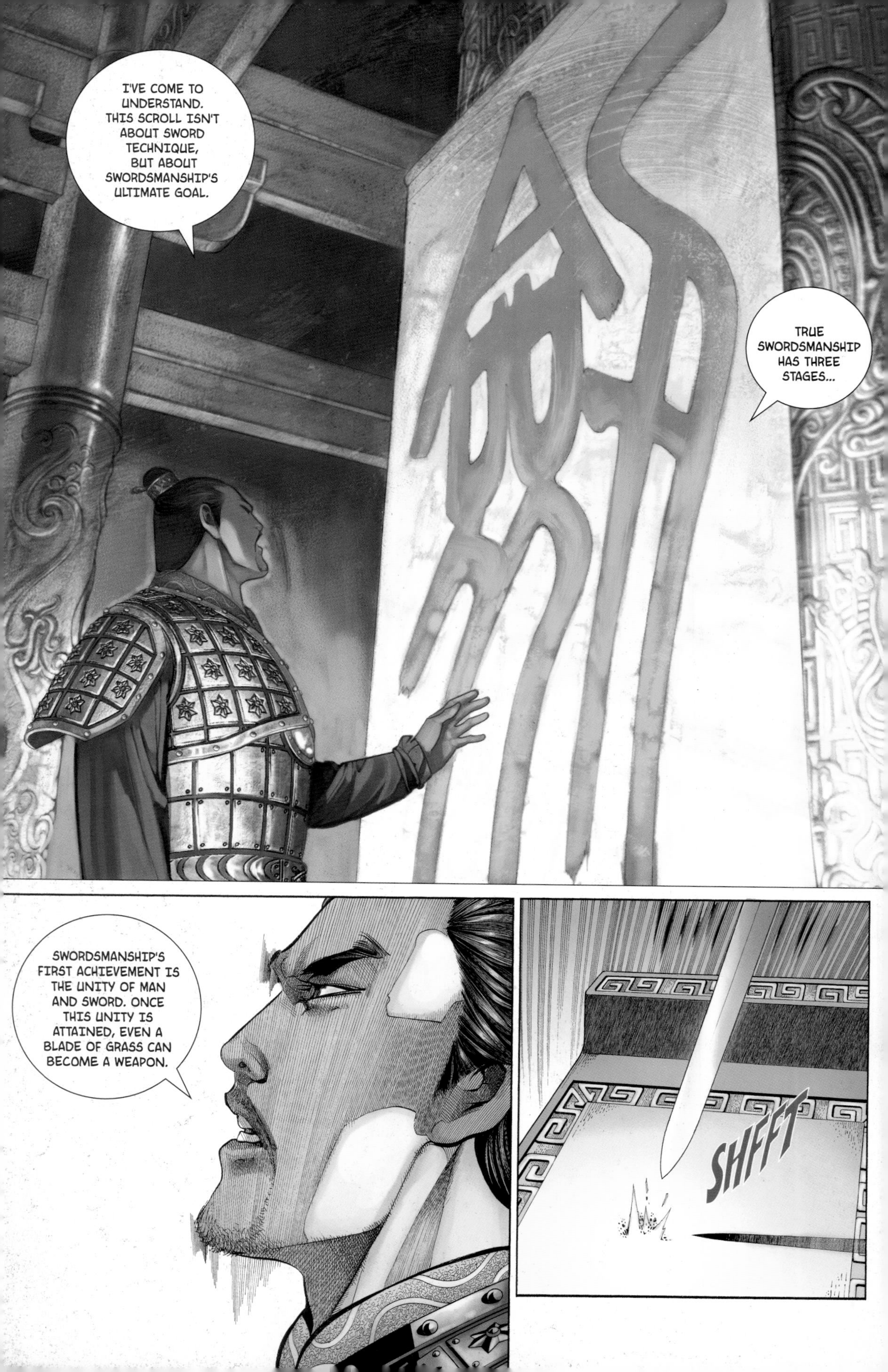
I'VE COME TO UNDERSTAND. THIS SCROLL ISN'T ABOUT SWORD TECHNIQUE, BUT ABOUT SWORDSMANSHIP'S ULTIMATE GOAL.
TRUE SWORDSMANSHIP HAS THREE STAGES...
SWORDSMANSHIP'S FIRST ACHIEVEMENT IS THE UNITY OF MAN AND SWORD. ONCE THIS UNITY IS ATTAINED, EVEN A BLADE OF GRASS CAN BECOME A WEAPON.
SHFFT

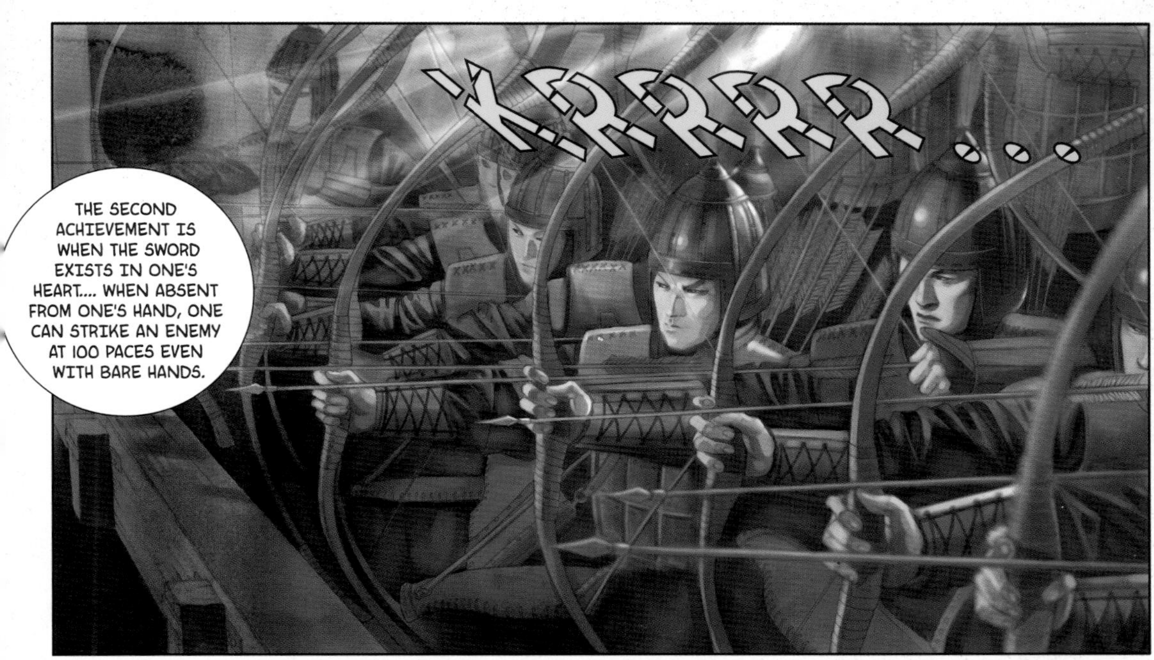
KRRRRR...
THE SECOND ACHIEVEMENT IS WHEN THE SWORD EXISTS IN ONE'S HEART.... WHEN ABSENT FROM ONE'S HAND, ONE CAN STRIKE AN ENEMY AT 100 PACES EVEN WITH BARE HANDS.

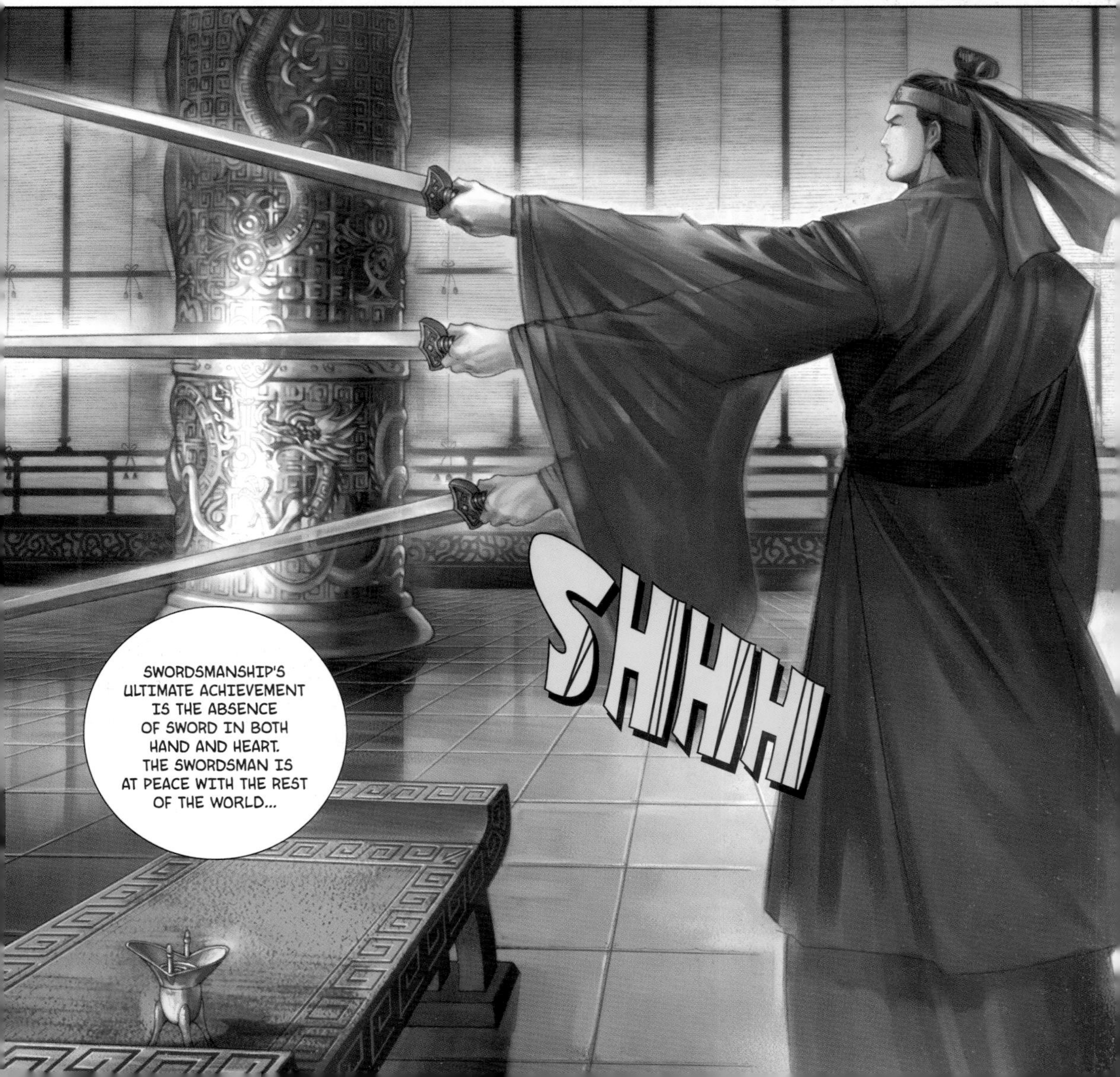
SHHHH
SWORDSMANSHIP'S ULTIMATE ACHIEVEMENT IS THE ABSENCE OF SWORD IN BOTH HAND AND HEART. THE SWORDSMAN IS AT PEACE WITH THE REST OF THE WORLD...

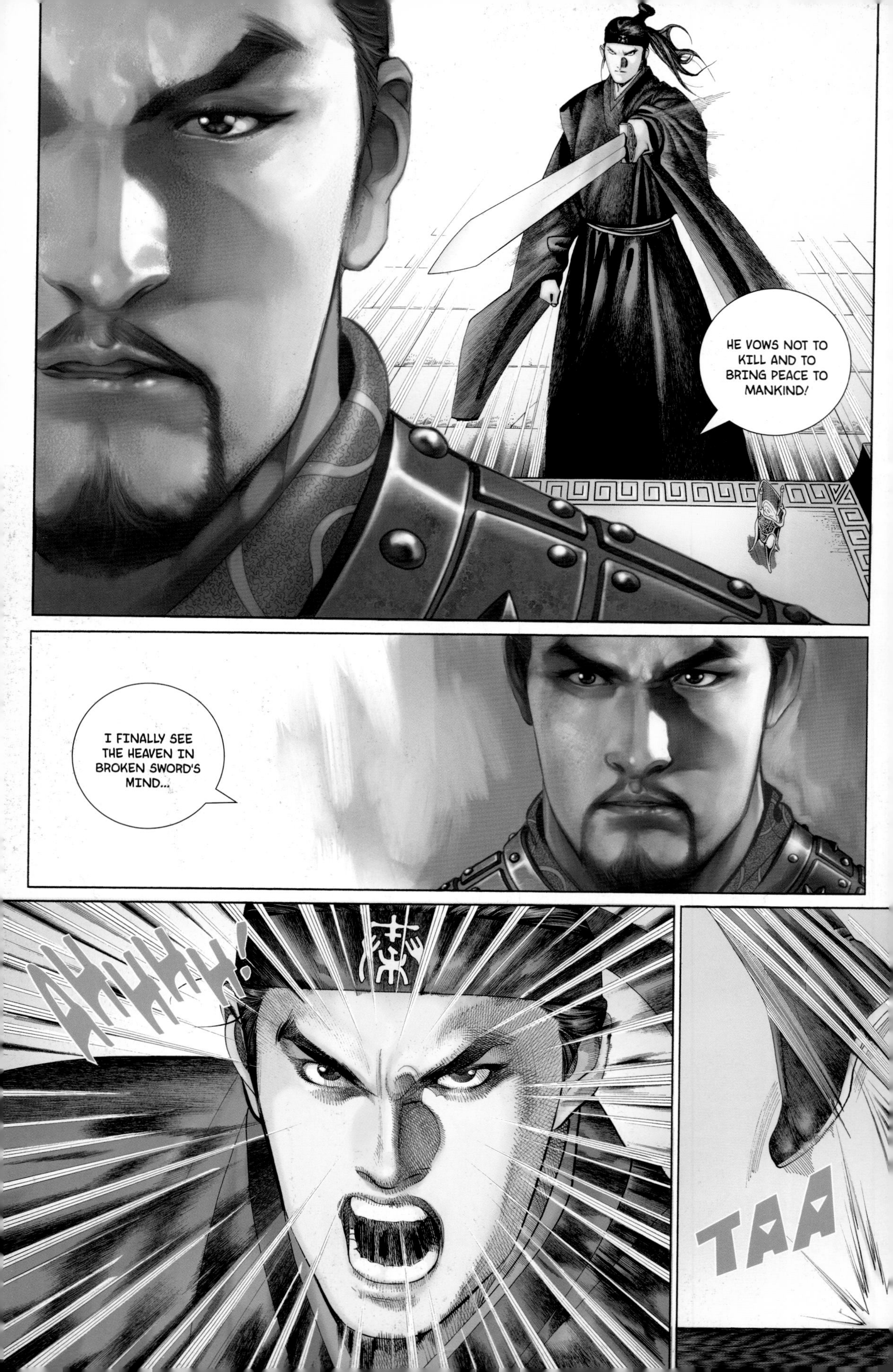
HE VOWS NOT TO KILL AND TO BRING PEACE TO MANKIND!
I FINALLY SEE THE HEAVEN IN BROKEN SWORD'S MIND...
AHHHH!
TAA

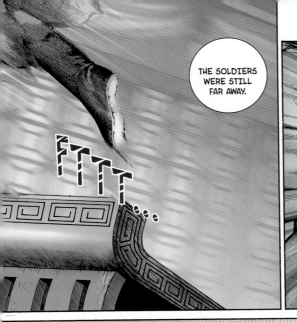

FTTT...

THE SOLDIERS WERE STILL FAR AWAY.

NO ONE COULD STOP ME.

SHMMM

I HAD THE UTMOST CONFIDENCE IN MY TECHNIQUE AND ABILITY...

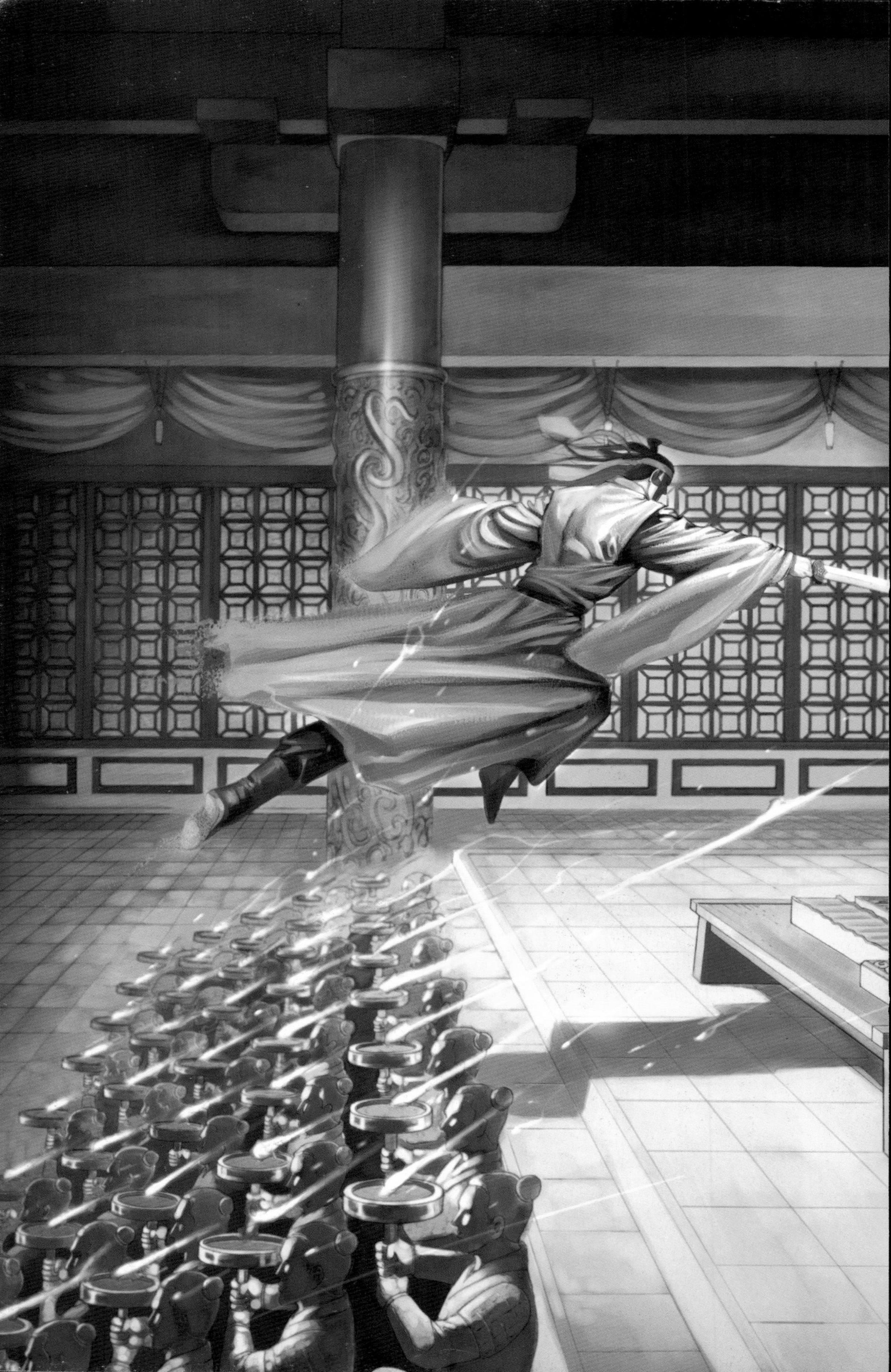

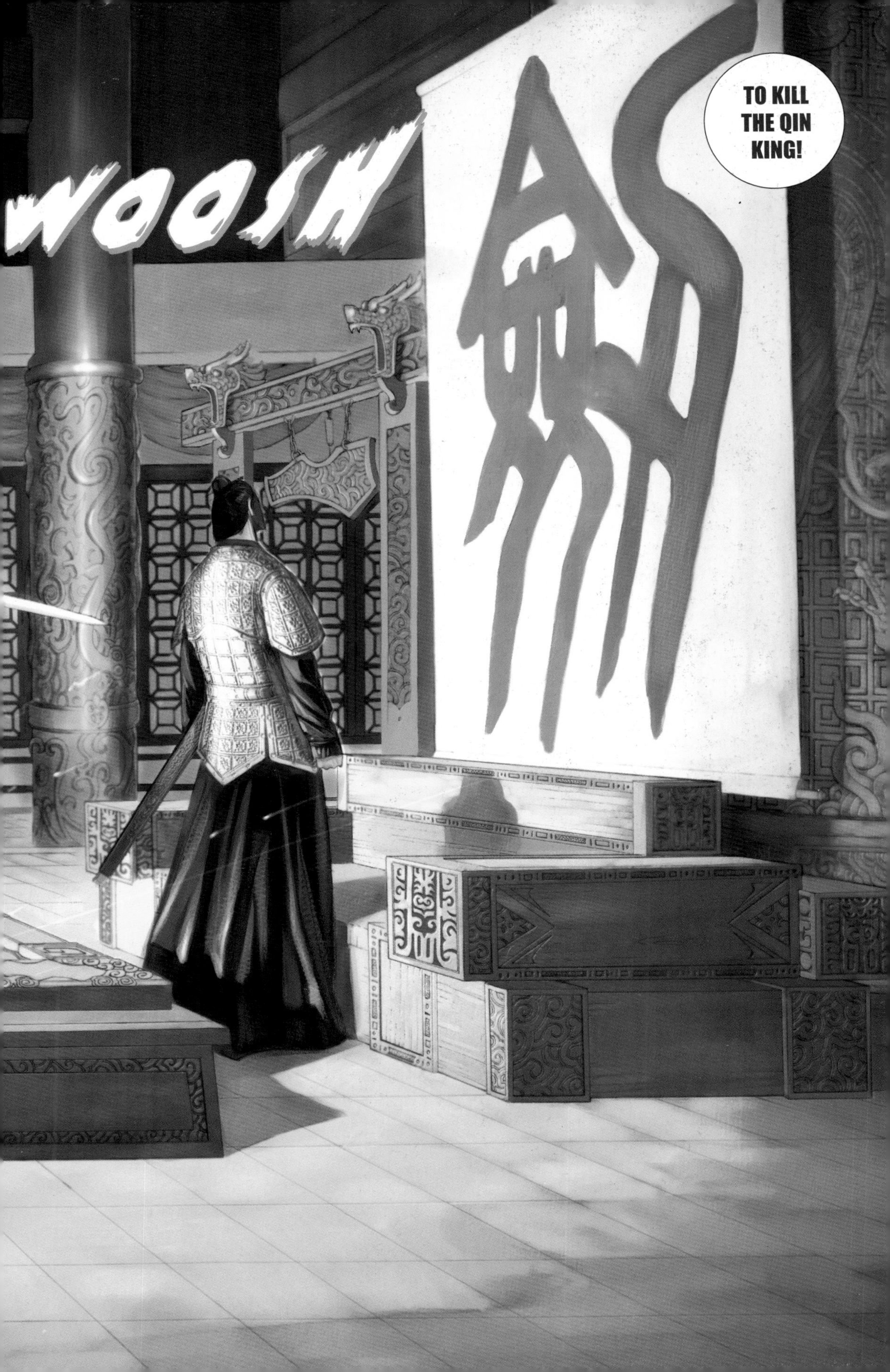
WOOSH
TO KILL THE QIN KING!

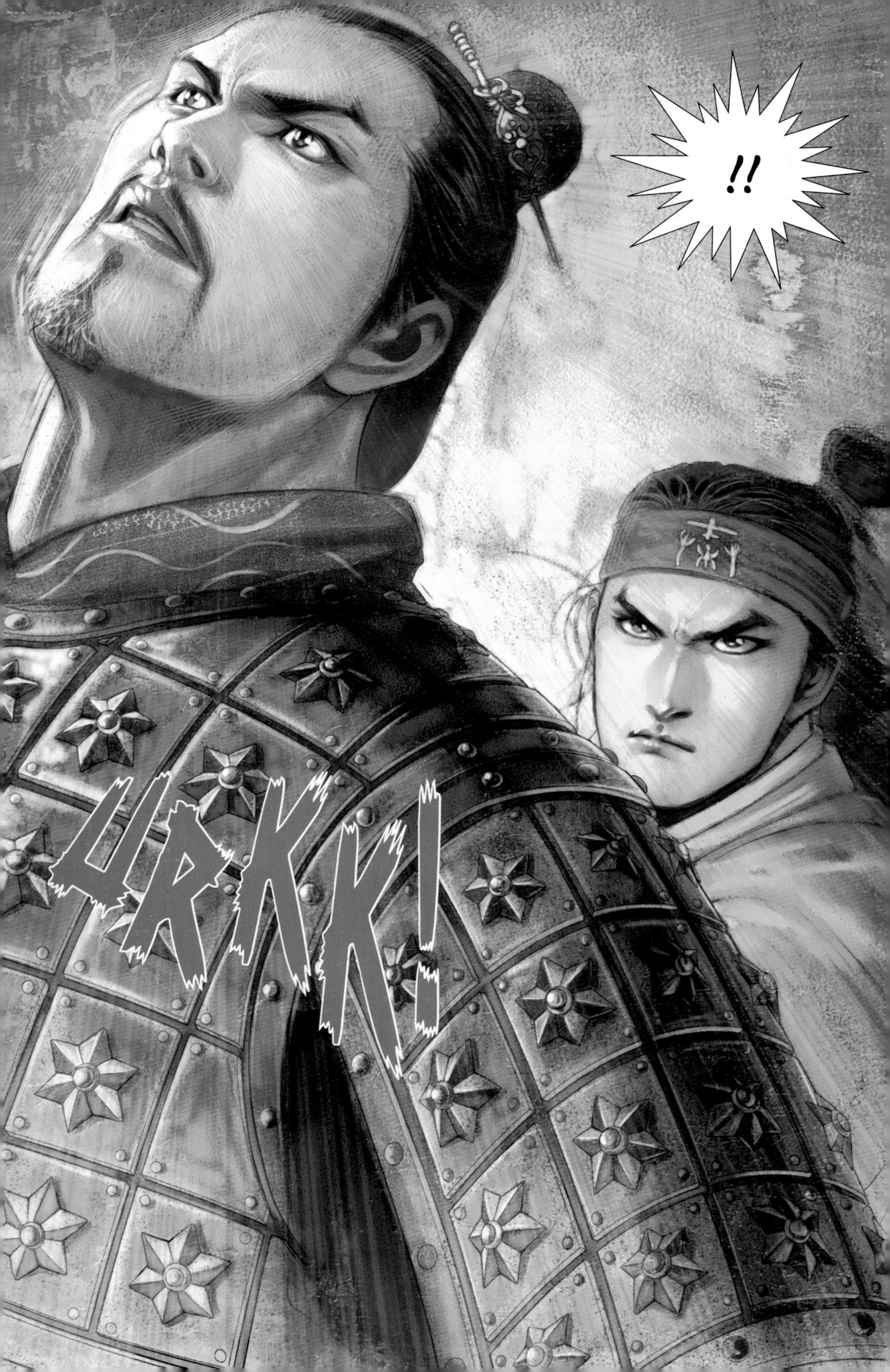
!!
URKK!

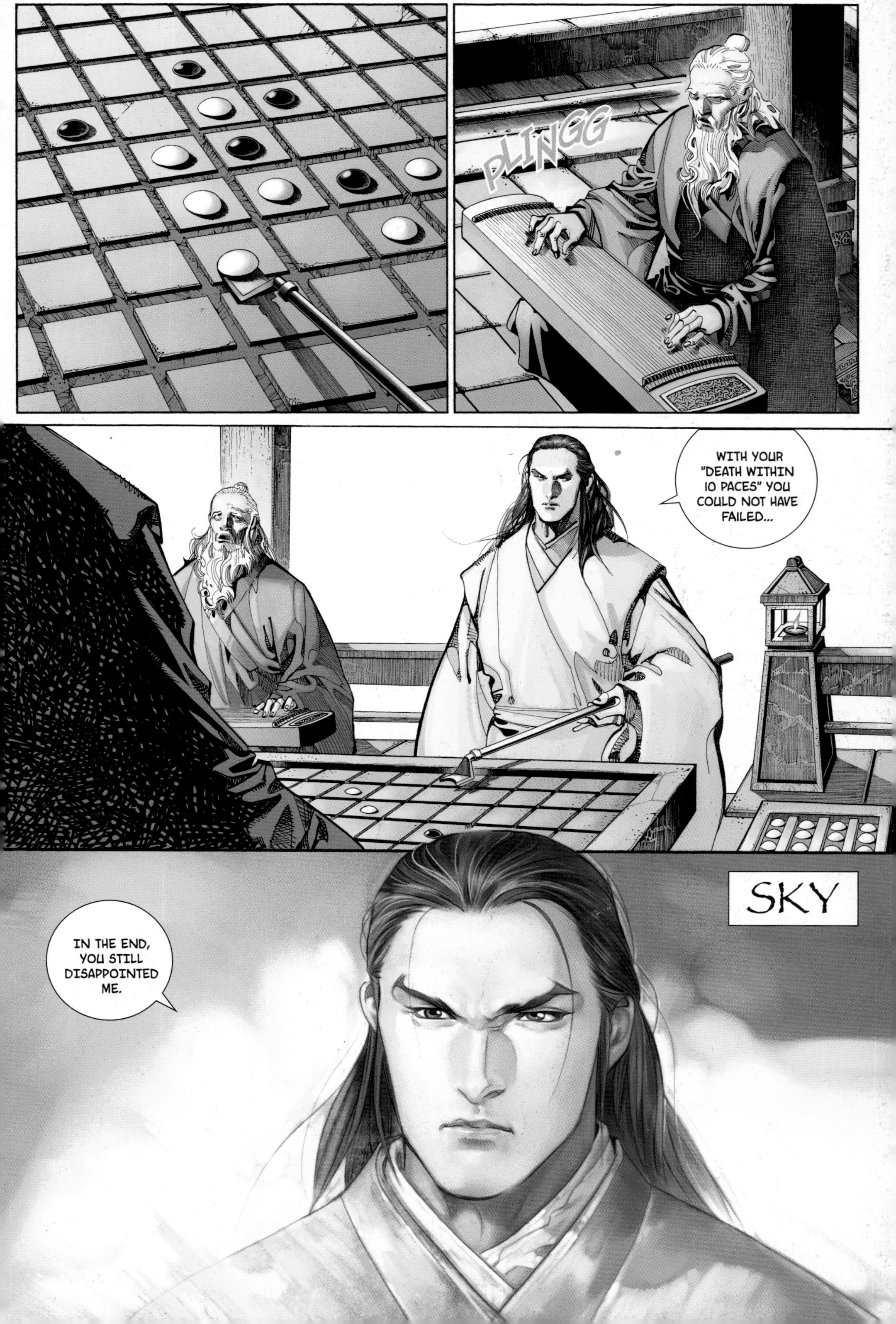
PLINGG
WITH YOUR "DEATH WITHIN 10 PACES" YOU COULD NOT HAVE FAILED...
SKY
IN THE END, YOU STILL DISAPPOINTED ME.

NAMELESS

I APOLOGIZE.

MY SWORD SWERVED...

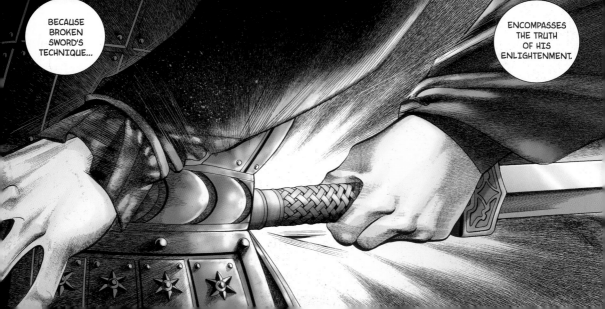

BECAUSE BROKEN SWORD'S TECHNIQUE...

ENCOMPASSES THE TRUTH OF HIS ENLIGHTENMENT.

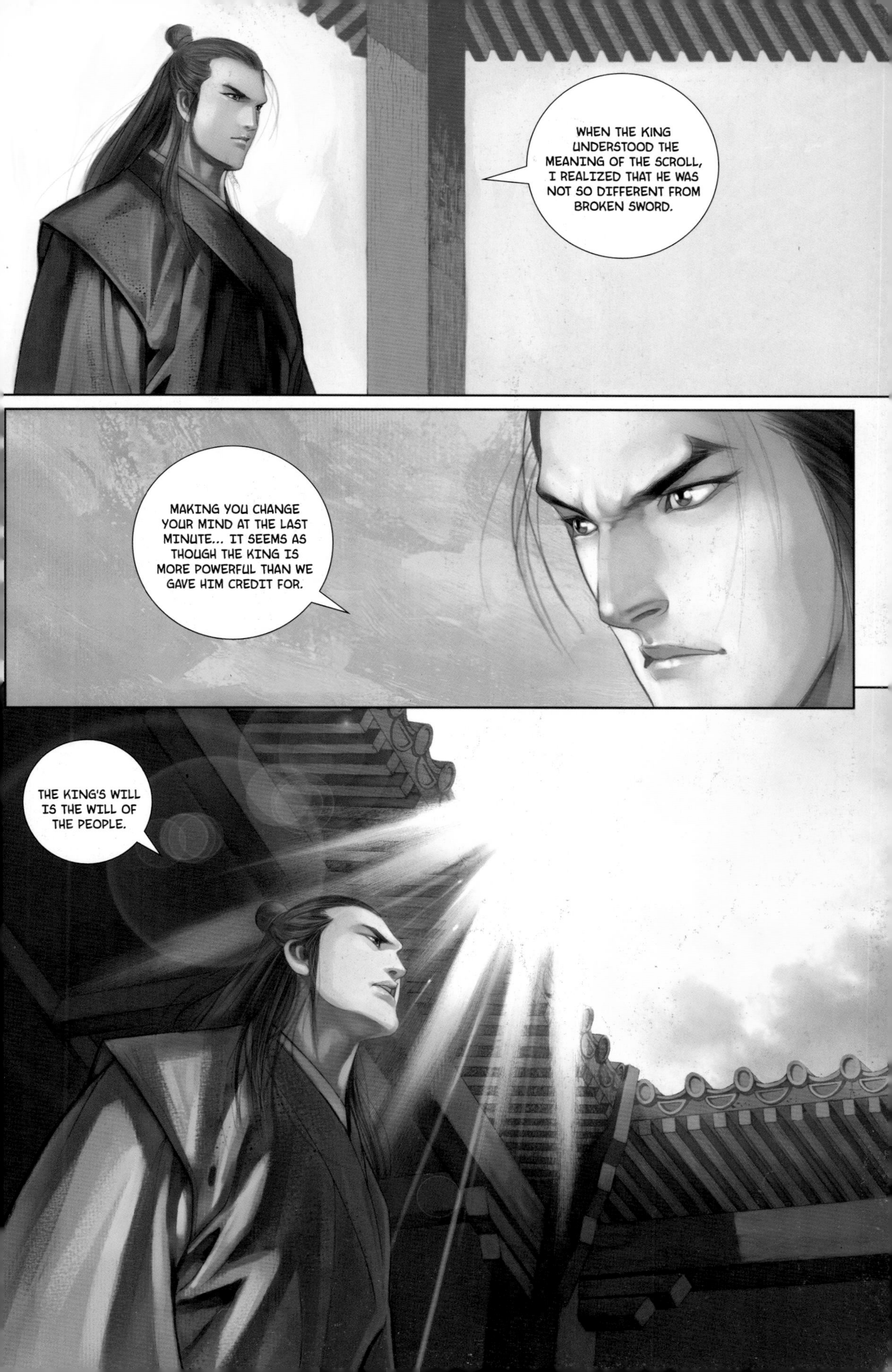
WHEN THE KING UNDERSTOOD THE MEANING OF THE SCROLL, I REALIZED THAT HE WAS NOT SO DIFFERENT FROM BROKEN SWORD.
MAKING YOU CHANGE YOUR MIND AT THE LAST MINUTE... IT SEEMS AS THOUGH THE KING IS MORE POWERFUL THAN WE GAVE HIM CREDIT FOR.
THE KING'S WILL IS THE WILL OF THE PEOPLE.

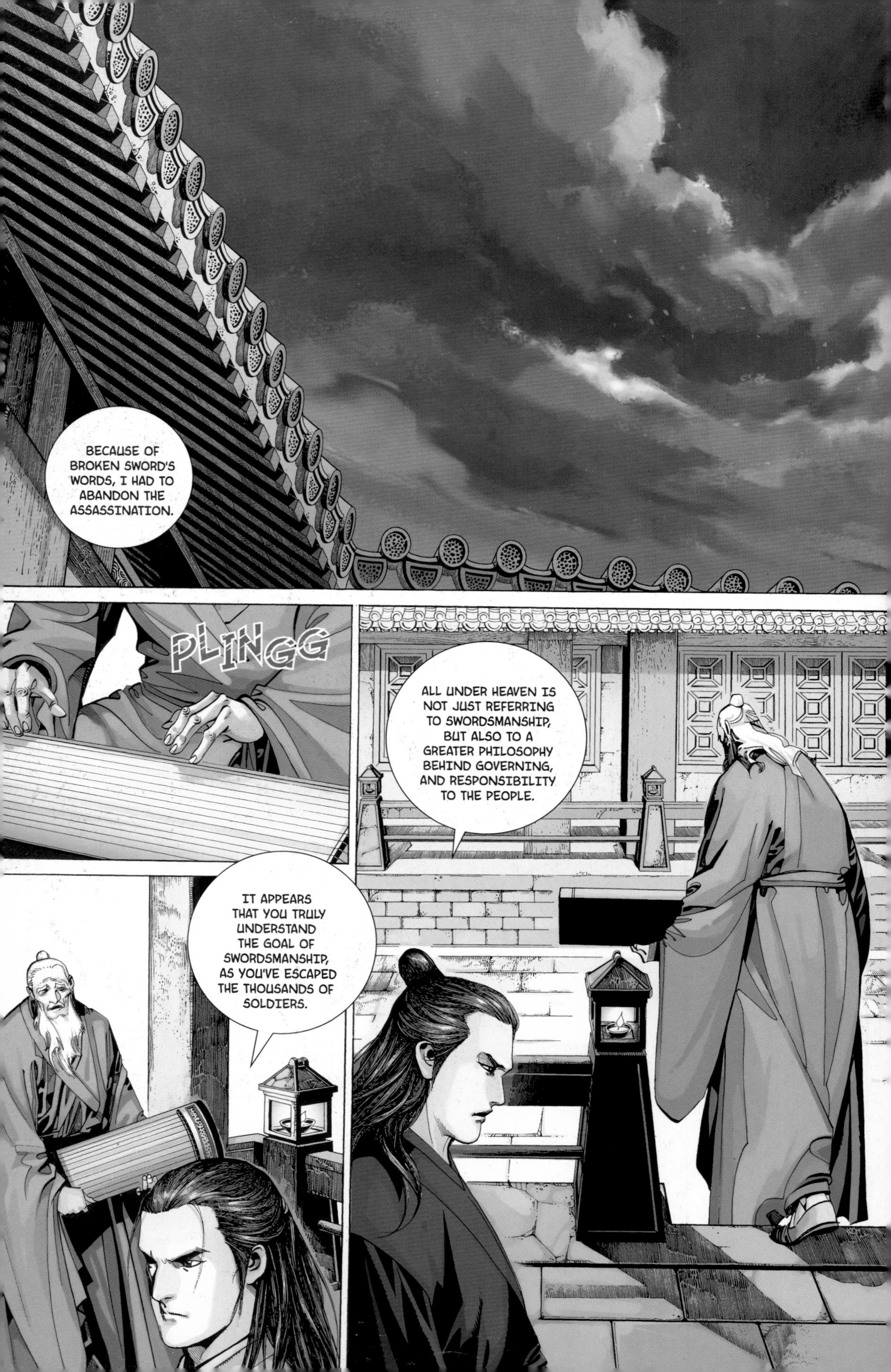

BECAUSE OF BROKEN SWORD'S WORDS, I HAD TO ABANDON THE ASSASSINATION.
PLINGG
ALL UNDER HEAVEN IS NOT JUST REFERRING TO SWORDSMANSHIP, BUT ALSO TO A GREATER PHILOSOPHY BEHIND GOVERNING, AND RESPONSIBILITY TO THE PEOPLE.
IT APPEARS THAT YOU TRULY UNDERSTAND THE GOAL OF SWORDSMANSHIP, AS YOU'VE ESCAPED THE THOUSANDS OF SOLDIERS.

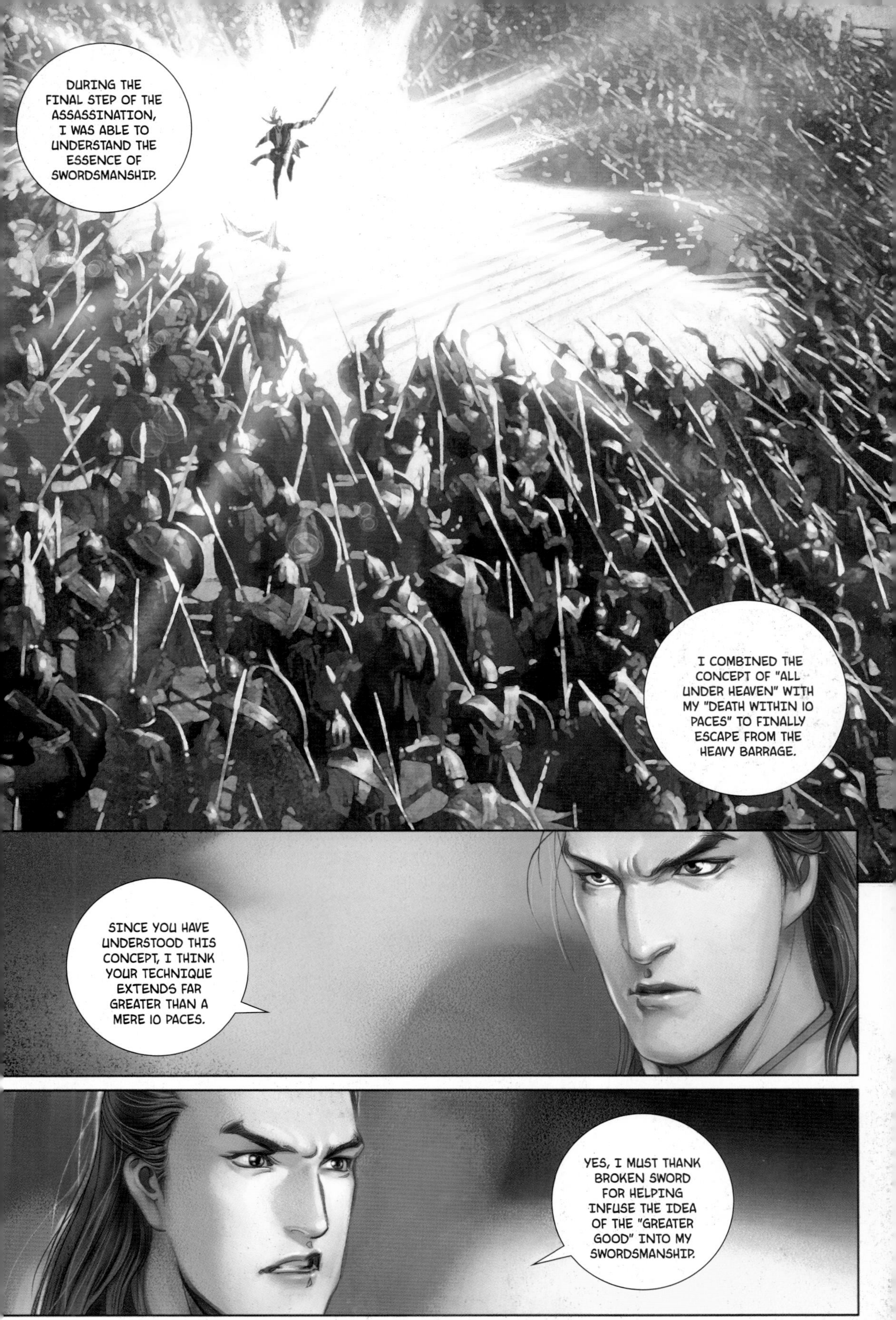
DURING THE FINAL STEP OF THE ASSASSINATION, I WAS ABLE TO UNDERSTAND THE ESSENCE OF SWORDSMANSHIP.
I COMBINED THE CONCEPT OF "ALL UNDER HEAVEN" WITH MY "DEATH WITHIN 10 PACES" TO FINALLY ESCAPE FROM THE HEAVY BARRAGE.
SINCE YOU HAVE UNDERSTOOD THIS CONCEPT, I THINK YOUR TECHNIQUE EXTENDS FAR GREATER THAN A MERE 10 PACES.
YES, I MUST THANK BROKEN SWORD FOR HELPING INFUSE THE IDEA OF THE "GREATER GOOD" INTO MY SWORDSMANSHIP.

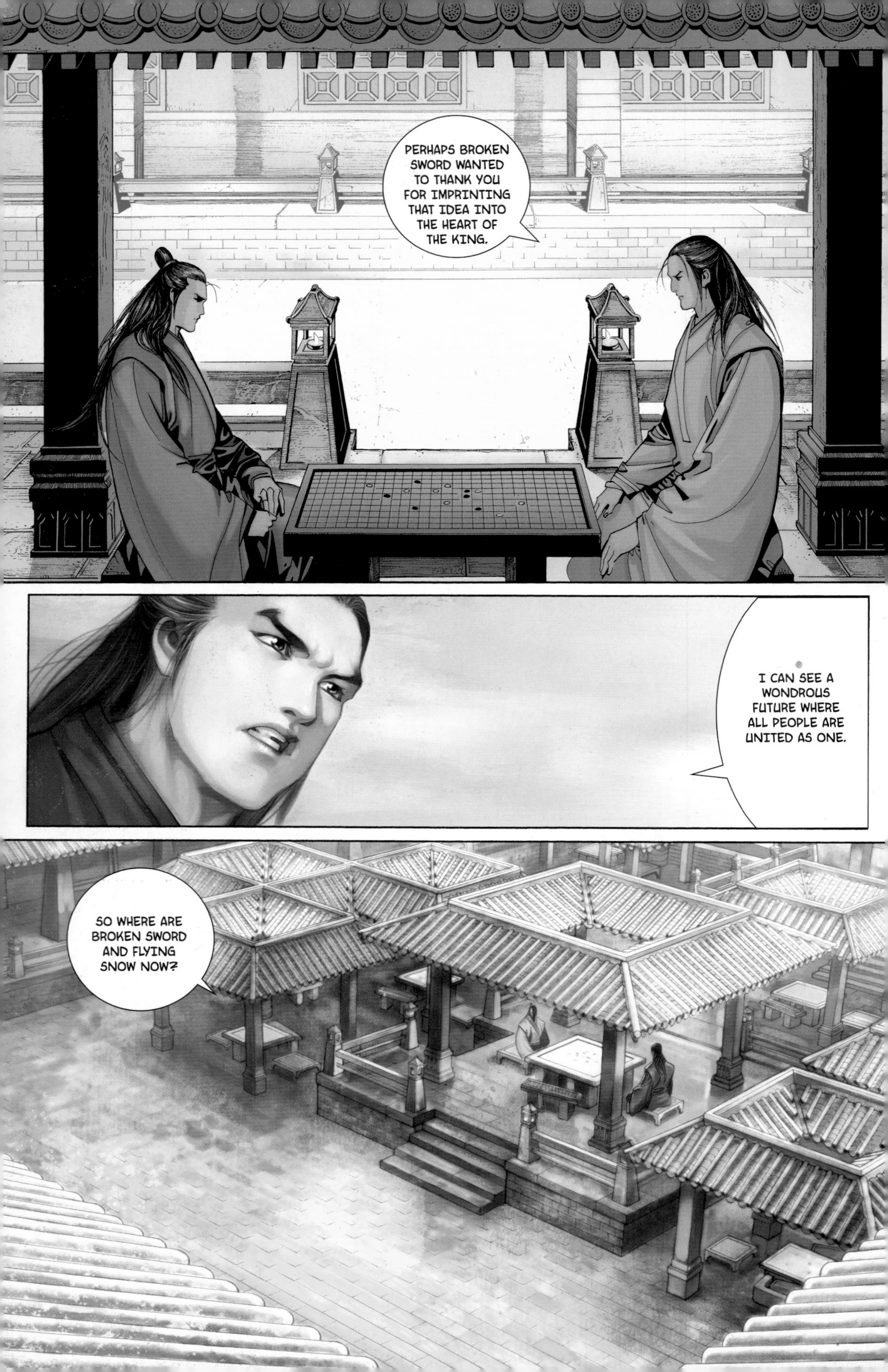
PERHAPS BROKEN SWORD WANTED TO THANK YOU FOR IMPRINTING THAT IDEA INTO THE HEART OF THE KING.
I CAN SEE A WONDROUS FUTURE WHERE ALL PEOPLE ARE UNITED AS ONE.
SO WHERE ARE BROKEN SWORD AND FLYING SNOW NOW?

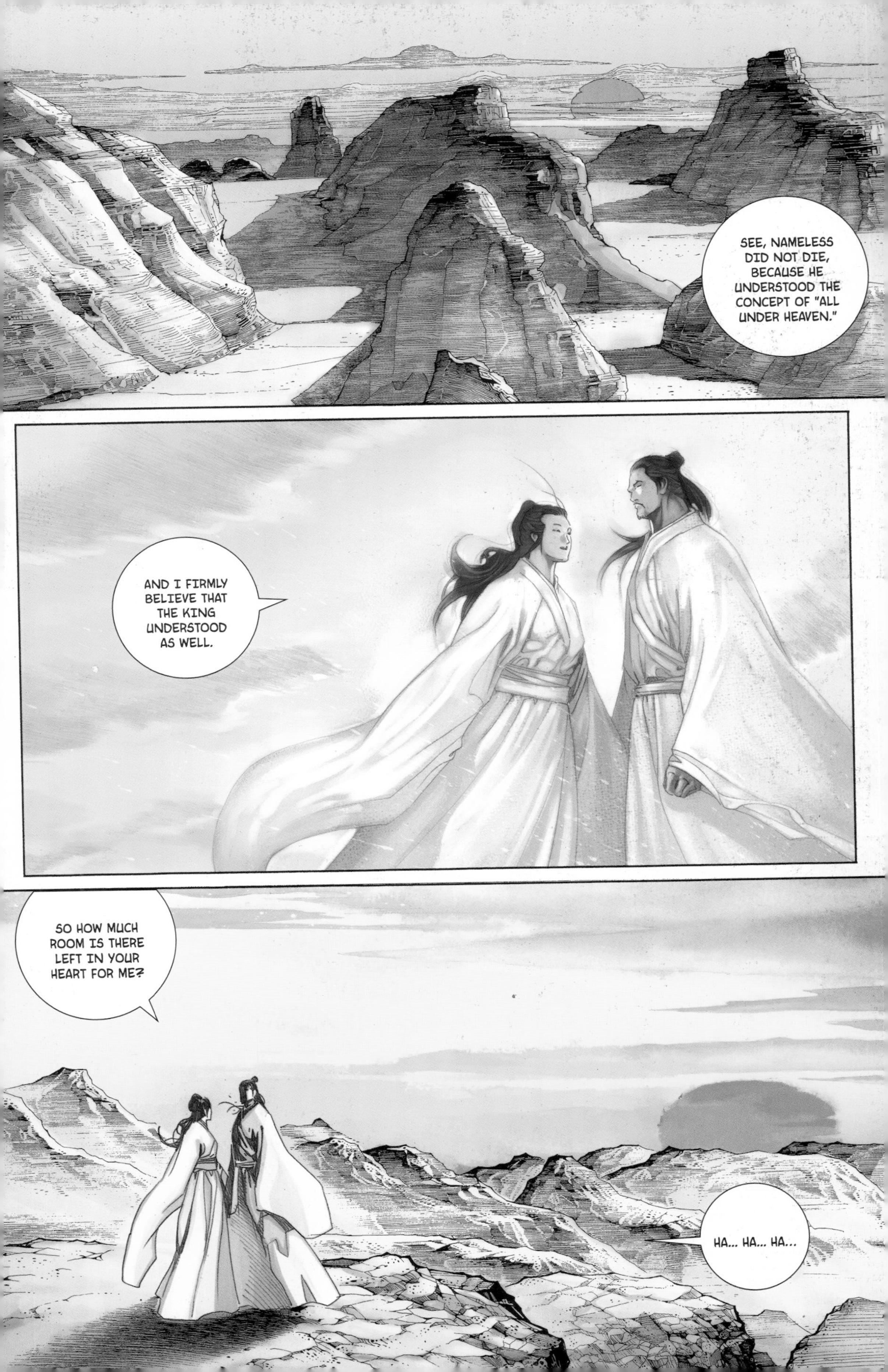
SEE, NAMELESS DID NOT DIE, BECAUSE HE UNDERSTOOD THE CONCEPT OF "ALL UNDER HEAVEN."
AND I FIRMLY BELIEVE THAT THE KING UNDERSTOOD AS WELL.
SO HOW MUCH ROOM IS THERE LEFT IN YOUR HEART FOR ME?
HA... HA... HA...

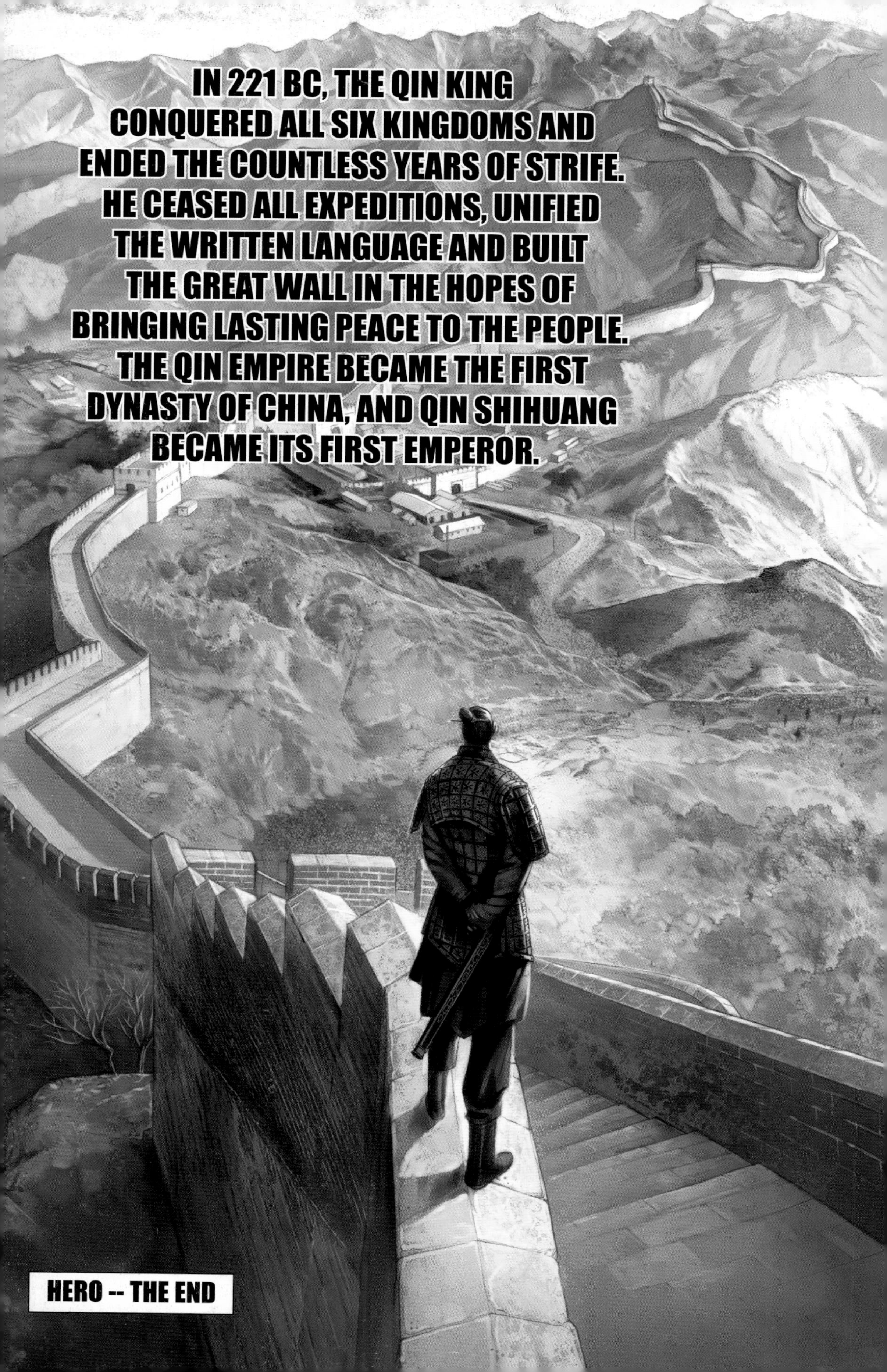
IN 221 BC, THE QIN KING CONQUERED ALL SIX KINGDOMS AND ENDED THE COUNTLESS YEARS OF STRIFE. HE CEASED ALL EXPEDITIONS, UNIFIED THE WRITTEN LANGUAGE AND BUILT THE GREAT WALL IN THE HOPES OF BRINGING LASTING PEACE TO THE PEOPLE. THE QIN EMPIRE BECAME THE FIRST DYNASTY OF CHINA, AND QIN SHIHUANG BECAME ITS FIRST EMPEROR.
HERO -- THE END

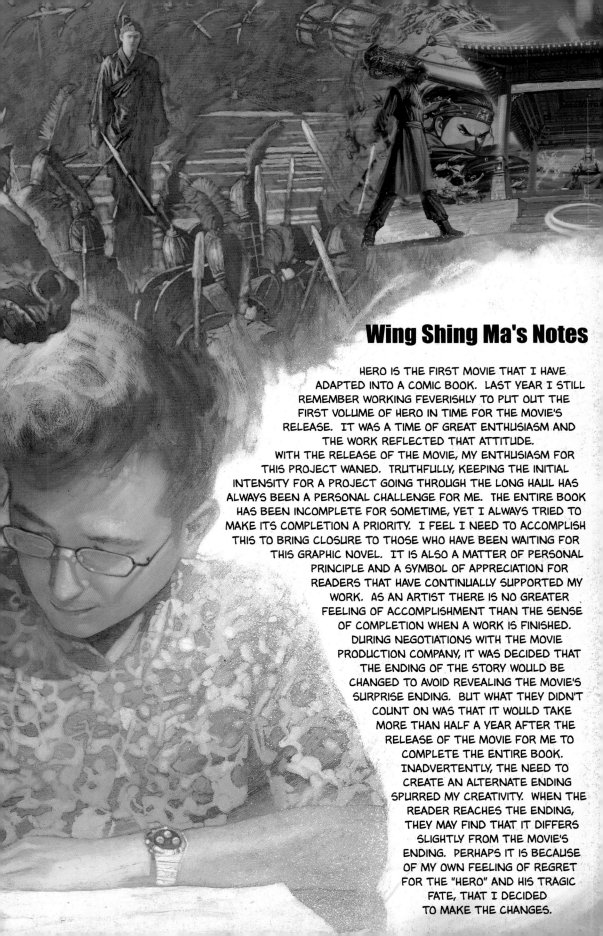

Wing Shing Ma's Notes

HERO IS THE FIRST MOVIE THAT I HAVE
ADAPTED INTO A COMIC BOOK. LAST YEAR I STILL
REMEMBER WORKING FEVERISHLY TO PUT OUT THE
FIRST VOLUME OF HERO IN TIME FOR THE MOVIE'S
RELEASE. IT WAS A TIME OF GREAT ENTHUSIASM AND
THE WORK REFLECTED THAT ATTITUDE.
WITH THE RELEASE OF THE MOVIE, MY ENTHUSIASM FOR
THIS PROJECT WANED. TRUTHFULLY, KEEPING THE INITIAL
INTENSITY FOR A PROJECT GOING THROUGH THE LONG HAUL HAS
ALWAYS BEEN A PERSONAL CHALLENGE FOR ME. THE ENTIRE BOOK
HAS BEEN INCOMPLETE FOR SOMETIME, YET I ALWAYS TRIED TO
MAKE ITS COMPLETION A PRIORITY. I FEEL I NEED TO ACCOMPLISH
THIS TO BRING CLOSURE TO THOSE WHO HAVE BEEN WAITING FOR
THIS GRAPHIC NOVEL. IT IS ALSO A MATTER OF PERSONAL
PRINCIPLE AND A SYMBOL OF APPRECIATION FOR
READERS THAT HAVE CONTINUALLY SUPPORTED MY
WORK. AS AN ARTIST THERE IS NO GREATER
FEELING OF ACCOMPLISHMENT THAN THE SENSE
OF COMPLETION WHEN A WORK IS FINISHED.
DURING NEGOTIATIONS WITH THE MOVIE
PRODUCTION COMPANY, IT WAS DECIDED THAT
THE ENDING OF THE STORY WOULD BE
CHANGED TO AVOID REVEALING THE MOVIE'S
SURPRISE ENDING. BUT WHAT THEY DIDN'T
COUNT ON WAS THAT IT WOULD TAKE
MORE THAN HALF A YEAR AFTER THE
RELEASE OF THE MOVIE FOR ME TO
COMPLETE THE ENTIRE BOOK.
INADVERTENTLY, THE NEED TO
CREATE AN ALTERNATE ENDING
SPURRED MY CREATIVITY. WHEN THE
READER REACHES THE ENDING,
THEY MAY FIND THAT IT DIFFERS
SLIGHTLY FROM THE MOVIE'S
ENDING. PERHAPS IT IS BECAUSE
OF MY OWN FEELING OF REGRET
FOR THE "HERO" AND HIS TRAGIC
FATE, THAT I DECIDED
TO MAKE THE CHANGES.

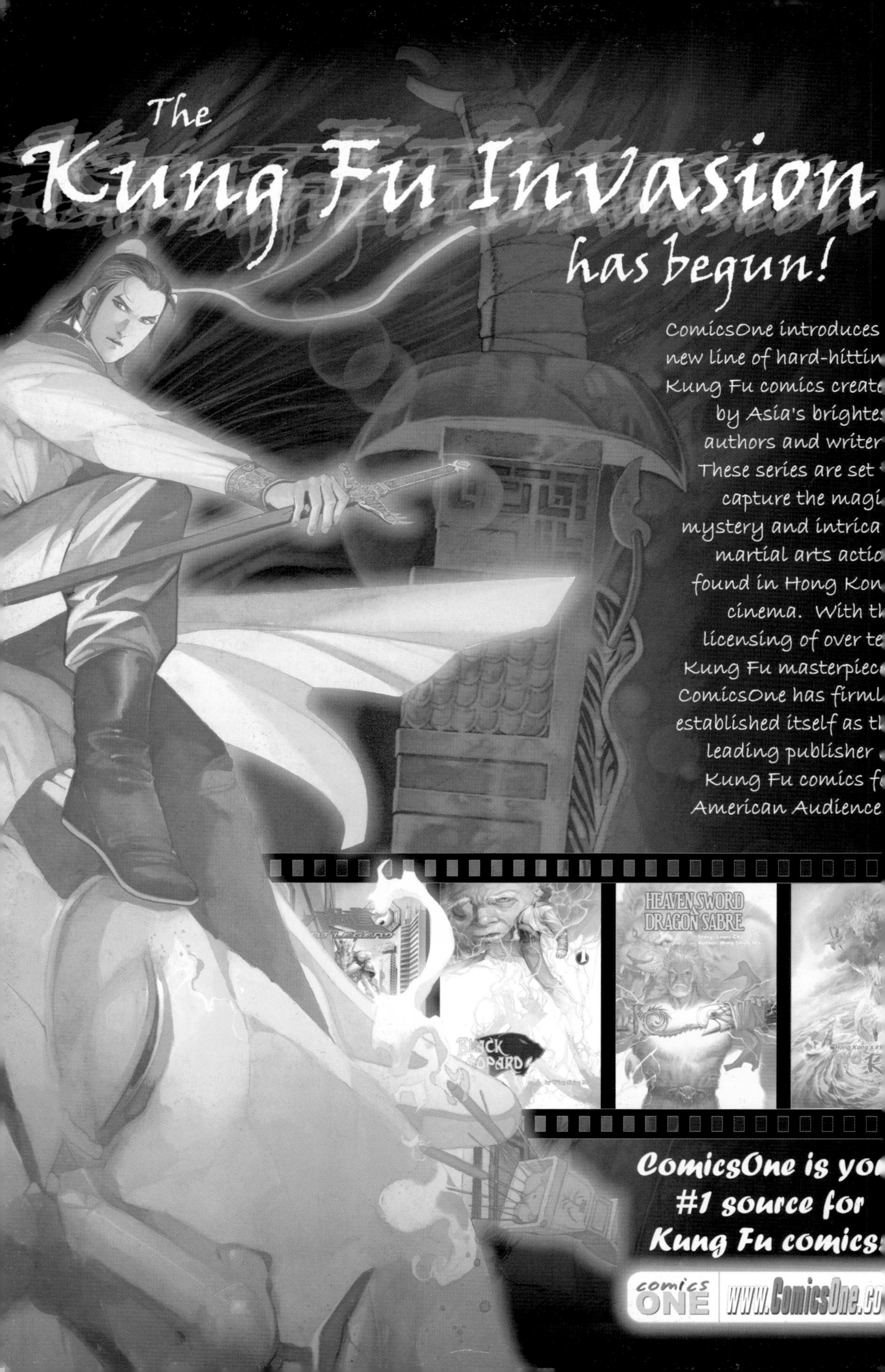
The
Kung Fu Invasion
has begun!
ComicsOne introduces
new line of hard-hittin
Kung Fu comics creat
by Asia's brighte
authors and writer
These series are set
capture the magi
mystery and intrica
martial arts actio
found in Hong Kon
cinema. With th
licensing of over te
Kung Fu masterpiec
ComicsOne has firml
established itself as t
leading publisher
Kung Fu comics f
American Audience
HEAVEN SWORD & DRAGON SABRE
ComicsOne is yo
#1 source for
Kung Fu comics
comics ONE
www.ComicsOne.co

HEAVEN SWORD & DRAGON SABRE

Heaven Sword and Dragon Sabre is an epic adventure set against the backdrop of the Mongol invasion in ancient China. The story follows WuJi Chang's growth as a Kung Fu master amidst the frenzied pursuit of two ancient and powerful weapons: Heaven Sword and Dragon Sabre. In order to unite his country and overthrow China's Mongol oppressors, WuJi must develop his own formidable powers while understanding both swords' relationship to his parents' legacy.

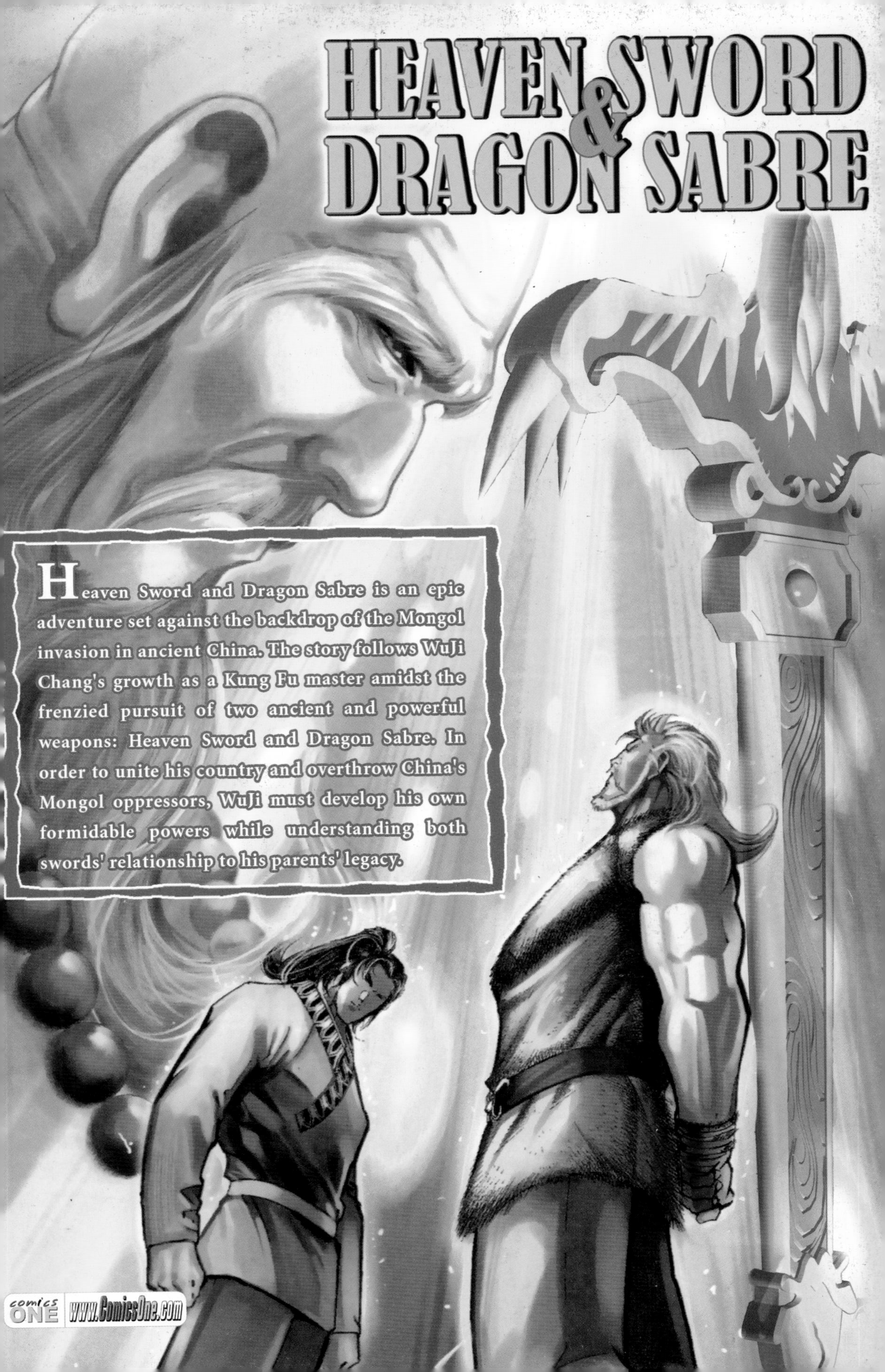

comics ONE www.ComicsOne.com

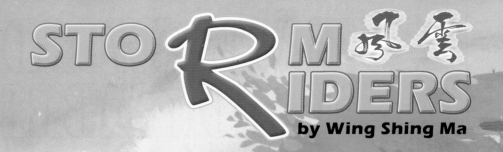

STORM RIDERS 風雲

by Wing Shing Ma

Storm Riders: Invading Sun wraps up loose ends and spirals forward with a whole new story arc as strange alliances are born and torn asunder. The long awaited return of Conquer is finally at hand and the greatest test of might for Wind and Cloud is upon them! Will the sins of the Master finally come to an end?

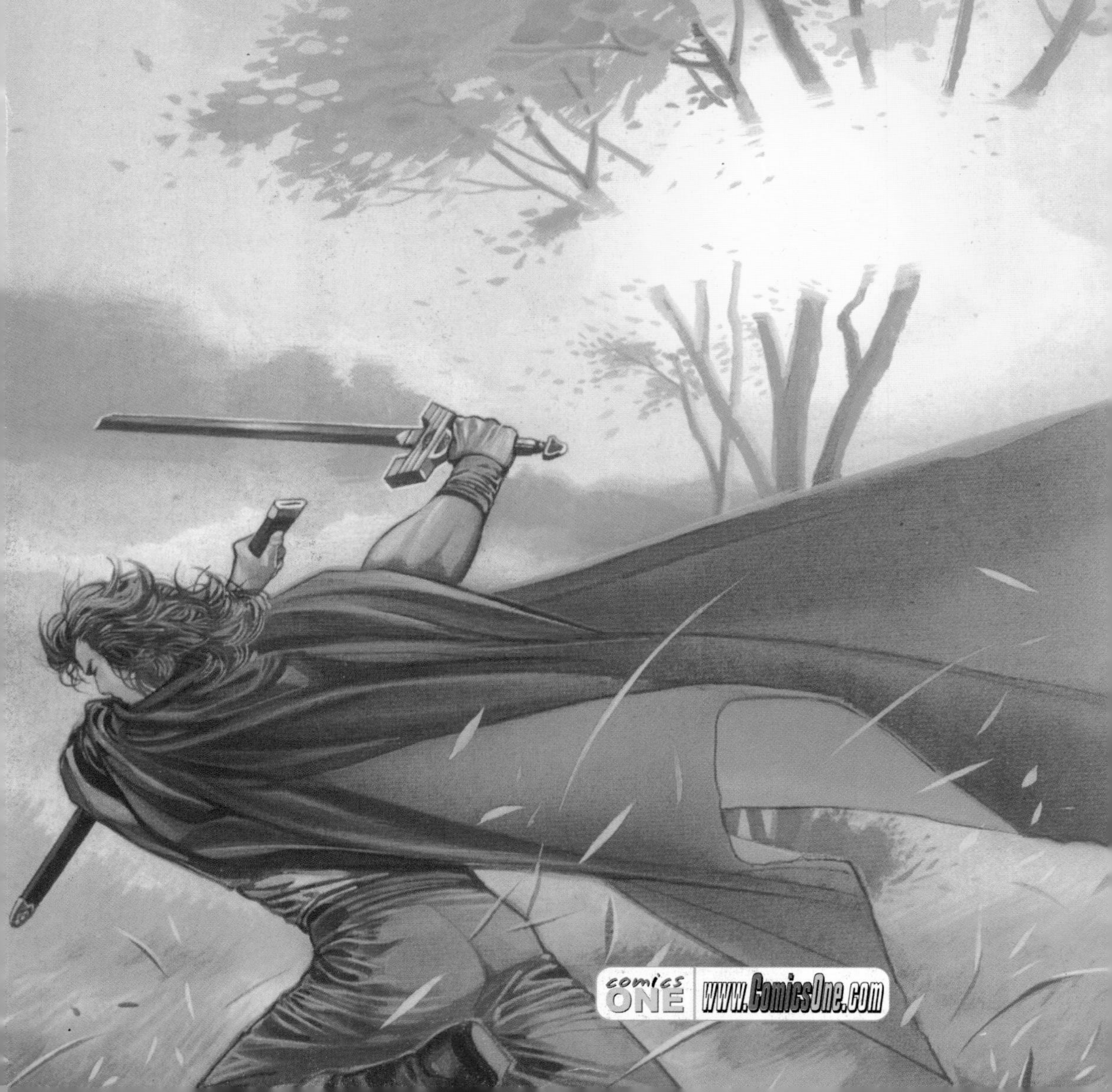

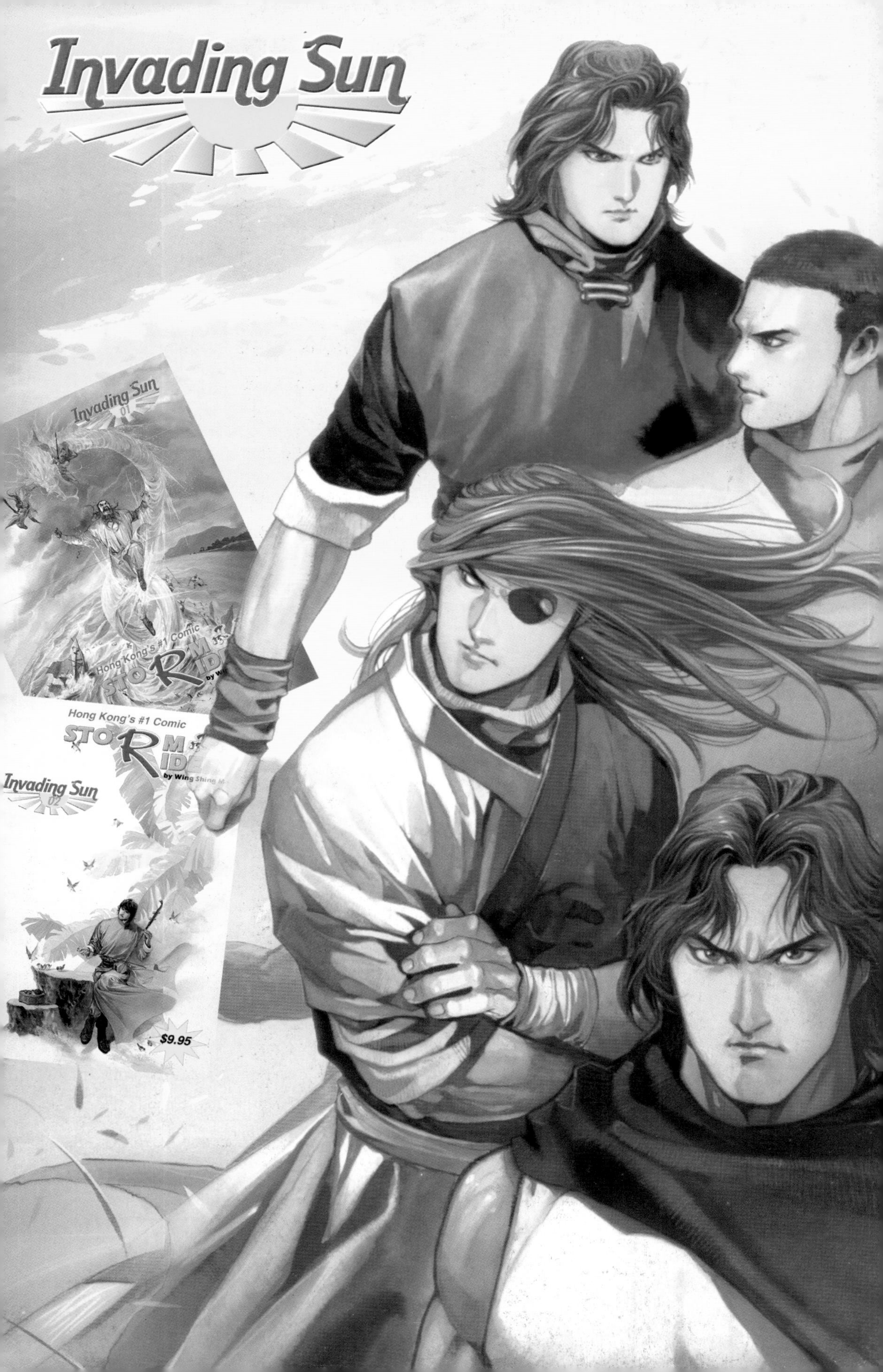
Invading Sun
Invading Sun 01
Hong Kong's #1 Comic
STORM RIDERS
Hong Kong's #1 Comic
STORM RIDERS
by Wing Shing Ma
Invading Sun 02
$9.95

STORM RIDERS 風雲
Merchandise

Hero Sword

Hero Sword: Master swordsman Nameless of the Storm Riders series, passes this potent yet modest sword to his devoted and skilled student Jien-Chen. The straight sword has always been the weapon of the scholar and ComicsOne's 9-inch Hero Sword is definitely a distinguished way of opening your mail. It ships in a fine wood box perfect for displaying and comes with a jeweled scabbard and a red tassel bound to the hilt. Get yours today!

Snowy Saber: One of the most powerful weapons in the entire kung fu world is now available from ComicsOne as one of the most powerful letter openers in the world. Wielded by main character Wind from the popular Storm Riders series, this beautifully crafted 9-inch letter opener is the perfect replica, complete with scabbard and cloth-wrapped hilt. It ships in a fine cherry colored box perfect for displaying. Get yours today!

Snowy Saber

Destiny

Destiny: The perfect complement to the Snowy Saber and Hero Sword, this curved stainless steel blade is 9 inches long and comes with an ornately detailed scabbard. Store this powerful weapon in its decorative cherry box until the time comes to strike down your enemies or open that ever-menacing utility bill. Get yours today!

Mini Snowy Saber

Mini Snowy Saber: From the pages of Storm Riders comes main character Wind's family blade. Our mini Snowy Saber is the perfect trinket to spruce up your key chain and ward off any would be assailants.

Flame Kylin Sword

Flame Kylin Sword: Young Master Duan-Lang inherits the Flame Kylin after his father's tragic demise. This Duan family heirloom comes in two different flavors. Choose from the jade colored scabbard with a bronze blade or the silver scabbard with matching blade. The Flame Kylin Sword is 5.5 inches lo[n]g and comes with an elegant red tassel. While the Flame Kylin makes a great letter opener, the sword and scabbard can also double as hairpins.

Please visit our web site for order and weapon information at www.comicsone.com or www.comicsworld.com

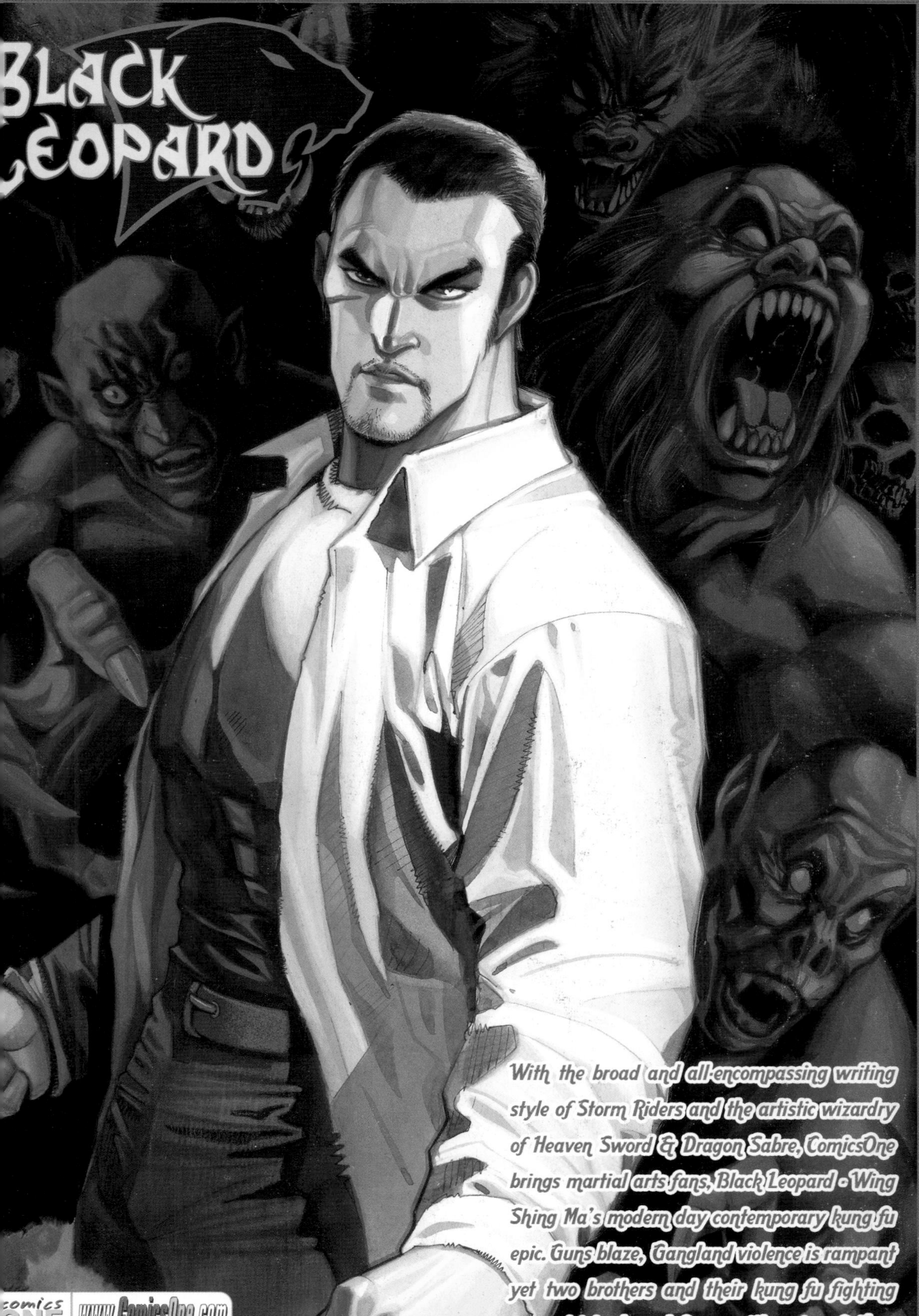
BLACK LEOPARD
With the broad and all-encompassing writing style of Storm Riders and the artistic wizardry of Heaven Sword & Dragon Sabre, ComicsOne brings martial arts fans, Black Leopard - Wing Shing Ma's modern day contemporary kung fu epic. Guns blaze, Gangland violence is rampant yet two brothers and their kung fu fighting compatriots show defiance with an iron fist!
comics ONE
www.ComicsOne.com

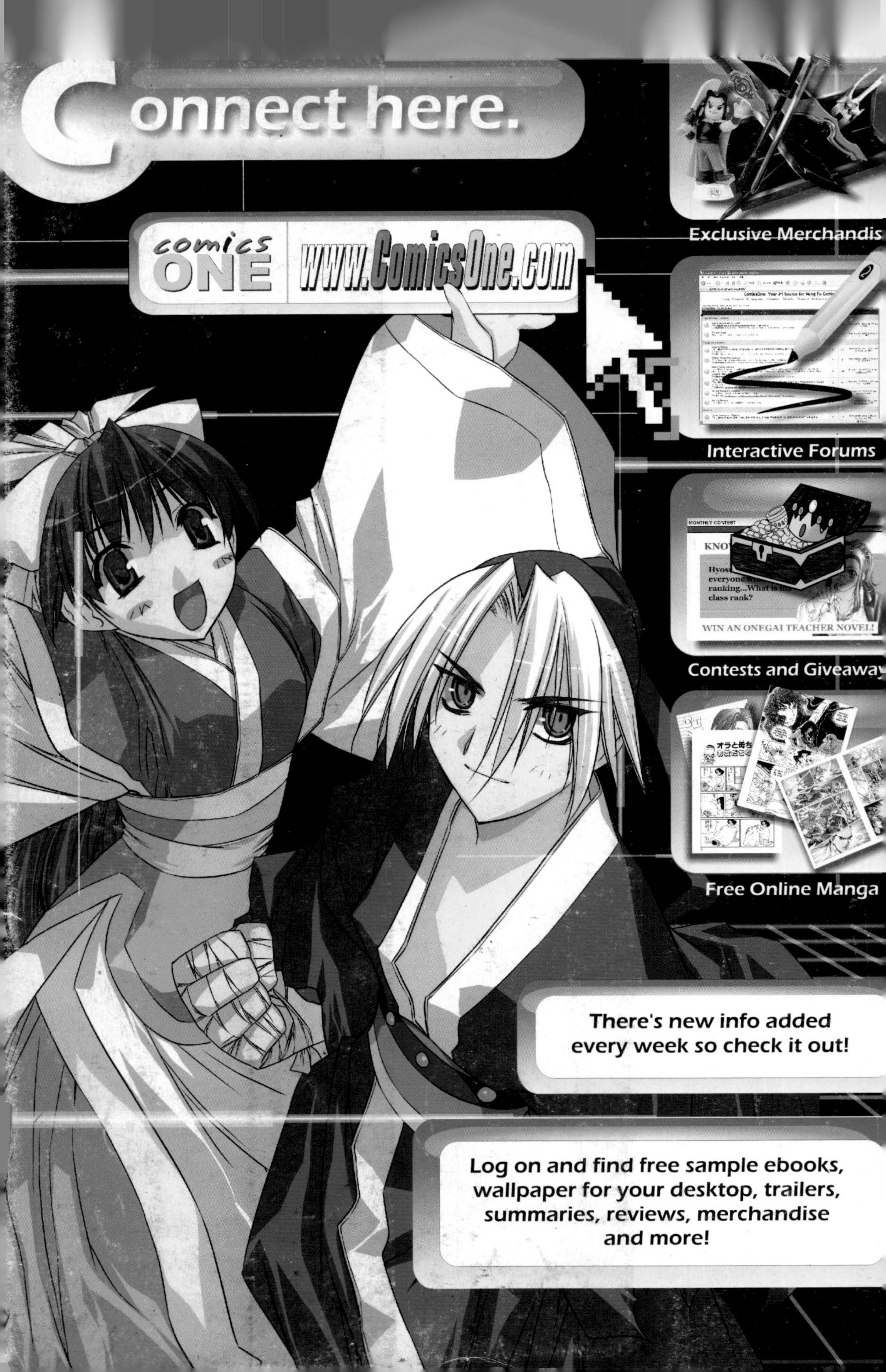
Connect here.
comics ONE
www.ComicsOne.com
Exclusive Merchandis
Interactive Forums
MONTHLY CONTEST
WIN AN ONEGAI TEACHER NOVEL!
Contests and Giveaway
Free Online Manga
There's new info added every week so check it out!
Log on and find free sample ebooks, wallpaper for your desktop, trailers, summaries, reviews, merchandise and more!